Theological Audacities

Princeton Theological Monograph Series

K. C. Hanson, Charles M. Collier, and D. Christopher Spinks,
Series Editors

Theological Audacities

Selected Essays

FRIEDRICH-WILHELM MARQUARDT

Edited by Andreas Pangritz and Paul S. Chung

FOREWORD BY H. MARTIN RUMSCHEIDT

TRANSLATED BY DON MCCORD, H. MARTIN RUMSCHEIDT, AND PAUL S. CHUNG

PICKWICK *Publications* · Eugene, Oregon

THEOLOGICAL AUDACITIES
Selected Essays

Princeton Theological Monograph Series 137

Pickwick Publications
An Imprint of Wipf and Stock Publishers
199 W. 8th Ave., Suite 3
Eugene, OR 97401

www.wipfandstock.com

ISBN 13: 978-1-60608-943-9

Cataloging-in-Publication data:

Marquardt, Friedrich-Wilhelm.

Theological audacities : selected essays / Friedrich-Wilhelm Marquardt ; edited by Andreas Pangritz and Paul S. Chung ; with a Foreword by H. Martin Rumscheidt ; translated by Don McCord, H. Martin Rumscheidt, and Paul S. Chung.

Princeton Theological Monograph Series 137

xiv + 264 p. ; 23 cm. Includes index.

ISBN 13: 978-1-60608-943-9

1. Christianity and other religions—Judaism. 2. Judaism—Relations—Christianity—1945-. 3. Barth, Karl, 1886-1968. I. Title. II. Series.

BX4827 B2 M37 2010

Manufactured in the U.S.A.

Contents

Acknowledgments

THIS BOOK IS THE RESULT OF A JOINT TRANSATLANTIC EFFORT IN translating the theology of Friedrich-Wilhelm Marquardt, former Professor of Systematic Theology at the Free University in Berlin, into (American) English.

The first initiative to compose this anthology of essays by Friedrich-Wilhelm Marquardt in an English translation came from Rudolf Weckerling (Berlin; born 1911). He was once a "young brother" of the Confessing Church in Germany. After World War II Weckerling—together with Eberhard Bethge, Dietrich Bonhoeffer's friend and biographer—became a member of the *Unterwegs-Kreis* (underway circle) in Berlin, a circle of "Dahlemites" (the radical wing of the former Confessing Church).

He later became Bethge's successor as the student's chaplain at the University of Technology in Berlin-Charlottenburg, while Friedrich-Wilhelm Marquardt was student's chaplain at the Free University in Berlin-Dahlem. Weckerling together with Marquardt accompanied the first German student group on its journey to the state of Israel in 1959. He later served as a minister in the Protestant congregation in Beirut (Lebanon), in Liberia, and in Berlin, where he is living today in his blessed age of 98. He encouraged the translators and editors of this volume to undertake the task of translating and editing the essays contained in this anthology. Without his initiative and encouragement the project would not have become possible.

The editors thank Mrs. Dorothee Marquardt, Friedrich-Wilhelm Marquardt's widow, for giving her permission to use the essays for translation into English.

The translators have worked in joyous and voluntary spirit.

Most of the essays contained in this volume have been translated by Don McCord, retired pastor in Morristown, New Jersey, who in the early sixties lived as a "fraternal minister" in Berlin. During that time he participated in the *Unterwegs-Kreis* and became acquainted with Marquardt and Weckerling. He translated the following essays: "'Enemies for Our Sake': The Jewish No and the Christian Theology," "Elements Unresolved in Leo Baeck's Criticism of Adolf von Harnack," "Martin Buber as a Socialist Zionist," "Why the Talmud interests me as a Christian," and "The Secretary of the Church Administration. From Barth's Pastorate." In addition he translated the essay "Friedrich-Wilhelm Marquardt—a Theological-Biographical Sketch" by Andreas Pangritz, an introduction into Marquardt's life and work.

Two essays have been translated by H. Martin Rumscheidt, Professor of Theology Emeritus at Atlantic School of Theology in Halifax, Nova Scotia. Since the seventies he knew Marquardt and shared in his interest in Barth studies and in a renewal of the relationship between Jews and Christians after the Shoah. He translated the essays "The Idol Totters: The General Attack from the Epistle to the Romans," and "Theological and Political Motivations of Karl Barth in the Church Struggle." In addition, Martin Rumscheidt revised the translation of the essay "Enemies for Our Sake."

The essay "First Report on Karl Barth's 'Socialist Speeches'" has been translated by Paul S. Chung, Associate Professor of Mission and World Christianity at Luther Seminary, St. Paul, MN.

The translations have been controlled and revised in comparison with the German original versions by Andreas Pangritz, Professor of Systematic Theology and director of the Ecumenical Institute at the University of Bonn, Germany. His student assistants Sabine Neuhaus (Aachen) and Cornelia Sahamie (Cologne) have been of great help in this process. Ralf H. Arning (Berlin), who also contributed to revising the translations, completed the editing work in order to get the manuscript into shape according to the style of the publisher. He also prepared the index of names.

The editors are especially grateful to Christian Amondsen, assistant managing editor at Wipf and Stock Publishers for accepting the volume in the Princeton Theological Monograph Series, and Dr. K. C. Hanson, editor, and Diane Farley, editorial administrator, for their help in getting the volume edited and published.

Paul S. Chung, St. Paul, Minnesota
Andreas Pangritz, Bonn, Germany

Foreword

"Cross Over to Macedonia and Help Us!"
What Is the Help Friedrich-Wilhelm Marquardt May Bring Us Over Here?

H. Martin Rumscheidt

AMONG THE AIMS OF THIS SELECTION OF TRANSLATED ESSAYS BY Marquardt is that having "come across" (in the literal sense of having been brought here) in translation, he may also "come across" (in the colloquial sense of being understood), he will be of help on our shores in the work of theology we do. It is the editors' wish that "translation" will turn into "transposition": a crossing over in several aspects.

The call to the apostle Paul to cross over and come across to Macedonia came to him in a dream (Acts 16:9); the subsequent narrative there identifies the help he brought. In borrowing the words of that apostolic call, there is no intentional or unintentional bestowal of apostolicity on Friedrich-Wilhelm Marquardt. But there is a definite proposal in the use of that verse: He has things to bring that definitely help us on this side of "the great pond"—as Europeans affectionately call the waters that must be crossed over en route to the Americas. Andreas Pangritz' introductory essay sketches at greater length what Marquardt's help to us here may look like.

Let us then suppose that Friedel—as his friends used to call him— had been called to "cross over" and, heeding the call, had come and is now among us. What help does he have in his satchel?

In 1995, Pangritz published an article on the need for a transformation in the relation between Christians and Jews; he quotes these words by Marquardt: "The sense that Christian theology has been fundamentally battered by Auschwitz has called into being a broad, and from the outset, interdenominational movement of theological conversion in the United States of America. But here in Germany we present ourselves remarkably insensitive in that aspect."[1] It appears that Marquardt had in mind what was happening in the then nine years old Annual Scholars Conference on the Holocaust and the Churches, founded by Franklin Littell and Hubert Locke and the endeavors by Jewish scholars to develop a Jewish theology after Auschwitz.

What had been missing, in my experience, from that interdisciplinary, international and interdenominational movement was the necessary interchange between Christian and Jewish theologians without which *Christian* theology cannot enter upon the radical conversion that the Shoah demands. For nearly four decades I have been held in the grip of the question of what has to change in Christian faith and theology so that it may still—or once again—be believable after the Shoah. In my own participation in the Annual Scholars Conference and in other theological Christian-Jewish encounters, I cannot detect in that "movement" the radical approach to the relation between Christians and Jews after Auschwitz found in Marquardt's work. That the movement existed cannot be denied, of course. But neither can I ignore the steadfast demand, if not even challenge issued by Ken Dollarhide, a theologian of North American aboriginal peoples' origin and a convert to Judaism, who for close to two decades has called for a genuinely and rigorously *theological* collaboration of Christians and Jews that builds on the foundational work of the late Paul van Buren for the sake of reframing Christian theology after Auschwitz.

In relation to that challenge, it is necessary to note that North America and in particular the United States and its sizeable Jewish population offers what may indeed be called a providential context for such theological collaboration of Jews and Christians. In that context, for example, exegetes of the sacred texts and experts in how they have been interpreted, used and abused, over the course of centuries could exchange their knowledge and, in so interchanging, create the very fertile space for that utterly necessary movement of theological and eccle-

1. Andreas Pangritz, "Umkehr und Erneuerung: Helmut Gollwitzers Beitrag zur Veränderung des christlich-jüdischen Verhältnisses," *Berliner Theologische Zeitschrift* 12.2 (1995) 270. The citation is from Friedrich-Wilhelm Marquardt, "Hermeneutik des christlich-jüdischen Verhältnisses: Über Helmut Gollwitzers Arbeit an der 'Judenfrage,'" in *Richte unsere Füße auf den Weg des Friedens,* ed. Andreas Baudis et al. (Munich: Kaiser, 1979) 141.

siastical conversion. Are there obstacles for such ex- and interchange and how could Marquardt help us?

It has been an aim of the still continuing inter-church and inter-faith conversations in North America to foster tolerance for, and a much deeper and more nuanced knowledge of, one another. It is surely good and to be wholly embraced when people of "other" faiths and the activities grounded in their faith are honestly valued and—what is perhaps more important still—protected by law. Tolerance *yes*! It is an as such laudable virtue. But Friedrich-Wilhelm Marquardt demands much, much more from the conversation between Christians and Jews. To approach what he demands here I draw on the challenge Rabbi Irving "Yitz" Greenberg issues to those conversations. "No statement, theological or otherwise, should be made that would not be credible in the presence of burning children."[2] In these words, where the commanding voice of the Shoah is powerfully present, the conversion, repentance and renewal of Christian theology Marquardt calls for is paraphrased and the responsibility for credible faith assertions today is signaled. But tolerance is simply incapable of something like that; repentance is not in its genes. A genuinely integral Christian *metanoia* in the presence of Jews who in their flesh and memory still bear the hell of "the final solution of the Jewish question," in the presence of the people on whom for centuries the Christian peoples and their churches have placed the burden of anti-Judaism, can only be a radical hermeneutical *and* existential process. Women and men in North America have entered upon the road to such a *metanoia*, but, as I see it, that road can only benefit from the precise orientation Friedel Marquardt has provided for it.

Where does that road lead or, more accurately, where does it begin today? Several outstanding North American Christians have shown that it is necessary to travel it. They are convinced that the so-called "Jewish question" is in fact a question for and about Christians. I have in mind such people as James Carroll, Franklin Littell, Krister Stendahl, Leonard Swidler, and the already mentioned Paul van Buren; others follow in their footsteps, for example, in the Annual Scholars Conference on the

---

2. Irving Greenberg, "Cloud of Smoke, Pillar of Fire: Judaism, Christianity, and Modernity after the Holocaust," in *Auschwitz: Beginning of a New Era? Reflections on the Holocaust*, ed. Eva Fleischner (New York: Ktav, Cathedral of St. John the Divine, 1977) 23.

Holocaust and the Churches, searching for the road to the conversion of Christian theology.

I will speak only about two points in Marquardt's thought which help us on this continent to set our feet firmly on that road.

On November 9, 1998, on the occasion of the sixtieth anniversary of the pogrom known as *Kristallnacht*, Marquardt addressed a gathering in the North German town of Greifswald on "Jewish Challenges to the Church's Confession that Jesus is the Christ." In the talk he refers to Schalom Ben-Chorin who had been Marquardt's partner for many years in Jewish-Christian dialogues in Germany. Ben-Chorin speaks about the *Heimholung*, the repatriation, so to speak, of the historical Jesus back into the Jewish people, a sort of "rediscovery" on the part of the Jewish people of the radical critic Jesus of Nazareth, a man from and of their people. Marquardt takes up this notion of *Heimholung*.—Here he is really of help in my judgment.—The road to the utterly necessary movement of theological conversion and renewal requires the repatriation into Christian theological and ecclesiological life and work of the Jesus whom the Jewish people have brought home, *heimgeholt*. And this is necessary for the sake of the promises of the Holy One to the descendants of Abraham, Isaac and Israel, promises which by divine grace are addressed to other nations through the Jew Jesus, one of those descendants.[3] If there is to be a road of conversion and renewal, it cannot lead around the acknowledgment that the Jesus Christians speak about is utterly and in his essence a Jew and of the Jewish people of the first century CE Roman province of Palestine.

Three years before that, Marquardt had given an address titled "Evangelische Freude an der Tora"—Protestant delight in the Torah. He describes the aim of that address as follows: "As a Protestant Christian I simply want to begin in your hearing and in a loud voice to praise the Torah and build into that praise as much delight in the law as I, a novice in *Simchat Torah*, can possibly do."[4] And he touches upon something that surely aids the well-known Anglo-Saxon predilection for the

---

3. Marquardt, "Jüdische Herausforderungen an das Christus-Bekenntnis der Kirchen," in his *Auf Einem Schul-Weg: Kleinere christlich-jüdische Lerneinheiten* (Berlin: Orient & Okzident, 1999) 279–300.

4. Marquardt, *Evangelische Freude an der Tora* (Tübingen: TVT Medienverlag, 1997) 24.

pragmatic but also on what may give new vigor to the movement of theological conversion.

I describe this by means of another quotation from that talk at the German *Kirchentag* in 1995.

> Through its ordinances and with its exacting demands law makes *doers* of us and confers on us a correspondingly upright consciousness of ourselves: We can do something. We are not simply puppets manipulated by higher powers and forces. That the God of Israel makes doers of us through the Torah is, in my view, the most beautiful thing we can thank Him for: Every lethargy, every melancholy, indifference and moroseness is ended. Having no accountability leads very quickly to meaninglessness. Wherever the Torah claims us as doers, it confronts the nihilism that exclaims: There's nothing I can do. The Torah opposes anti-revolutionary laziness.
>
> Of course, the Torah also makes doers of us in a grave sense. Judgment according to works also belongs to it; at the end God will ask us: And what have you *done*? The question won't be: Did you believe?—what did you believe?—what did you think?—which *Weltanschauung* did you embrace? God asks: What did you do or not do? At the last judgment God engages us as doers. But how good it is that even here and now God makes doers of us with the Torah, helping us already here and now to avoid the potential embarrassment of replying then that "we lived by faith alone without the works of the law." *That* answer God does not want to hear from us then. And that is why the Torah is so good: It prepares us even here and now for meeting God on the level where He will engage us as doers of His ordinances and as witnesses of His law.[5]

The notion of the law making doers of us brings to mind a word by another who "delighted in the Torah," one who really did cross over to the real Macedonia: the apostle Paul. When he writes to the sisters and brothers in Rome: "Do not go with the flow of this age but be transformed by renewing your mind that you may show what God wills: the good, what God delights in, the perfect" (Rom 12:2; transl. altered), he has the Torah, the "law" in mind in describing God's will in those three terms. "Doing" the Torah is living life set free from the structures of "this age" or, in Paul's words "from this body of death" (Rom 7:24). Here Marquardt takes up Karl Barth's insistence that Law is Gospel or that

5. Ibid., 28–29.

Torah is grace. We may now rephrase something cited above: Through its ordinances and exacting demands grace makes *doers* of us and confers on us a correspondingly upright consciousness of ourselves . . . Grace opposes anti-revolutionary laziness. And this is where Marquardt's engagement with Barth's political ethics is rooted. What attracted him was Barth's articulation of the theological motivation that prompts what churches and individual Christians say and do, or don't, in the concreteness of their actual existence. The significance of Barth's political ethics as Marquardt presents it in his work lies in the fact that for Barth "wherever we speak 'theology' we also implicitly or explicitly speak 'politics'" (as Barth put it in a letter to students in Holland in February 1937) or, in other words, theology is really something to be done. Some of the chapters included in this anthology show Marquardt's interpretations of Barth's theological-political thinking. Here, too, Marquardt is of help in reclaiming for both theology/religion and politics/state what is readily lost in a rigorous church and state separation. And here too delight in the Torah calls us back into the conversion of theology and its individualized ethics of inwardness or good conscience.

On the road to the conversion and renewal of theology and church after the Shoah, the road where the presence of burning children is acknowledged, tolerance—if it is modest and gracious—will gladly help lead us far beyond itself. Where Friedrich-Wilhelm Marquardt's help begins is in the notion of *Heimholung*, our being repatriated into God's covenant by the people to whom Jesus and Paul belong, the people from which they "crossed over" to the various "Macedonias" to help us. This radical notion of *Heimholung* is the gate through which theological conversion has to pass for then it can discover the delight in the Torah that erupts in *Simchat Torah* and that makes us doers and believers of the law.

PART ONE

The God of Israel and Christian Theology after the Shoah

1

"Enemies for Our Sake"

The Jewish No and Christian Theology

We will not have Christian anti-Judaism behind us until we are theologically able to do something positive with the Jewish No to Jesus.

I

Again and again this No was and is for Christian theologians an occasion for their thesis about the "end of Israel." According to the different positions regarding the Christian meaning of the Hebrew Bible, theological traditions cannot come to agree even about the value of pre-Christian Israel in the history of salvation. All the more, a majority of Christian theologians are convinced that, after Jesus' death and resurrection, Jewish Israel has become meaningless for theology and the history of salvation, and has nothing more of importance to say to our understanding of God and our faith.

The fact that this Christian anti-Judaism is expressed in many different levels of argumentation does not change a thing in regard to this almost unbroken conviction shared by scholarly theologians.

The most important argumentation today—important because it is unconsciously taken for granted—rests on a simple relativization of Israel in salvation history. It dismisses Israel as merely another phenomenon in the general history of religion, thereby eliminating it from the realm of the theologically normative. And yet, this position should not be regarded simply as an inevitable result of the historical point of view, which itself is an inevitable aspect of scholarly theology as well. Rather such historricization of Israel often implies an evaluation—loaded with theological affect—of Judaism as a form of paganism. This tradition includes in its unbroken line the recent generations from Adolf von Harnack to Paul Althaus[1] and Günter Klein,[2] to name but a few names as examples. According to this line of argumentation, the Jewish No to Jesus Christ means the end of the particular election and calling of Israel and that the chosen people has been relegated back into the world of the gentiles.

One can debate the value of this argument for a long time. To give it the most favorable interpretation, this "re-paganizing" thesis is only an auxiliary phrase to give some kind of Christian basis for a historical, and therefore categorical, i.e., *a priori*-binding universalism within scholarly theology. This is demonstrated in every case where—as for example in Gerhard Ebeling[3]—"justification by faith alone without the works of the law" is seen as the valid precondition par excellence for a theology that practices historical criticism without prejudices and is therefore, under present-day circumstances, genuinely scholarly. The Reformation principle *sola fide* [by faith alone] allegedly "destroys" the salvific value of every specific history, leads into the ambiguity of everything historical and therefore into what is truly historical, which, given that it is historically relative, no longer knows any sacred space. Above all, it "demolishes" any reliance on history that might make the decision of faith unnecessary and thus leads into the arena where the notion that good works save us is overcome. To put it another way, present-day Protestant theology seeks its self-justification in the context of an understanding of reality in which, as a result of the formation of categories, everything historically outstanding and unique is, if not excluded outright, certainly pre-determined for relativization or even destruction.

What has up to now scarcely been recognized are the consequences of this connection of the central doctrine of Protestant the-

---

1. Cf. Paul Althaus, *Die letzten Dinge* [The last things], 6th ed. (Gütersloh: Bertelsmann, 1956) 313 (with quotation from Th. Kliefoth).

2. Cf. Günter Klein, "Römer 4 und die Idee der Heilsgeschichte" [Romans 4 and the concept of salvation history], in G. Klein, *Rekonstruktion und Interpretation: Gesammelte Aufsätze zum Neuen Testament* [Reconstruction and interpretation: Collected essays on the New Testament] (Munich: Kaiser, 1969) 162.

3. Gerhard Ebeling, "Die Bedeutung der historisch-kritischen Methode für die protestantische Theologie und Kirche" [The meaning of the historical-critical method for Protestant theology and church], in G. Ebeling, *Wort und Glaube* [*Word and Faith*], (Tübingen: Mohr, 1960) 1ff., especially 45.

ology (construed in a very existentialistic way), on the one hand, and the understanding of what is truly "scholarly" as regards its capacity to understand and grasp the concept of Israel and Judaism, on the other. What can one understand and grasp theologically about a people that is constituted in history by the law and its works, that is, by the Torah, a people that exists in history principally and in actual fact in segregated particularity and therefore amalgamates "faith decision" and "historical certification" into one whole?[4]

It is more than likely that the effective grounds today for the general resistance of scholarly theology to any understanding and overcoming of theological anti-Judaism even after 1945 can be found in the modern fusion of the Protestant doctrine of faith and the theory of what constitutes scholarship. For general and widespread anti-Judaism in exegesis, doctrine, and practice is not just the subjective conviction of individual scholars or merely the result of particular research in exegesis or dogmatics. It is cemented methodically because it guarantees "the method."[5]

This is not the place to pursue this alarming point of view in detail. But we must name it simply because it may from the outset exclude a new Christian position towards the Jewish No and rob it of any scholarly significance and, secondly, because if one seeks to establish a new position, one needs to be aware of this.

We ought not to deceive ourselves: if our observation is correct, what we have here, given its presupposition and result, is simply a modern, "scholarly" objectivized replay of the old Christian anti-Judaism. The language about the hardening of the heart, rejection, disinheritance, and cursing of Israel as the divine answer to the Jewish No to Jesus Christ, was also not left confined to the domain of prophetic preaching in early Christian history and the Middle Ages. The preaching of God's No against Israel was translated against the Jews in the form of every known social, economic, political and physical manner as well. The word of faith was integrated into the whole social and intellectual system and stamped Judaism as a provocation. It "disturbed" the entire

---

4. Cf. Friedrich-Wilhelm Marquardt, "Erwählung und Normalität" [Election and Normalcy], *Emuna: Blätter für christlich-jüdische Zusammenarbeit* 4 (1969) 41ff.

5. Charlotte Klein's perceptive and eye-opening study *Anti-Judaism in Christian Theology* (Philadelphia: Fortress, 1978) could be strengthened and further developed in light of this perspective.

understanding of the universal reality then no less than today in that it could be subsumed or relativized neither in the social nor in the ecclesiastical realm. So it could be tolerated only in negating its independence, which affected, then as now, not only its theological meaning, but also its political and physical existence.

Those less determined in such a total theological negation of Judaism than those in the two traditions mentioned above were concerned with developing an auxiliary construction in both a salvation-historical and a systematic-political form. They sought to honor Israel's meaning prior to the birth of Christ and to see the Judaism, which repudiated the gospel, in the light of a great salvation-historical future. But that, too, is finally based more on not knowing what to do with present-day Judaism "between the times."

Of interest in this connection is a remarkable, but little known concern of Luther's. Given the historic uniqueness and specific nature of Judaism, he was prepared to revise his concept of the "two kingdoms" and the anti-Judaic implications that arose from the basic distinction between law and gospel into a "three kingdom" concept. In his "Instruction to the Christians on how to submit to Moses," he experimented with the following ideas: "There are now two kingdoms: the secular in which the sword rules, and is seen outwardly; and the spiritual where the spiritual rules alone with grace and forgiveness of sins; this kingdom is not viewed with physical eyes, but is grasped alone by faith. But between these two there is yet another kingdom, set in the middle, half spiritual and half secular, which encompasses the Jews with the law and external ceremonies, showing them how they should conduct themselves before God and humankind in their behavior in the world."[6]

Luther's readiness to allow changes in his own system of reality and in the construction of his own method is important. For it makes it difficult to maintain a simple dialectic in distinguishing between the divine kingdom and the secular kingdom in order to make room for Judaism without forcing it to be assimilated into the system. It is true that the description of the Torah in Luther's denigrating expression "external ceremonies" is insufficient. But the kingdom, which encompasses the Jews, remains also for him a kingdom of Jewish service "to

---

6. "Eine Unterrichtung, wie sich die Christen in Mosen sollen schicken," in Martin Luther, *Ausgewählte Werke* IV, ed. Hans Heinrich Borcherdt and Georg Merz, 3rd ed. (Munich: Kaiser, 1957) 181–82. —Trans. Andreas Pangritz.

the world," thus a kingdom with a specifically Jewish mission, which is neither comprised in the secular nor in the spiritual rule of God, but rather "is set in the middle."

Luther did not do any more work on this idea about a "third kingdom" of the Jews, so it is difficult to gauge its possible further ramifications. But the attempt acts as something of an unredeemed promise, a pledge to make room for Judaism systematically in the creation of theological categories. To be sure, what Luther points to here has yielded only ambivalence in the position regarding Judaism, as is shown by the unsatisfactory "half spiritual, half secular" that overlooks the indissoluble connection between law and covenant. In case of doubt, such an ambivalent position regarding Judaism generally turns into an anti-Judaic direction, as it did with Luther, another reason why we need to overcome the overtly negative and especially the ambivalent half/half positions. Precisely this forces upon us the conviction that we will have anti-Judaism behind us only when we are able to learn to do something positive with the Jewish No to Jesus Christ.

II

In Jewish self-understanding the No is an act of faithfulness to the Torah.

1. Therefore, for Jews this No has a thoroughly positive value. They would have to understand it as betrayal of God if they responded other than with a No to Jesus Christ. The hardness of the contradiction between Jews and Christians cannot be stated any clearer than in this very clear Jewish confession of faith. That is why Christian reactions are easy to understand that either set an opposite confession of faith, well-founded all along the line, against this confession and answer the Jewish No to Jesus Christ with a Christian No to Judaism—or else dispute the necessity of a logic and theology according to which loyalty to the Torah implies the rejection of Jesus Christ. In the first case the law is subject to radical criticism, in the second a different relationship between Jesus and the law is proposed.

In both cases, however, the question has to be raised whether Christians ever have exposed themselves to the Jewish No and have borne the pain of this contradiction. It might be that we have to face a "God against God" situation in the depth of the Jewish-Christian contradiction, which we can only suffer and come to terms with as an *Anfechtung* [trial or affliction], such as Luther had to learn in his experience between law and gospel, focused as it was on the dimension of the individual. It was this dimension to which Karl Barth pointed when he spoke of the "ontological impossibility" of the rupture between church and synagogue; this was a phrasing molded by historical *Anfechtung*. This makes one realize how little the well-known forms of Christian anti-Judaism seem to be marked by historical *Anfechtung*, above all their present day forms in the situation after Auschwitz, and therefore how questionable their theological seriousness is. Conversely we may say that no Christian pronouncement about Judaism can be taken seriously that expresses itself—whether in total negation to the Jewish No or in an ambivalent relationship to Judaism—only on the level of historical or objective consciousness, thereby claiming a "position," without being tried and afflicted by God through the existence of the Jews. According to the Reformers, "the proper way to study theology" [Luther] is only possible in *Anfechtung*; more than ever this insight should be a valid criterion today especially in the Christian relationship to Israel and should somehow be recognizable in the content and form of Christian utterances about Judaism.

2. It does not make much sense in this context to concern ourselves overly with the reasons for the Jewish rejection of the so-called "historical Jesus." Despite good scholarly investigation, they remain difficult for us to comprehend. All the documentation that has come down to us is from early Christian writings; we do not have any of the contemporary Jewish pronouncements. All the answers we can bring forward are conclusions that can be drawn in various ways.

Therefore it is necessary to distinguish between historical reasons for the Jewish rejection of the historical Jesus and the No of the Jewish confession of faith. For essential aspects of this No can have no meaning for the rejection of the "historical" Jesus: above all not the monotheistic confession expressed in every Jewish life in the daily prayer of the *Shema Yisrael* [Hear, O Israel!]; it does not affect Jesus of Nazareth, it affects Christian theology. We must also ask whether the Messianic question about Jesus could historically have played such a role as it does at the heart of the Jewish No we confront today. Every answer depends very much on the contents of the very diverse constructions of the historical Jesus. Bultmann, among others, portrays Jesus as having no consciousness of being the Messiah.[7] But even in the question concerning the historical Jesus' understanding of the law, there are considerable contradictions among the various theologians and their constructions. It is well known that Jewish scholarship concerning Jesus' understanding of the law portrays him as not at all atypical and outside the realm of Judaism, unlike the Christian presenters, especially again in Germany, for whom it still seems to be a conviction not to be abandoned. This conviction is once again codified *a priori* through a method in which the "historical" Jesus is discovered by excluding what in the New Testament is known as "teachings of the community," but also what may be recognized as "Jewish."[8] What is preprogrammed in the method is that the "historical" Jesus discovered by means of it is of necessity atypical in a Jewish context, even anti-Jewish. These results do not lead very far in understanding historical reasons for the Jewish rejection of Jesus, and serve rather to give even greater necessity for repeating and firming up the principal No of the Jews over against contemporary Christianity.

The decisive opposition therefore is not to be sought between Judaism and Jesus if it is the "historical" Jesus one has in mind. Concerns about "bringing Jesus home" back to Judaism demonstrate this as well. And Christian polemics has to learn from this at least that the difference of faith cannot be historicized in terms of the relation of "the Jews" to "Jesus." That "the Jews" "did not recognize" their Messiah, and therefore "delivered him to the cross," is in historical perspective an impossible, unverifiable claim, and should finally disappear from sermon, lessons, and catechetical instruction.

---

7. Cf. e.g., §4 in Rudolf Bultmann, *Theologie des Neuen Testaments* [*Theology of the New Testament*], 6th ed. (Tübingen: Mohr, 1968).

8. Cf. Rudolf Bultmann, *Die Geschichte der synoptischen Tradition* [*The History of the Synoptic Tradition*], 4th ed. (Göttingen: Vandenhoeck & Ruprecht, 1958) 132ff., 222; Ernst Käsemann, "Das Problem des historischen Jesus" [The Problem of the Historical Jesus], in E. Käsemann, *Exegetische Versuche und Besinnungen* I (Göttingen: Vandenhoeck & Ruprecht, 1960) 205; also Eduard Schweizer, "Der Menschensohn" [The Son of Man], *Zeitschrift für neutestamentliche Wissenschaft* 50 (1959) 201, says: There is relative "certainty that we have before us a *logion* [word] of Jesus, when this can be explained neither from late Judaism nor from the situation of the early community."

The opposition is rather between Judaism and the gospel that arose in response to Easter, between Judaism and Christian confession of faith and Christian theology.

Here, too, the intersection, viewed historically, is more questionable than certain. Does the apostle Paul really play the divisive role, which until now both sides, the Jewish no less than the Christian, have attributed to him?

Indeed Paul is the earliest Christian writer of the New Testament, and yet his relationship to Jesus is already determined by the full weight of the Christian creed. In addition Bultmann can rightly name him "the first Christian theologian," and it is precisely his relationship to Judaism that carries Paul to the lofty heights of a spiritual reflection that is not easily reconnected to real Judaism and must first go through a whole series of levels of abstraction. Without a doubt he initiated a history of profound anti-Jewish consequences to this very day, a history, which runs from Marcion to Augustine and Luther, and finally to today's theological anti-Judaism.

But on the other hand, there is now a lot under way on both sides in regard to Paul. Although it has not yet come to "bringing Paul back home" to Judaism, there is nevertheless a certain reintegration into the Judaism of his time. And recently there has begun on the Christian side an effort at theological "reparation," like the one Catholic New Testament scholar Franz Mussner proposed in a very exciting way in his commentary on Galatians,[9] the epistle that still serves as a never-ending source of anti-Judaic Christian theology. In both Protestantism and Catholicism, there are under way several wide-ranging new interpretations of Paul's theology. In addition to the already tried and tested German works by Günther Harder and Otto Michel, there are those by Georg Eichholz and above all Markus Barth; they set themselves against the widespread anti-Jewish exegesis of Paul. Not accidentally these are scholars who are involved in the contemporary Jewish-Christian dialogue, who live in relationship to living Jews and for whom this relationship has repercussions on their exegetical work.

---

9. Franz Mussner, "Theologische 'Wiedergutmachung' am Beispiel der Auslegung des Galaterbriefes" [Theological "reparations" on the example of the commentary on Galatians], *Freiburger Rundbrief: Beiträge zur christlich-jüdischen Begegnung* 26 (1974) 77ff.

This means, however, that today Paul is once more an open case. Because it is unavoidable in Christian-Jewish relations to refer to Paul, given his great authority and his impact in history up to now, discussing him can only take place in an openness that does not let itself be intimidated by a commonly accepted view achieved however arduously by so many New Testament scholars.

3. We called the Jewish No to Jesus Christ an act of confession. This must be shielded against possible Christian misunderstanding. Just as there is no Jewish theology comparable to Christian theology, so there is also nothing such as a Jewish doctrine or normative creed. What we call "confession of faith" is for Jews a unity of prayer, day-to-day conduct, and martyrdom. The daily prayer of the *Shema Yisrael* and the daily performance of the acts of justice prescribed by the Torah have their apex in the *Kiddush Hashem*, the hallowing of the divine name in the sacrifice of life. What we, drawing on the thought-forms of history of religion and philosophy, call "monotheism," claiming it to be something uniquely Jewish, is—if we ignore those thought-forms—actually the lived unity of prayer, day-to-day conduct, and martyrdom. It is not a theory, not a theological statement or creed. If abstract language has to be used at all, it is an "ethical monotheism," as Leo Baeck emphasized again and again.[10] Hence, it is not so much a theory about the uniqueness and oneness of God but rather a self-unification or integration with the God of Abraham, Isaac and Jacob always to be accomplished anew by every Jew and by the people of Israel as a whole. There is a twofold identification taking place: In that Israel unifies itself with its God, it identifies him ever anew as the God of the covenant and itself as God's people. Thus, it is more a historical self-identification that takes place here than a theological-theoretical truth to be analyzed, criticized, formulated or discussed.

In principle, this may be true for Christianity as well—if only we were rid of our wretched differentiation between "confession" and "confessing." Here the difference between Judaism and Christianity is to be found in what historical identity means here and there. The Christian confession is essentially provoked by ever changing theological heresies and is an answer to false doctrine or teaching. (Of course, there is al-

---

10. Cf. Leo Baeck, *Das Wesen des Judentums* [*The Essence of Judaism*], 2nd ed. (Frankfurt am Main: Kauffmann, 1922) 83 etc.

ways an ensemble of political and social factors at play as well, which, however, is said to be of no decisive significance, as the resistance of the Confessing Church and the Barmen Declaration would indicate.) On the other hand, both everyday experience and the experience of the historical process and its affects on the bare life and survival of the Jewish people enter into the *Shema Yisrael* and its meaning. What moves a Jew every day in the *Shema Yisrael* is certainly not chiefly the invocation of the oneness of God, as if in opposition to the Christian doctrine of the Trinity. Rather it is the attempt to throw oneself into the transcendence of the God of Abraham, Isaac and Jacob, in order to be able to stand the needs of daily Jewish existence in everyday world history and to be able anew to exist safely and self-consciously in faithfulness.

There are consequences to be drawn from this difference for an understanding of the Jewish No to Jesus Christ. The depth and foundational nature of its meaning cannot be comprehended in an isolated historicizing observation of the relationship to the earthly Jesus or from the conflict with Paul and its pre-suppositions and consequences. That is, isolated, historicizing grounds do not get to the substance of this No and its grounding in Jewish self-understanding. However necessary they are for our modern historicizing consciousness, diverse historical-exegetical corrections do not yet create the cognition we need in Christian-Jewish relations.

To put it briefly: Israel's conflicts for survival have throughout left their mark on Israel's faithfulness to the Torah. That is true in New Testament times before and after 70 CE, in the fight against Rome and for the maintenance of the unity of the people, which Jewish-Christians rebuffed politically. And it is true in the ages of Islamic and Christian imperialism and their demands up to the modern imperialisms of capitalism, fascism, and communism. For Jewish Israel all of these struggles had the inner dimension of a struggle for the First Commandment and, conversely, the First Commandment was for Israel, in its lack of worldly power, the only possibility of resisting.

We Christians must learn to comprehend the Jewish No in this context. It cannot be separated from the whole history Israel was sucked into. Nor can it be separated from the part of the historical processes dominated by Christians in the West and in the European colonies. This No is addressed to us Christians in our relationship to Judaism, and only then is it addressed through us to Him, Jesus Christ. It is quintessentially Jewish thought—analogous to the confessional structure of unifying oneself [with God]—when Jews ultimately cannot know Jesus Christ apart from Christians, and when it is not possible for them to make a distinction between Lord and servant, between the believers and Jesus Christ. The covenantal understanding of the God-humankind relationship is the basis on which Jews refuse to follow a Lord whose servants beat them. And it has nothing to do with historical psychology, but indeed with faithfulness to God, that Jews reject the pagan dualism, which would be the precondition for a "pure" relationship with Jesus, untouched by any historical experiences. The protest of the Jewish No is directed against this dualism.

What does this mean for Christians? We will have to speak about something basic in a moment. But given the way things are, a difficult and bitter psychological effort will be required of us first: we need to acknowledge that the inner logic and consistence of the Jewish No is directed against us and that it is rooted there. But more than that, we must also recognize the uncontested theological content, the truth that is contained in this No. We need to do this even when it is directed against the total corpus of our theological insights.

We, especially in the Protestant tradition, are not used to taking psychological points of view as somehow objectively important. Our anti-psychological tradition teaches us to distinguish and keep separate the "matter" of theology from that of history and psychology. This is one of the reasons for the general refusal to offer any "theological reparations" to Judaism that Franz Mussner spoke of. That is precisely why we must speak of it here. In Jewish covenant existence and therefore in Jewish experience and the corresponding logic there is no such pure "matter." The conditions of a life in covenant with the God, to whom the Hebrew Bible witnesses and who, according to orthodox Christian self-understanding is the father of Jesus Christ, contradict strongly this pagan separation between the ideal and the real, between origin and history, between the norm and the actual. We cannot therefore allow Christians, ourselves as well, to use this separation, not even in the re-nowned difference between the *iustus in spe* and *iniustus in re* ("righteous according to our hope, unrighteous in reality"), as long as it serves as psychological self-justification.

So, Christians need to learn that it is in God's name that the psychological vehicles are contested, by means of which they—even when they admit their historical failure—think they can still confront Jews with a pure "matter." Apart from the problems relating to content, this attitude bristles with so much naiveté and psychological ignorance, even insensitivity, that there ought to be no cause for pride. It is precisely this psychological insensitivity that renders us unreceptive to what "matters." We can no longer afford it and justify it in any form simply because it makes us theologically unobjective.

The difficulties into which we are plunged are serious indeed and we do not know in advance how we shall save our skins. But though there may be many things, even important things in life about which we do not dispute: *de fidei est disputandum*—there must be disputes about faith!

This not only presupposes that one keeps oneself generally open for arguments in matters of faith but also that one can indeed and truly be touched. No one can really stand up for the truth who is not open to question, sensitive and vulnerable in the very depths and able to become uncertain in his/her own self-understanding and creed. If the Jewish No to Jesus Christ were really faithfulness to the Torah, then that would concern not only some favorite faith notions about the meaning and essence of the law but also touch and rattle the content and historical character of the Christian Yes to Jesus Christ. It would touch the very foundations of Christian theology, possibly even the doctrine of the Christian church. And finally, the good Lutheran perception of the church's and her teachers' capacity for error has to become concrete actuality.

In fact, church and theology have to this very day sought refuge in tabooing the Jewish No and, like untouchables, have kept everything essential at bay. That is completely understandable from the perspective of psychology and sociology of religion, but after all it is a religious reaction and it is more than questionable whether it is an attitude guided by truth.

Psychological and sociological reservations always point to questions of power that are played out in individuals as well as in collectives and institutions, not least in the drive for self-preservation and the desire for power on the part of scholarly communities with their common convictions. And especially the Christian-Jewish relationship has always been, materially and historically, a field of power struggle, at least from the Christian side: There is no other explanation than that most of the time this relationship has been pushed to the very threshold of being and non-being; today "enlightened" scholarly theologians and "convinced" Christians still let themselves be carried away using language of destruction that makes someone like David Flusser call for the police.[11] These power structures turned the famous Christian-Jewish dialogues of the Middle Ages into a farce. This too is an experience that is part of the Jewish No. Above all else, renunciation of power born in the depth of the soul would not only be a physical but a truly intellectual and scholarly pre-condition for opening ourselves to Judaism and learning to see it as it is rather than our concepts would like it to be. It would be a renunciation also of those more subtle forms of power that function today even where a Christian-Jewish dialogue is affirmed and a high degree of willingness to learn is demonstrated.

For example, in his answer to Helmut Gollwitzer, Gershom Scholem showed how strongly even a renunciation of the anti-Judaic tradition and the appeal and reference to "original Christianity" will meet Jewish defensive reaction as long as the difference between tradition and origin is supposed to give grounds for a better Jewish standard in the dialogue. Jews feel themselves coerced by this to forget the integrity and the connection of their experiences with anti-Judaism without having what is originally Christian offered to them as a reality on which they can rely.[12]

Something similar occurs when theologians participating in dialogue devalue the Jewish "bringing Jesus home" as a theological liberalism left behind long ago, indicating thereby that the only item up for discussion with Jews is the Christian creed in its full scope and weight.[13] As in the Middle Ages, the theme of the dialogue is dictated

---

11. David Flusser, Besprechung von Charlotte Klein, *Theologie und Anti-Judaismus* [Review of Ch. Klein, theology and anti-Judaism], *Freiburger Rundbrief: Beiträge zur christlich-jüdischen Begegnung* 27 (1975) 138ff. Cf. 139: "Has anyone every thought that such words and similar sayings are subject to police arrest, or that they, naturally indirectly, incite to murder?"

12. Gershom Scholem, Zum Verständnis der messianischen Idee im Judentum. Mit einer Nachbemerkung: Aus einem Brief an einen protestantischen Theologen [Toward an understanding of the messianic idea in Judaism: With an afterword: From a letter to a Protestant theologian], in: *Über einige Grundbegriffe des Judentums* (Frankfurt am Main: Suhrkamp, 1970) 168ff.

13. Cf. in this context the strange saying by Julius Wellhausen, *Einleitung in die drei ersten Evangelien* [Introduction into the first three gospels] (Berlin: Reimer, 1905) 114–15: "The historical Jesus, not just in recent times, is elevated to a religious principle

already before the question can be raised and weighed whether "bringing Jesus home" in the Jewish context might be and mean something very different from theological liberalism. Renouncing power would imply renouncing a historical consciousness purely analogous to the European-Western experience.

And again something similar happens when—though not in the historical, but even more in the full theological sense—the message is sent to Jews that they, as Jews and in their own identity, can make an impression on the Christians when they—as each of us—do not deny their part of the guilt in the death of Jesus Christ, when they would not put the blame historically on the Romans but freely accept and confess their responsibility. Precisely in so doing could they substantiate for us their No to Jesus Christ most impressively.[14] That is the way we would like to have it and, as far as we are concerned, it would also be right and proper *sub specie Dei* [under the aspect of God]. But should it not unsettle us theologically when Jews insist that things must be correct historically if they are to make sense theologically? And is it not really our hunger for power that is unmasked when we—let us be honest here: on the highest theological level—were once again to treat the historical connection simply as a "Gordian knot" to be cut in order to be able to discuss things only "under the aspect of God?"

The confessional structure of Judaism we spoke about balks at such examples from recent years and puts us before the immense difficulties, even *aporiae* of the Christian-Jewish relation. We are made to recognize that the thought-form of the "original source" [*Ursprungsdenken*], which is so familiar to Protestant theologians who in principle reduce

---

and set against Christianity. There is sufficient reason to distinguish his intentions from his results. Nevertheless one can not comprehend him without his historical results, and if one separates him from them, one cannot do justice to his meaning . . . Without the gospels and without Paul, Jesus continues to be held fast in Judaism (!), to which he clinged, although he grew beyond it (!). There is no way back to him [a historical Jesus], even if we wanted to."

14. Cf Hans Joachim Schoeps, "Möglichkeit und Grenzen jüdisch-christlich Verständigung" [Possibilities and boundaries of Jewish-Christian understanding], *Theologische Literaturzeitung* 79 (1954) col. 73ff. In col. 74 Schoeps quotes a comment by K. Barth to his draft of a *Theologie des Judentums* [Theology of Judaism]; Barth asks, whether a "Theology of Judaism" also and particularly in these times (namely in the year 1934) ought to culminate in the proof that Jesus had to be crucified and that therefore the responsibility for the crucifixion *had* to be taken even today by any singular Jew.

their thinking to the *solus Christus, sola fide, sola gratia* [Christ alone, faith alone, grace alone], is or can be an expression of power here as well when we seek to separate history and its results form the source and origin.

Thus, we have to learn a mode of thinking and practice a way of acting that does not control its origin and that cannot claim to have the purity of its origin. We do not have power over our "matter;" no: we are beggars. This applies particularly to the relation between the origin and effects of Christian theology. And therefore, in face of the Jewish No to Jesus Christ, we possess no superior possibilities, no better knowledge, and do not occupy a more advanced historical level. On the contrary: The Jewish No shakes us only the more strongly in our beggar-poverty and powerlessness.

III

We should learn to consider the Jewish No to Jesus Christ, as far as its substance is concerned, as enmity for our sake.

1. In Romans 11:25ff., Paul had a positive evaluation in mind of what we horribly are used to call "Jewish unbelief" (that is, in Jesus Christ). The Jewish rejection of the gospel made room for the entry of non-Jews into the salvific activity of God. If "the" Jews had followed Jesus Christ, the world mission and the building up of the ecumenical enterprise would have become a "purely Jewish" thing. It would have remained entirely in Jewish hands. But now their No forced God to achieve the divine goals through other means. God took things back into his own hands in order himself to enter humankind in Jesus Christ and thus to promote the divine goals in a new way. It happened that, against their will, the Jewish No served God's own good purpose nonetheless. God did not at all reject his people but assigned the new world historical movements to the meaningful context of the history of Israel and thus justified the people of Israel.

Christian theology has sometimes interpreted that unanticipated goodness of the Jewish No as something predestined. According to that position, the Jews had to say No according to God's will and, even against their will, had to serve as a demonstration of the superiority of the divine will and the fact that it alone is efficacious. Their No belonged to the divine necessity in which the sending of Jesus Christ was grounded.

To be sure, this predestinarian interpretation misses the aspects of the will that are at work in the unwillingness of Jews. Therefore one does not even ask about the will in the Jewish unwillingness, given that, as unwillingness, it is already deprived of power and made meaningless by God's will.

But now Paul has communicated his explanation of the salvific meaning of the Jewish No with thoroughly rational intent in order to create understanding, so that we Christians "might not think ourselves wise." Thus, the "mystery" of the Jewish No is intended to create a foundation of understanding precisely for us Christians. And it is not only from the structure of the Jewish confession of faith described above that the Jewish No is directed at us, but also from the apostolic proclamation. So, it might well be good advice to be attentive not to only the will of God but also to the willing in the Jewish unwillingness toward Jesus Christ in order to become really "wise."

2. It cannot be our intention to discuss yet again in well-known academic fashion the anti-Christian positions of Judaism in their "for" and "against." There has been enough controversial theology about such issues as monotheism vs. the doctrine of the Trinity, collective vs. individual Messiahship, covenant law vs. cheap grace etc., with what thus far have been historically fruitless results. Jewish and Christian skepticism about dialogues of this type, such as Karl Barth's, is justified. Skepticism is apt here especially because the well-developed forms of thought in the various dialogues in the Western world and its differentiation of concepts and its antitheses, its syntheses and dialectics, paradoxes and utopias, seem to be so completely worn out that they and their compulsion to progressive abstractness do not allow openness for a possibility of encounter, for a biblical "recognition." In addition, all such scholarly endeavors fail because the social context is being lost more and more, from which these Western forms of thought have emerged and which they mirror. Therefore, within a church and an unrepentant Christianity, without an inclination to offer a theological reparation, academic attempts remain a game with glass beads and of necessity provoke such protests as that by Scholem against Gollwitzer.

For the time being, we therefore see our task in expressing how much the Jewish No affects us, accepting the uncertainties it creates for us, and in shedding the armor of our well-structured self-evident truths and self-understandings. May the Spirit grant the Christian consciousness to be convulsed, which thinks of itself as "immediate" but is in truth altogether mediated, for there are today no greater opponents to the Spirit than the forms that have grown up and developed to protect us from such convulsions but that only blind us to movements in reality. I have in mind the kind of tremors Zionism has created in Judaism for more than a hundred years but that have barely registered any aftershocks in Christianity. This holds Christians in a fatal historical imbalance and inequality over against the history of Israel.

We inquire therefore about the positive in the Jewish No. We start from our consternation and that way seek to grasp the Jewish "enmity" as intended "for our sake."

IV

1. Were the Jewish No to Jesus Christ really faithfulness to the Torah, it would not automatically mean that we who confess Christ are all unfaithful. But it would mean that "God knows thousands of ways to save from trouble" and that we ought to be able to recognize most clearly and embrace at least two of them in their distinction and difference theologically. God would then be God differently to Jews and differently to non-Jews. That is, God would reveal himself to each of them through different meanings of the law and necessarily also through different meanings of Jesus Christ.

Some time ago, Markus Barth, drawing on much preparatory work on the law, came to the following conclusion that may possibly shake up not only exegetical knowledge but also the whole structure of doctrine in the Christian tradition:

> The connection that is evident in the Pauline epistles between Jesus Christ, the Holy Spirit, and the fulfillment of the law forces one to rethink once again all the Augustinian, Thomistic, Reformation and later teachings about the law. The main cause for this is the following: According to Paul, God's holy, just and good law (Rom 7:12.24) is given solely and alone to the People of Israel. Every attempt to declare it as being valid for everyone

(even if only, according to the formulation of my father [Karl Barth], as the "form of the gospel"), is disputed radically by Paul. In Romans 4 and Galatians 3, the apostle declares emphatically that the law is given only to Israel; for only where promise and covenant are given first does God also give the law. So the covenantal love of God is the ground and basis of the law. But if there is no law without covenant and promise, it is nonsense to attempt—in the name of Jesus Christ, as a pedagogical preparation for him, or as a test of true righteousness—to impose the law on those, who "are far from the covenants of the promise" (Eph 2:12), to say nothing of requiring of them individual works of the law as a substitute for complete obedience.

According to Markus Barth, the law is wholly an instrument of the missionary calling of Israel among the nations, for the sake of which it has been elected. The law helps Jews to live as reflections of the righteousness, truth and faithfulness among humankind. The law threatens them with a curse (different from God's anger directed to all sinful humankind), if they break God's covenant and transgress God's law. The law determines them to be a light among the nations, and to spread the voice of God from Zion everywhere. Jesus Christ is *the* Jew who fulfills this determination of every Jew through the law, and he does that as the image of God, as the one subject to God's curse, as the light of the world. He is and does this all as a Jew for all Jews.

The difference in the relationship to the law has an effect on the different meanings that Jesus Christ has for Jews on the one hand and for non-Jews on the other. "According to Galatians 3:13–14 and 4:4–6, the coming and work of the Messiah has different effects for Jews and gentiles. While those under the law are redeemed from the curse, those outside the law receive the blessing of God and adoption as children." For the sin of non-Jews is not the transgression of the law and breach of the covenant, but pagan godlessness and idolatry. Gentiles must first get to know God and become God's children. Therefore Jesus Christ gives into their heart the Holy Spirit of adoption as children and that is for them the decisive work.[15]

---

15. Markus Barth, "Exegetische Anfragen an das Gesetzesverständnis Luthers und Barths" [Exegetical questions about the understanding of the law in Luther and Barth], in Bertold Klappert, *Promissio und Bund: Gesetz und Evangelium bei Luther und Barth* (Göttingen: Vandenhoeck & Ruprecht, 1976) 256ff.—Trans. Don McCord and Andreas Pangritz.

2. This perspective on Pauline theology must be discussed, and not only exegetically. In terms of doctrine it means nothing short of an earthquake. It shatters the whole structure of our Western fundamental and universal theology, so bound to the thought of a conceptual unity that it leaves no room methodologically for the actual *polymerōs* and *polytropōs*, that is, for the multiplicity of forms of divine speech (as in Heb 1:1). The subjection of theology to the laws of conceptual logic and identity of consciousness has long ago robbed God's universal activity of mercy of its character as event [*Ereignischarakter*] and subsumed it under a universalism that simply claimed an *a priori* and, to a large extent, ideological validity.

Much worse, however, is the fact that behind this coercive conceptual unity there is a practical idolatry, namely turning Jesus Christ into a law, which as such is the target of the Jewish No. To be sure, the confession of Jesus as Lord and God has nothing to do either historically or dogmatically with the heinous "elevation" of a human being to the status of divinity. The language of general history of religion, which speaks in this way, conceals rather than characterizes what is specific in the Christian confession of faith. But it cannot be denied that the theological reflection of old and of more recent times has much too quickly and too frivolously ontologically trivialized the actuality, the polemic, and the protest, which created the need, for example, for the so-called *Hoheitstitel*, the Christological titles of Jesus signaling his "elevated" status. The *pathos* of today's often repeated claim that the designation "Christ" for Jesus was even for Paul no longer a "title," that is, a functional determination of his actual historical activity, but his proper name, personalizes that designation and removes Jesus from the conflict. What is conflict and open process is turned into victory, movement filled with counterclaims into ontology and imperial reign, function has become person, being and power. But wherever this happens, what is decisive in what those titles point to is always lost: the surprising event and the mercy that cannot be earned, in short: the encounter with Him, or: the *humilitas*, the humility, in which he reveals himself and which is the inner connection of his activity on earth and from heaven (for that which we call "revelation" is not a formal designation about his becoming present to us, but the content of the narrative about the humility of the Lord, who comes to us sinners, in order to communicate with us). Events that can be reported, became and become in theological

Christology so quickly the law of a "new being." So Jesus is deprived of his future, and torn out of his *kairos*, the moment of danger, change and transformation, which happens whenever and wherever he appears. Someone like that is not the Jesus Christ of the Bible, for the biblical Jesus Christ in person appears only in an effective *peplērōtai ho kairos,* "the moment is fulfilled." He cannot be overpowered by the conformism of person and being without losing his identity.

That manner of making a law of Jesus Christ occurs every time "faith in Him" is made into a requirement and precondition of the participation in His salvation. This naïve and formalistic logic is for the most part not aware that it conceives the reality of the mercy of Jesus Christ as a kind of apodictic or casuistic commandment, and demands that one relate to the Savior as to a new law. How such a relational requirement between him and the participation in his salvation tears apart the person of Jesus Christ, who not only brings, but is, salvation!

Turning Jesus Christ and faith in Him into a law deprives him of his divine identity and autonomous activity so that he can be transplanted into our legalistic consciousness. The most radical conclusion from this is that the only thing that is really real is what I genuinely experience in my consciousness. Faced with the Jewish No, the conclusion arrived at with this more than questionable psychology and theory of knowledge is one of utterly primitive logic: they don't believe in Him, therefore He has nothing more to do with them. This seemingly persuasive and certainly historically still effective logic represents nothing that can be called true but only sectarian psychology and ghetto spirit.

It may seem paradoxical, but it has deep theological meaning, when the "Jews of the law" resist such a Jesus Christ turned into a law. In so doing they function in a threefold sense as advocates of pure grace.

In the first instance, they say that the law into which Jesus here appears to be forced, has really nothing to do with the essence of the Torah of Israel, for the Torah is not a "way" on which one could strive for "salvation," as has always been claimed by modern Christian theology. The Torah of Israel is already grounded in salvation, namely in the covenant that God has made with Israel, in the calling of Israel, and in the promise that is added to this calling. Israel with its law already comes from salvation. Therefore the Torah—contrary to an ineradicably false judgment of Christian polemic—knows no logic of requirements according to which participation in salvation might only be constituted by human intention and activity. If the relationship to Jesus Christ is grasped in such a psychology and logic, another law reigns—seen from the perspective of the Torah—namely a pagan law, according to which salvation is constituted along with faith since a gentile cannot conceive of anything real without the fetish of ego-consciousness. Israel stands as an advocate of God's free grace and sole activity in opposition to this unreasonable pagan demand of an ego-law associated with the proclamation of Christ.

Secondly, no Christ transformed into a law could ever be recognized as the one who brings and fulfills the messianic Torah and as Messiah. Pressed into such a narrow understanding of an ego-identity, Jesus cannot be recognized as the one, to use Luther's words, who has been sent *mutare totam creationem* or *mutare totum mundum*—"to transform the whole of creation, the whole world." In addition, such a Christ—far from being the one who "fulfills" the Torah—would have to be one who destroys the holy, righteous and good, God-given and grace-filled Torah, one who dissolves the structure of the Torah with a pagan legalism and its psychology and mentality. It is faithfulness to the Torah when no door is opened for this pagan problematic to enter into the Jewish context of service.

Thirdly, with this allergic reaction against what is pagan in the church's proclamation of Christ, Jews give Jesus back to us, until we are able to know and to say better what it is we have in him. Tied up in the corset of the conditional logic of faith, Jesus lacks what is precisely the most decisive in him and what the church's Christology can and must affirm: his essential unity with God. For what he lacks there is the very freedom of the creative mercy, the transcendence and superiority, wherein he cannot allow himself to be subject to conditions. It is, therefore, finally the Jewish understanding of God in light of which an understanding of Christ conceived in this way appears unbelievable. And the Jewish No is a protest against the idolatry of Jesus Christ that rules in the pagan transformation of him into a law. So it is faithfulness to the First Commandment, which expresses its protest in the Jewish No.

In relation to this we ask whether this conditional logic really expresses the intention of the New Testament confession of Christ. The answer is: Certainly not! Therefore, it is all the more on target that the Jewish No is directed against an exegesis of the (mainly Jewish) New

Testament under the categories of conditional legalism. This protest also touches the exegesis and doctrine of Reformation theology. Despite its insight concerning the fact that there is no salvation in good works, its teachings about the law only sharpened the conditional logic of the medieval ethic and transformed it into an existential logic, a logic of the "way to salvation." Knowing that neither belief nor unbelief are achievements or spiritual attitudes, is a long way from knowing that the understanding of salvation as an "answer" to a question addressed to us for our "decision" on a "possibility" offered us, is not a departure from but an intensification of the law of conditional logic. For our purposes, it is of greater significance that Christians have not learned to attribute to others, let alone to "the Jews," what they indeed recognized as "pure grace" for their own self-understanding. What anti-Judaism does not want to admit, namely that for Jews, too, nothing but the self-evidence of the merciful God is at issue, is what the Jewish No protests *for*. This No resists the usurpation in effect in the conditional logic that considers itself able to represent God's decision about how God will relate to humankind. It resists the "only one way" pressure implied by this logic, which denies the possibility of God's many ways of acting. It resists the confusion of how humans form their values and God's word. It resists the insertion of any intermediate instance able to judge between God and humankind, and the human arrogance contained therein. And thus the Jewish No calls into question the idea of justification that claims to be able to know the score of God's final decision out of the perfection, either from a Gnostic perspective—*ēdē gegonen* ("it has already happened") or from a Christological perspective—*tetelesthai* ("it is accomplished"). The Jewish No with its rejection of every arrogance of power is directed radically against the preconditions of power that lie in the Christian proclamation of the once and for all transformation of everything that has already and decisively been achieved. The Jewish No denies the completeness of the world and, accordingly, the right to those ultimate logical or factual judgments. *Therefore, the Jewish No attacks the practice of Christian anti-Judaism through Christianity's very theology, it attacks this theology through that theology's very logic, and it attacks this logic through this logic's very ontology. And in this it is faithfulness to the Torah of the free and transcendent God, the God of the First Commandment.*

An interjection. We present the Jewish "enmity for our sake" as an attack on the thought forms and methods, the theoretical presuppositions, and formalized results of Christian theology. And thus it is an attack on our theological workshop, our means of production, that is, the field for which we as theological workers are responsible, reflect on, and where, in principle, we can change something. The categories of universalism and dualism, *a priori* definitions, and historical differentiations and procedures of exclusion, but also the ideologizing of our understanding of academic scholarship through forms of theological legitimation, etc.—none of this is found in the Bible. They possess no other dignity and necessity than that of our choice and our rejection. For that we alone are responsible as good or bad craftspeople of our academic discipline.

But now there exist today much more radical attempts to get rid of Christian anti-Judaism. The "Holocaust" theology developing in America in recent years sees in Auschwitz and in the emergence of the state of Israel not merely a crisis of Christian theology and its means of production but, in part, a collapse of Christian dogma itself. Sometimes the question is already being raised about revising the New Testament *kerygma* [proclamation] itself. Some scholars are reflecting on a direct historical line from certain New Testament expressions and structures to the crimes of the Third Reich and to the absence of Christian resistance, or at least to the ineffectiveness of Christian resistance against the Reich.[16]

It is indeed impossible to remove oneself from these radical propositions, if only for the reason that it ought to shame German theologians that such efforts of repentance and of "reparation" that must also be achieved precisely in academic theology, are undertaken today not in Germany but, vicariously in our place, in America. The fact that in the USA the Vietnam experience forms the background for discovering and working on the "death and resurrection" of the Jewish people as a *scandalon* for Christian theology, shows just what dimensions of reality itself are called into question theologically. Theological anti-Judaism has

---

16. Cf. Nathan Peter Levinson, "Der Holocaust und seine Lehren heute" [The Holocaust and its message for today], *Freiburger Rundbrief: Beiträge zur christlich-jüdischen Begegnung* 27 (1975) 24ff.; Alice and Roy Eckhardt, "Christentum und Judentum: Die theologische und moralische Problematik der Vernichtung des europäischen Judentums" [The theological and moral problematic of the annihilation of European Judaism], *Evangelische Theologie* 36 (1976) 406ff.

certainly to do not only with the relationship of Christians to Judaism, but is an indication for the blindness against reality as a whole, the reality of God, but no less to the reality of the world.

This more radical American probing corresponds more appropriately to the challenge posed to us since it considers from the outset and in a completely different way the practical-historical level where the Christian message has its effects—much more than we are doing with our more limited theological-theoretical considerations.

Nevertheless, we think that our considerations, not intended to contradict the American ones, are more appropriate for our situation here today. It is true that Christianity has throughout its history used the theological disputes as an alibi, in order to remain in power and to spare the *schēma tou kosmou toutou*—the "form of this world" any of those transformations that are contained in the confession to Christ, in the heart of Christian faith (even according to Luther: *mutare totam creaturam, mutare totum mundum*! [to transform the whole of creation, the whole world]). It can be a sign of timidity in face of radical trans formation to keep on calling for theology since we know that this too can still be covert form of self-assertion and striving for power. In the working group "Jews and Christians" at the *Deutscher Evangelischer Kirchentag* [German Protestant Church Congress] we have long since come to the insight that it is not on the theological but on the practical political level of common prophetic witness against the *kosmos houtos* [this world] that alienation and guilt between Christians and Jews can be overcome.

But it was precisely theological anti-Judaism, which caused or at least legitimized in history the enmity against the Jews that has had such deadly consequences. And now it is once again theological anti-Judaism that prevents the churches from getting beyond general declarations against anti-Semitism and from bringing about transformations in Christian substance. In addition we are aware of the continuing connection between life and thought, which prevents us from throwing theology on the scrap heap.

But above all: none of us could and would assume responsibility for destroying and dissolving the Christian *kerygma* and *dogma* [proclamation and doctrine] in which our identity as Christians is constituted. Responsibility for this *kerygma* and *dogma* is not ours to take on. We are subject to them in a manner like Israel in its faithfulness to the Torah:

it is not open for discussion; our whole effort consists in attempting to subordinate ourselves to them again and again in a free, new insight. *In* this our identity we are asked for repentance and to this repentance belongs the historical structure of our consciousness existing between *kerygma* and *dogma*. Simply to throw them away serves practically no one, since having no history produces only acts of barbarism and new destructive anger, which quickly flash over from something spiritual into something physical. For the time being, we do not wish or are able to follow a certain nonchalance of the just named American considerations concerning this subject.

However, we must take the attack on the theoretical household of our theology more seriously because it is here that we can and must do something. And opening ourselves ever more attentively to the Jewish No will take care of the collapse of our theological constructions. It is not a matter of attending to an abstract "Judaism," nor (in an air of "concreteness") of picking out this or that Jew whom we choose and claim as a new kind of "Jewish protégé" for our theological conscience, but rather of opening ourselves to the Jewish No in which Jews and their Judaism are present to us. The theological means of production are dependent, in their quality and efficiency, on the conditions of production. And to the conditions of production of Christian theology today it belongs that Israel does not die, but lives, and—alongside Christianity—proclaims the glory of the Lord.

V

Nothing human has final or ultimate validity. Everything exists on the boundary. This is true for the Christian Yes in the form of the church's insight. This is true as well for the Jewish No. It has a transitional character not only according to Christian doctrine regarding salvation history, but also according to Jewish self-understanding. It is a judgment about the "not yet" of fulfilled time, and as such a judgment concerning its coming fulfillment through the Messiah. Over against the Christian proclamation about the fulfilled time in Jesus Christ, the Jewish No means a waiting and watching for what might come from it in the world, how it breaks through, what it brings about. But in this waiting and watching the Jewish No represents something decisive par excellence: an "eschatological *proviso*" on the historical level. Here we come to the depth of the position, to the *dignity of the Jewish No.*

The tension between the "already" and the "not yet" of realized salvation is an indispensable moment in the evangelical understanding of justification. It is alive in the individual who, under the promise of the word of God, is both justified and sinner at the same time. But the *proviso* of God's judgment and will is a reality not only in the individual. God's will points to the new heaven and the new earth. God's justifying activity has world-historical dimensions. It divides itself on the level of world history into the witness of the church and the witness of Israel as Yes and No. God's Yes and No are not, however, torn apart in a dualistic fashion. It can therefore only be testified to by the church and by Israel "at the same time."

It is a loss of both eschatology and the reality of God, when the *simul iustus—simul peccator* ("justified and sinner at the same time") of the Reformation understanding of justification is not held as something transitory, but is understood as the ultimate and final determination of the relationship between God and humankind. The charge of just such a lack of eschatological content has to be brought against Karl Barth when he teaches that Israel is a continuing witness to God, but only in the negative form of a witness to unbelief and God's anger. Here Barth misses the will in the Jewish unwillingness and he obscures the insight that the witness of the Jewish No has its roots in the judgment and will of God itself. God has "not yet" allowed the completion of all things, and thereby, just according to the understanding of the Reformers, has "still" reserved for himself everything decisive, the last things, the realization of reality, and has withheld it from us both, Christians and Jews. Israel is the witness in world history of the "not yet" of the divine will. With its No Israel represents the eschatological *proviso* of God himself. It resists the Christian *pathos* about the end of time, the final truth and judgment. It exists as the ferment of the decomposition of all false perfections. With its confession to the transcendence of God *in spite* of Christ—Israel testifies not to an idol-like abstract "God above God," nor to a "hidden God," but to the eschatological *proviso* in God himself, which is not abolished even in the sending of Jesus Christ and which Paul proclaimed with the thought about the eschatological subjection of Jesus Christ, "so that God might be all in all" (1 Cor 15:28).

And Israel's No is a witness to God's freedom before himself and to the *proviso*, which God still upholds before himself and his aims.

Christians need this witness in order for their "unbelieving" brothers [and sisters] in the world to become aware of them. Particularly we theologians need this witness so that we do not confuse the "at the same time" of justification in a pagan way with a logical unity, and above all in order to allow God to be *God in all of his freedom*, that is, to allow God truly to be God. Anti-Judaism, as the non-recognition of the divine positivity of the Jewish No and as attempt not to allow God to be living against God, is a lie—in Jesus' sharp conclusion that whatever is not the truth is a lie—that contradicts the gospel all along the line. By ousting Judaism from the circle of what is normative in a Christian sense, anti-Judaism can only come to be a half-truth—and thus a whole lie. For it refers only to half the witness of the God of Abraham, Isaac and Jacob, as it is witnessed by the church, and it excludes the co-witness of the "simultaneously" witnessing Israel. Only through consideration and appreciation of the Jewish No can Christian theology become true.

But more than that: With its No Israel makes itself into the advocate for every human No to the God who is revealed in Jesus Christ. If one sees the deepest secret of serious atheism as an intellectual, spiritual and practically lived-out keeping the wound of the incomplete, not yet ready world, of the not yet truly human humanity and the not yet experienced "Behold! The dwelling place of God is with humankind," and "God with us," then every serious atheism has its biblical justification in the Jewish No. To say it more precisely: in the Jewish No atheism can come to its seriousness, because here it sees itself really related to the real God and receives its own truth in the openness of God toward himself, in God's own "incompleteness." Here one would also seek and find the justification of non-biblical religion in the face of the Christian message. Moreover, here atheism and religion would become serious, because they could find in the Jewish No their representative for the expectation and future of the Yes and therefore for the expectation and future of their own end and error. It is just in the expectation and future of their own end and error that they are what they are and in this expectation and future their protest against that which is opposed to salvation and opposed to truth becomes forceful and powerful. The dignity of the Jewish No consists in bringing both, the Christian Yes and the non-Christian No, to their *raison d'être* in the reality of God by contesting both their final and ultimate validity in the name of the still living God. Let humankind honor this dignity! Let Christian theology subject itself to this No!

2

Elements Unresolved in Leo Baeck's Criticism of Adolf von Harnack

I

ADOLF VON HARNACK WAS THE MOST IMPORTANT AND MOST ESTEEMED Protestant theologian of the last decade of the nineteenth and the first decades of the twentieth century: as church historian and teacher of the history of doctrine. In the winter term 1899/1900 he gave a lecture at the University of Berlin for auditors of all faculties that very quickly became famous and widely circulated under the title: *Das Wesen des Christentums* [the essence of Christianity].[1] Leo Baeck, the leading Berlin rabbi, answered scarcely a year later in a review, about which I want to meditate here. Baeck's book, *Das Wesen des Judentums* [*The Essence of Judaism*], published in 1905, can also be seen as an answer to Harnack's *Das Wesen des Christentums*. It was necessary, because Harnack, as so often theologians of his (and our) time, found it proper to present *the picture of Jesus and the Christian gospel* against the dark background of an understanding of Judaism that for Jews already at that time, at the beginning of the twentieth century, had to be perceived as a provocation. When I speak of Leo Baeck's criticism of Adolf von Harnack, I am speaking at the same time of a challenge to Christian theology by a Jew, which still today is not superfluous.

I am not giving a historical contribution, but simply speaking of the things that mattered then and unfortunately still matter today. For,

---

1. Published in English under the title *What is Christianity? Sixteen Lectures Delivered in the University of Berlin during the Winter Term 1899–1900*, trans. Thomas Bailey Saunders (London: Williams & Norgate, 1901).

although we are separated by more than eighty years from the encounter of that time—and what years these were, when measured by the relationship between Christians and Jews in Germany!—Baeck's criticism from that period so long ago could be and must be applied today nearly unchanged to quite a lot of great Protestant theology.

But what am I talking about as an *encounter* at that time? Let me make a couple of historical remarks before I get to the things that really are of interest to me. There was no encounter between Harnack and Baeck at that time, neither intellectually, as far as I know, nor biographically. I am not schooled in either Baeck or Harnack and have not worked on the sources, so I am not able to say with certainty whether, for example, Harnack ever reacted to Baeck's review of his lecture, nor whether there was any reaction to any of the Jewish reviews of his book. Leo Baeck's name does not appear in the great biography on Harnack by his daughter Agnes von Zahn-Harnack. This is at least an indication that a reference by Harnack to Baeck, if there was one, was not worth being registered biographically [*buchenswert*] (in terms of Thomas Mann). But that is naturally already an important historical aspect that compels us to place the relationship between Harnack and Baeck in the deep "unrelatedness" of Christian theology and Jewish thought—still at the beginning of the twentieth century, in a time of relative emancipation of Judaism in Germany, and with such a good representative of *liberal* theology and mind as Harnack was. It was not just Christian dogmatism of a traditional *orthodox* origin, which closed, mildly put, if not *blinded* our theology in regard to Judaism in history and the present. Even such a scholarly and humanely liberated Christianity as Harnack incorporated, such a decidedly historical-critical theology as his kept in regard to Judaism a limitation of knowledge, more yet, excluded Judaism from the sphere of ordinary interest and scholarly curiosity. While curiosity has been passed on to us since the classical period as the basis of scholarly capacity, it is Judaism where even such an important scholar as Harnack finds his personal limits, more yet, the limits of his scholarly capacity. One could and would have to make a special study of the relationship between liberal theology, the so-called theology of cultural Protestantism, and Judaism comparing the traditional theology of the nineteenth century with its liberal opponents, in order to come to more precise historical concepts. Liberalism was as little immune to the general anti-Judaic evil of the day as the conservative Christianity of the

Bismarck era. But Harnack was head and shoulders above his "school." Soon after his call to Berlin he became something like a *praeceptor Germaniae* [teacher of Germany], at least a bright star of German academia and its universities. One might have thought that in this esteem the greatest openness and circumspection would have been combined. But in regard to the Jews, who paid attention to Harnack's scholarly production, there was no evidence of such an openness.

How differently that looked from the other side! I mention only a few randomly selected *Jewish references* to Harnack's most famous work, *Das Wesen des Christentums*, which in addition to the review by Leo Baeck we are dealing with here, appeared in rapid succession. After Baeck's review had been published in the *Monatsschrift für Geschichte und Wissenschaft des Judenthums* in 1901, the year after the publication of Harnack's book, the great and detailed review by J. Eschelbacher was published in the same journal in 1902 and 1903 under the title *Die Vorlesungen Adolf von Harnacks über das Wesen des Christenthums* [Adolf von Harnack's lectures concerning the essence of Christianity], a work covering no less than 127 pages! The same author was thereafter continually occupied with Harnack. Two additional titles were published by him: *Das Judentum im Urteil der modernen protestantischen Theologie* [Judaism in the judgment of modern Protestant theology] (1907) and *Das Judentum und das Wesen des Christentums* [Judaism and the essence of Christianity] (1905). In 1902 F. Perles published *Was lehrt uns Harnack?* [What does Harnack teach us?] (published again in 1912 in his *Jüdische Skizzen* [Jewish Sketches]). Likewise in 1902, M. Schreiner published *Die jüngsten Urteile über das Judentum* [The latest judgments about Judaism]. And while Leo Baeck was not satisfied with his review on Harnack, but felt compelled to offer his counter-treatise *Das Wesen des Judentums* (first edition 1905, second 1922), other comparable attempts appeared soon: S. Mandel's *Das Wesen des Judentums* (1904), even before Baeck's work and with the same title; S. Kaatz' *Das Wesen des prophetischen Judentums* [The essence of prophetic Judaism] (1907) and the work by M. Stein *Judentum und Christentum* (1906). And these are only a few randomly selected examples.

The strong Jewish interest in Harnack's book is easily understood. Harnack was one of the most prominent Protestant and Christian theologians of his time; and as a theologian at the same time the very "pinnacle" of German academia in general—the last time that a theologian could be seen as the representative of the whole of academia [science and humanities]. He was this not only because of the social and academic positions he soon had attained, but as a scholarly and intellectual "type." As far as his position was concerned, it was Harnack who on August 4, 1914, crafted Kaiser Wilhelm II's "Appeal to the German Nation" [the appeal to war]. His lectures in the winter term of 1899/1900 at "Unter den Linden" [avenue where the University of Berlin is located—trans.] on "The Essence of Christianity" were open to students of all faculties. They were expressly structured and formulated in a generally intellegible way, therefore with public appeal and quickly and widely circulated. So Harnack's works affected Judaism as intellectual and social forces in the public, which could be and, for Jews, had to be discussed. That does not mean that the intensity of Jewish concerns was above all motivated by *intellectual* politics, by defense of Judaism against a supremely powerful Christian voice. Harnack's lectures were of course rather challenging in their content as well.

Thereto I want to make the following remarks in advance: Leo Baeck began his review with a brief demonstration of respect for the scholarship deposited in Harnack's book, saying: "Everyone who possesses enough scholarship as to be able to have esteem for scholarship, will take this book into one's hand with respect." But then Baeck's whole review served, to put it briefly, *to call into question* Harnack's scholarship with unyielding toughness; we will see in which way this works. In contrast to Eschelbacher's Jewish-apologetic review, in which the author opposes Harnack's anti-Judaic judgments point by point with the help of material from Jewish tradition, Baeck aims at the center. He does not to speak as a Jew to a Christian, but as a person "who possesses enough scholarship as to be able to have esteem for scholarship" to the scholar. He aims at the very nerve of Harnack's work, and he does it in such a way that, as far as I can see, hardly one of the Christian critics of Harnack's (who were not cautious at all) can match Baeck in methodologiical sharpness. Pointedly expressed: With his review Baeck undermines basically any possible respect for Harnack's scholarship. And that is something quite different from the intellectual politics of a minority against a dominant representative of the majority. Rather here speaks a superior scholar; I am stimulated by this element of doubt about Christian scholarship. It is a provocation.—Today still, in the so-called Jewish-Christian dialogue, insofar as it is concerned with theology and scholarship, it is not a question first of all of religious contradictions, but rather of a much *too limited* concept of scholarship on the part of Christian theology.

But first let us consider a further aspect of possible Jewish interest in Harnack.

He was not only a recognized scholar; he was at the same time thoroughly in dispute, so much so that in the year 1888 his call from Marburg to Berlin became a full-blown national affair, which finally had to be decided by Bismarck and the emperor personally. It was a problem of the kind that still today one might label "academic freedom." The Protestant churches had deep reservations about Harnack's attitude to central doctrines of the Christian faith: the virgin birth, the resurrection, his understanding of the sacraments; these were stumbling stones already in the way of his call to Berlin. And *in* Berlin Harnack, in 1892, stood in the middle of the so-called "struggle about the Apostles' Creed." That was the question about whether the Apostles' Creed could be replaced in Christian worship and about the binding nature in worship and therefore in faith as well of the doctrine contained in this creed, that is about the binding nature of the uninterpreted literal reading of this doctrine. Harnack's critique of doctrine was less founded on the "world view" of the time, rather it was the result of his historical investigations. Whenever the "genesis" [emergence] of things is looked at more closely the question about their "validity" becomes more complicated, that is, whoever knows the process of the historical development of a doctrine has more difficulty answering the question of its validity for the church than someone who has less historical knowledge. One might therefore think that Harnack, precisely as a Christian critic of doctrine, could be "interesting" in Jewish eyes. The relevance that the *"problem of doctrine"* in religion has in Leo Baeck's *The Essence of Judaism* would make this plausible at least for Baeck.

However, this problem does not yet come up in Baeck's review under the name of doctrine. But in order to determine what it is that occasions the stimulus in Baeck's relationship with Harnack, it is important to observe that he portrays just Harnack, whom he must strike at the very heart of his scholarship, as a theologian who, despite his sharp criticism of Christian doctrine, represents Christian doctrine—just Harnack, who against the heaviest reservations and political resistance of the imperial church authorities could be called to Berlin only in the name of academic freedom! That paradox is what gives the relationship its particular seasoning. But perhaps we need to say here: Jewish interest especially in Harnack is, at least in Baeck, not an expression of intellectual politics of the few against the representatives of the many, as it is in Eschelbacher's review in defence of Judaism. Rather in Baeck someone is resisting *a dominating power hidden in scholarship* in the name of scholarship. Experiences of domination make sensitive to even the smallest, purely intellectual, purely scholarly forms of domination. An awareness of traits of power and violence in Christian doctrine had been awakened in German Judaism at the latest since Moses Mendelssohn. These traits were still present after the end of the dogmatic era of the Middle Ages in Reformation Christianity, even in Protestant theology, which had opened itself extensively to the Enlightenment of the eighteenth and the following centuries. I see the sharp stimulus in Leo Baeck's relationship with Harnack in this Mendelssohnian tradition of sensitivity to *intellectual* power as well.

I am deeply touched by this as a Protestant theologian. When I am asked to speak of something simply unresolved in Baeck's review on Harnack, I will have to speak of a lack of sensitivity to the trait of power, to the dominating nature of our theological scholarship expressing itself in an inability to perceive, in a repression of the knowledge of Judaism adequate to Jewish self-understanding, in a repression of any concern, any interest, any openness for such a knowledge. I cannot get rid of the feeling that this hidden problem of Christian theology at which Jews point us, might not be a problem of Christian theology alone, but perhaps a problem of Western science in general, which is not conscious of the repressive violence contained in its spirit, its methods, its contents, and of its blindness to the fullness of reality. It seems to me that an insensitive, unreflective scholarship is dangerous for all of us in the nuclear age. This is for me the timeliness of the theme.

II

Now, on to the details. Leo Baeck's review has the title *Harnacks Vorlesungen über das Wesen des Christenthums* [Harnack's lectures about the essence of Christianity]. It appeared in 1901, one year after the publication of Harnack's book. Baeck criticizes blow for blow. The main blow is at the beginning: "Contradiction between designation and content." Harnack expressly claimed to speak of Christianity solely "in a historical sense," using scholarly means, excluding religious-philosophical considerations and apologetic intentions. Baeck: "But that remains merely an ideal, about the brilliance of which the reader might rejoice." It did not succeed. Nothing came out but an *apologia* of Christianity and nothing but *polemics* against others, which always is included in apologetics. Baeck is not interested in the fact of the failure of Harnack's intention, but rather with the reasons for the failure.

He agrees with a principle of scholarly historical representation which Harnack stands for: historical representation must reduce the abundance of historical material to "the essential." But there are two forms of "essential": firstly that which was "at that time (in the past) the most important," and secondly that which the historian "today, from the vantage point of the knowledge achieved," regards as essential. "Harnack did not always keep these two forms strictly separated from one another." Furthermore Baeck holds it to be self-evident that, in every report of history the judgments and partisanship of the reporter are mixed in. All the more, therefore, he says, one should be concerned not to *confuse* one's own judgment with the judgment of the period of time past being presented. Actually today's standards of value are always different from those of the past. Harnack wanted to portray the "essence of Christianity," as he called it, "with a 'fresh view for that which is alive.'" It would have been better, suggests Baeck, if he had not viewed history with the eyes of an artist from today, but with the eyes of an earlier time in order to reconstruct the historical essence of Christianity from its history.

That is a basic theme of every historiography and has, it seems to me, nothing at all to do with Jewish-Christian distinctions. Baeck traces Harnack's method back to an *inherited error* of the theological school from which Harnack had descended: the teachings of the Protestant theologian Albrecht Ritschl, for whom theological statements, including faith statements, were *expressions of value judgments*. In Ritschl's school the correctness and even the truth of an expression of faith was derived from its value for a person or a group of persons. Something of a Feuerbachian projection of the thought onto the heavenly screen was in play, and Baeck pointed this out. Harnack's historical method appears to have been carried away from this systematic of value judgments. Baeck draws the consequences from this: Harnack portrays "my" Christianity, the Christianity of his value judgments, he does not portray "the" essence of "the" Christianity and not at all the essence of *historically* original Christianity.

Baeck seeks to show how it comes to this reduction of the historical to what is personally valuable. It is not simply a matter of personal taste. The error is one of method. Baeck observes, for example, that Harnack knows the whole range of concepts of the "kingdom of God," from the prophetic to the apocalyptic that the New Testament passes on as views of Jesus; but authentically "Jesuanic" are for him only statements about an *inward* coming of the kingdom in the soul, all the rest is to be seen as only using the language of the time, not Jesus's own understanding. At first Baeck seeks to instruct Harnack about an important aspect of content—an instruction that Christian theologians have not accepted to the present day. *A distinction must be made between the "kingdom of God" and the "days of the Messiah."* If there is something in Judaism like "political-eudemonistic hopes," which in stereotyped Christian expositions are connected with Jewish hopes concerning the kingdom of God, then it is neccessary to learn that these are at best connected with the "days of the Messiah" and not with the "kingdom of God."

More important, however, is a basic principle of Harnack's historical method quoted by Baeck: "It is also in similar cases regarded as wrong to judge outstanding, truly epoch-making personalities primarily on the basis of what they shared with their contemporaries, and to consign to the background what was unique and great about them." I want to reflect on this methodological criterion briefly, because it became the norm.

1. The criterion of historical method is here clearly at the same time a criterion of *bourgeois* self-understanding. One can hear in it Goethe's Suleika-word from the *West-Östlicher Diwan* [West-East Divan]:

> Volk und Knecht und Überwinder,
> sie gestehen zu jeder Zeit,
> höchstes Glück der Erdenkinder
> sei nur die Persönlichkeit.
> [People and slave and conquerer,
> they confess in every age:
> the highest bliss of the children of earth
> is only personality.]

Goethe expresses it ironically in the *Zahme Xenion* [Gentle Xenion] "The Pantheist":

> Was soll mir euer Hohn über das All und Eine?
> Der Professor ist eine Person, Gott ist keine."
> [What is to me your ridicule about the all and one?
> The professor is a person; God is not.]

The general concept of personality, elevated to an "outstanding, epoch-making personality," serves in any case as a *methodological analog to the understanding of Jesus.*

2. An essential characteristic of such a personality is his/her incomparability: *the "essential" is to be sought in that which is without any analogy.* Of course there is much that such a personality has in common with his/her contemporaries, but that which is in common is not what is essential about him or her.

3. Essential is, on the other hand, that which is *different, distinct,* that "which was unique and great" about the personality.

4. Baeck comments: That could be a "proper principle," if the purpose were to help establish a judgment today. But it is not appropriate for history. Might it not be the case that Harnack, when he declares the *inward* coming of the kingdom to be the exclusive intellectual property of Jesus, he has—*sit venia verbo*—"confused himself with Jesus"? The irony in this question is clear enough, irony not against the "person" of professor Harnack, but certainly against the usefulness of this criterion as a criterion of historical method.

5. In a transformation Harnack's criterion has set a precedent. Rudolf Bultmann, who edited the post-war publication of Harnack's *Wesen des Christentums* in 1950, as well as his students slightly objectified this criterion methodologically; they renounce the concept of "personality" and also the question of essence, that is, the question concerning the essential about Jesus. But in *similar structure* they seek to secure the historical about Jesus in their method. They are of the opinion that one would best meet the original "historical" Jesus in the traditional biblical material by freeing him from two relationships: from that which can be explained in the context of the creed of the Christian community about Jesus and from that which can be explained about him in the context of

Judaism. The "historical" Jesus is one who has nothing to do either with the church or with Judaism.

One could spend a long time reflecting on how to understand the way from the search for the personally "essential" Jesus to the search for the "historical" Jesus.—Although this would be very interesting to me, I am not going to pursue that question here. One could observe in it, *how bourgeois values become imbedded in "historical method,"* and this is a very interesting and important fact from the perspective of criticism of ideology. A slope—the essential is the personal, and the personal is the historical—can be traced from Harnack to Bultmann and Bultmann's students, and Mussolini's "Men make history" is not so far removed from such a view. More important is the fact that Baeck as a Jew can accompany this path only with irony, and I think that such Jewish irony has something very clear and telling to offer just against this slope of the historical. Once more from Goethe: Baeck asks whether all this might not be only "der Herren eigener Geist" [the own spirit of one's Lords].

6. The own spirit of one's *Lords*. For Baeck sees precisely that with such a method everything Jewish is *a priori* declared irrelevant for Jesus, that is, *formally, methodologically*—without even looking at the content and at possible comparisons between Jesus and Judaism, and therefore in a way that from the outset there is no need for any comparison of content. Jesus is, by this method, distilled and expelled from Judaism: the word "distilled" is used in Baeck's review on another place as well. Such a method documents repression and use of violence, and Baeck does not treat it with irony in order to "save" Jesus for Judaism. He was not yet a theologian "bringing" Jesus "back home" to Judaism. (Attempts at bringing Jesus back home to Judaism are something belonging only to the area after Auschwitz.) But at that time Baeck had already for a long time his special Jewish relationship with Jesus, with Paul, with the gospels. He had this as a historian, and his earlier ironic remark concerning Harnack's methodological premise is an expression of methodological, scholarly irony, in contemporary language: ideological criticism of the bourgeois value judgments in the historical method employed.

7. Now, only in passing, because I am really concerned with our present situation (and with what I have called "unresolved elements" in the title of the lecture): In the transformation of Harnack's criterion by the scholars succeeding him this leads to the no longer paradoxical, but

rather absurd consequence that it is no longer only the "essential" Jesus, but even the naked "historical" Jesus who is completely separated from Judaism.—Because this rule is practiced still today and students are taught it already in their preliminary studies, I want us to spend some more time here. One might consider whether this rule, used strictly as a means of heuristics, could possess a relative legitimation. It could initially be of help in order to roughly sift the material, but it would then have to be abandoned immediately in order to make room for examinations of the content. But this is unfortunately not the case. In all presentations making use of this rule Jesus remains, whenever it is relevant, *de facto* removed from Judaism, and that shows that the rule means more than merely a technical aid for the preliminary ordering of the material. There is a *system* bound up with this rule. And therefore Baeck's sensitivity about it was on target. Fortunately there are now— albeit only in most recent times—New Testament historians, Roman Catholic first of all, but also Protestant, who are allowing themselves to be called back to historical reason by Judaism.

III

If there were more time, it would be good to speak more precisely about the series of examples by which Baeck demonstrates how Harnack actually illustrates the message of Jesus nearly exclusively by using the value categories of his own piousness. And the *means* by which he excludes other possibilities of understanding are scarcely *aspects of historical evidence*, but again for the most part nothing but value judgments. It is the observation that Harnack again and again *claims* the "exceptionality" of Jesus in contrast to Judaism, *without giving evidence thereof* in comparison with Jewish material, which upsets Baeck. One example: Because Harnack's religion cannot affirm any ascetic attitude towards the world, he reinterprets any expressions of Jesus in this regard. Because he [Harnack] cannot do anything with world denial and escapism, with discussion of laws, and with the gospel of the poor, he projects, according to Baeck, *his* religion into the religion of Jesus. Baeck regrets the "modernizations" of the gospel taking place here, which "water it down" and "blur it." Again his No is at the same time a piece of ideological criticism of a portrayal of Jesus, which lifts him out of his own historical circumstances and *adapts* him to "modernity." In an attempt at historical interpretation Baeck explains, for example, that Jesus' word about "not resisting evil" is "not only conceivable, but necessary," for in the political situation of that time it might have been "an ethical necessity in the eyes of many and perhaps the best observers" in order to provide for the survival and continuation of Jewish life in the era of the Roman Empire. Harnack, on the other hand, *takes the political edge off* from this instruction and considers it to be directed only to individuals for their individual lives.

It is apparent that Baeck can read *the gospel* in a form that is *much more radical and therefore also much more political* than the way Harnack reads it. Baeck sees an essential lack of "historical clarity" just in the fact that Harnack pays "little attention to the influence that the series of political events that lead to the destruction of the Temple and the fall of Bethar might have exerted." "Too little consideration is given also to the whole temperature of the century in which Jesus lived." "In order to understand Jesus and his disciples and those times, one would have to feel as well in what kind of climate, socially and politically, the Jews in Palestine lived. One ought to know what kinds of people were shaped by the historical events of the time."

"Unresolved" elements in Baeck's criticism of Harnack! It is the *criticism of a presentation restricted to intellectual history* assigning Jesus to the world of theological ideas and thoughts. There is nothing materialistic there! "Materialistic" in the strictest sense of the word: In the sentence, "One ought to know what kinds of people were shaped *by* the historical events," Baeck has the consciousness codetermined by the political structure; people are creatures of their circumstances. And indeed, such an understanding of Jesus is missing from many historical presentations of Jesus on the part of Christians still today. But with that the spice of the gospel is missing as well!

Here Baeck comes to an outbreak of his whole revulsion—now not merely scholarly, but basically Jewish—against the course of Christian theology, to which Harnack forms no exception. Harnack understands, according to the pattern of liberalism, the concept of *God's righteousness*, supported in the New Testament especially by Paul, as something that exceeds our ethical obligations of *doing* what is righteous. According to this liberal understanding Jesus rejects any earthly achievement of righteousness, but he does not stand against "righteousness as such." For "Jesus was, together with all truly pious persons, firmly convinced that

God finally creates righteousness." I suspect that Baeck was irritated by this hesitant, postponing "finally." He comments on this sentence in the following way: "At most a sermon or a book of spiritual edification could argue in this manner." Methodologically, however, Baeck insists, it is impossible to exchange, as Harnack does, the ethical postulate of doing what is righteous with the divine attribute of righteousness, in order to leave to God the concern for what is righteous and to exist in ethical renunciation of righteousness. Baeck declares this transposition of the concepts of righteousness to be forbidden already from a purely logical standpoint: it is a *quaternio terminorum* [a logical fallacy].

But here Baeck goes beyond a criticism merely in terms of scholarly method and he applies a sharp *criticism of Christianity.* "One always knew which properties and names to attribute to God, but much less often one knew that among the properties and virtues of humankind were to be counted a number of things, as for example the liberation of the oppressed, the abolition of all slavery, the elimination of torture and tormenting of humankind, not even to speak of other things. The agonies of a millenium are the illustration of this history of theoretical and practical ethics." This is the *practical Jewish protest against the Christian theory about God.* Baeck calls this theory "the result of the Pauline *an-archia.*"

If Baeck were still alive, I would gladly have tried to show him how in the meantime a rebellious student of Harnack's, Karl Barth (against whom at the time Harnack had uttered the strange charge of "communist quietism"), has found the way precisely from God's justification to the realization of human righteousness: in that year 1938, critical for both Judaism and the Confessing Church. There is, therefore, logically or not, a way from the divine attribute to the human mobilization for freedom and justice. Baeck, however, could not realize this in Harnack, because Harnack himself did not perceive it; the divine made him ready to hope in God's future—but until that time to feel good in the world and not to change anything in it.

IV

Among many other aspects I come finally to a very exciting main thought of Baeck's that is presented methodologically but that at the same time, with respect to its content, is full of *utopia for a kind of Jewish-Christian encounter*, to which we today have perhaps come a bit closer, although it still lies afar off. Baeck reveals a nerve of the conditions for the possibility of a Jewish-Christian encounter, which might truly become an encounter—an encounter of those who are seeking one another and, if God wills, one day may also find one another.

The deepest methodological barrier opposing any honest encounter seems to have become clear to Baeck once again in Harnack. To the present day we do not even know the *point*, where we can be compared with one another and where we therefore could meet. More precisely: It is the Christians who rigorously and with a certain systematic stubbornness pass by the only thinkable *meeting point*.

It is true, in the sign of an unbroken feeling of superiority there may have been already a number of Christian theologians, who no longer carry in their hearts a horror picture of anti-Judaic prejudice: about Jewish casuistry of the law or about Pharisaism, which still according to Harnack thinks of "God as a despot," who "keeps watch over the ceremonial in his household." (Baeck doesn't hide his horror at this caricature that is a "pure invention." "This all is fully thought up and made up!" "What no one would dare to do in any other science that seems—when committed against the history of Judaism—to be unpunished and allowed." Here he charges Harnack simply with ignorance about sources that are completely open and available.) But still, already in Harnack's time there were Christian theologians who saw in Judaism elements of *ethical elevation* and of *religious value*. But it was Julius Wellhausen, an important Protestant scholar of the Old Testament at the turn of the century, who, according to Baeck, formulated a methodological rule enabling Christianity to do away with the competition of what admittedly was valuable in Judaism: "To be sure, there is in the Talmud everything that is in the gospel, but alongside that there is much more." Baeck's commentary: "Rarely a word, in which the importance of the tone stands in no proportion at all to the importance of the content, has been spoken with such a weightiness and repeated with such a reverent zeal like this sentence of Wellhausen's." Baeck's irony!

Since then Jews seeking to point us to Jewish thoughts corresponding to the gospel run up against the charge: these Talmudic thoughts, which can also be affirmed by us, have been intentionally "distilled" by the Jews (here we have once again the word "distilled"), but there is also a great deal in addition that is "Jewish", and therefore the whole is out of question.

Certainly it is true that the same wording in the gospel and in the Talmud does not necessarily indicate that the meaning is the same. Different contexts of one and the same truth can yield different contents of truth. This is the case between Judaism and Christianity simply because Christians had to and still have to interpret the old biblical truths in *pagan* contexts, and these contexts are different from those of Jewish life intellectually, but also sociologically and politically. First Baeck says, against Wellhausen, only: Christianity, too, has a lot of baggage to carry claiming great weight and yet not appearing to be essential. Then Baeck, however, sharpens his argument to the one task before us. We ought no longer to talk past one another. We ought not compare that which is non-essential in the other with that which is essential in ourselves and thus base our results and judgments on such an uneven comparison. Now comes the maxim that moves me very much: "Anyone who is interested not just in a banal aperçu, but rather is concerned with the accuracy and rationality of the content, will compare the gospel of the New Testament at best with the gospel of the Talmud, but not, however, as Wellhausen does, with the whole Talmud. One must examine how the various circles of thought as they are found in the synoptic gospels have found their ascertainment and expression in the Talmud. So one can gain a gospel according to the Talmud. And only this ought to be placed in parallel to the synoptics. Only so does one obtain a scholarly result . . ." "The result would turn out, by the way, even more gripping, if one were to make the expressions of the Talmud in the style of the New Testament; the equality of the spoken forms would make the equality of the content even clearer."

I would like to stop for a moment at the expression "gospel of the Talmud." In the context of the history of our mutual missings this formula is a star glowing in the distance. Just in the expression "gospel" of the Talmud Leo Baeck has crossed the boundaries and made a giant step toward us Christians. Conversely it must still today come as something foreign for the most Christians of traditional shape to hear Jews talk about themselves by the concept of a "gospel," a good, joyful and liberating message. Even today we Christians have not yet existentially grasped the *simchat tora*, the joy in the law. There gleams in this expression a happiness, a joy in being Jewish, while most of us

Christians have thought that we alone possess the privilege of freedom and joy! Baeck instructs us that we are not able to see the "gospel" of the Talmud, because we never have understood the difference between Halacha and Haggada. We read the Haggada as fairy tales, not comprehending that *here* something comparable meets us in Judaism, Jewish theology, speech and story about *God*. It is, to be sure, a very different form and language of theology, but it is theology nevertheless! Because we—in our academic seriousness, which does not appreciate "stories"— do not understand Haggada, we are not able to understand Halacha either. We do not understand how both belong together and what Halacha means, as long as we read and judge it in isolation and compare and measure its "law" with our "gospel." Rather we should read it in its own context, along with the Haggada, where the story is told about the depth of Israel's faith, which gives the Halacha of everyday life the basis, essence and depth of the eternal. If we Christians understood the Haggada, then only we would know what the "religion of the law" (as we have negatively characterized it) really means in terms of religion. Then we would not have the need to pounce on the legal parts of the Torah, in order to comb through them and examine the "absurdities" (the things we, in ignorance, consider to be absurd) with a magnifying glass and then to define that which is really ridiculous as something "typically Jewish." This is what still happens with Harnack's disciple, the great Rudolf Bultmann, and with his disciples. (In the "Jesus" books of our great Protestant theologians one finds in the description of the Jewish law and Torah a passion for digging out single ordinances of the law that give the impression of being merely ridiculous.) And this is what happens in systematic theology as well: "the law" is pretended to be the religion of Israel, it is not understood as the instruction for the realization, use, and testimony of religion. The Christian identification of Jewish law with Jewish religion in general is the result of the fact that we are not able to discern and relate Haggada and Halacha with one another. Since we Protestants above all do by no means want to respect the doing so highly, we ascribe to the Jews the doing as their only religion. What nonsense! Nonsense already over against the Hebrew Bible, where election and covenant are the basis from which the instruction emerges. Leo Baeck presented this so movingly in *The Essence of Judaism*. The fact that also in what we name the "Old Testament" Torah is *both* history and law combined, indivisibly interwoven in one another, so that they cannot be torn apart by historical-critical manipulation, has not lead us Christian theologians to think about the precise meaning of this indivisible interwovenness in Judaism.

If we would think about it, we would no doubt come to the place where we would have to seek and recognize the inner connection point between history and law *in the Jewish people itself*. Then we would have to learn all over again the meaning of the sentence of Leo Baeck's in *The Essence of Judaism,* which has become for me the center of the Christian attempts at understanding in any encounter with Judaism: "Where the modern tendency dominates, to calculate the value of a religion arithmetically, one will hardly be able to do justice to Judaism or to the Bible." And if we were to ask him, why not?, he would answer with the core sentence, "The best in Judaism are, much more than the teachings, the living people." To grasp that, is the unresolved element in Baeck's criticism of Harnack and also of Christian theologians to the present day and therefore also of us. To understand that would be for us Christians a "star of redemption" from our narrow-mindedness. Baeck ignited it as a light for us: The best in Judaism are, much more than the teachings, the living—we have to underline and emphasize that—the *living* people!

3

Martin Buber as a Socialist Zionist

I HAVE NOT CHOSEN THIS THEME. IT WAS GIVEN TO ME BY THE JEWISH Adult Education Center.[1] I am not sure what the expectations were, nor in what connection the special question about Buber's socialism might stand. But I gladly accepted the task and would like to attempt this evening to sketch at least a few outlines of what socialism in connection with Martin Buber's work might mean. I will do this by inquiring about a few critical historical dates important for the socialist movement in Europe and Palestine and then in the state of Israel, and then by asking how Buber reacted to these dates. I have the hope that thereby we might succeed in discovering more precisely, on the basis of the historical material, at least a few of the major concepts of what one might name Buber's socialism.

I

The very early Martin Buber had a preference for the word "revolution." Already in 1903 he planned to write something intended to be a cultural-philosophical work bearing the name "The Creation of Redemption

---

1. Letter quotations are taken from the first two volumes of Martin Buber, *Briefwechsel aus sieben Jahrzehnten* [Correspondence from seven decades], vol. 1, *1897–1918*, vol. 2, *1938–1938*, vol. 3, *1938–1965* (Heidelberg: Lambert Schneider, 1972–1975). The lectures: "Warum muß der Aufbau Palästinas ein sozialistischer sein?" [Why must the upbuilding of Palestine be a socialist one?] and "Rede auf dem XII. Zionistenkongreß in Karlsbad" [Address to the Twelfth Zionist Congress in Karlsbad], as well as the "Kongreßnotizen zur zionistischen Politik" [Congress notes on Zionist politics] are to be found in M. Buber, *Der Jude und sein Judentum: Gesammelte Aufsätze und Reden* [The Jew and his Judaism: Collected essays and speeches] (Cologne: Melzer, 1963). The work *Pfade in Utopia* [*Paths in Utopia*] is to be found in M. Buber, *Werke*, vol. 1, *Schriften zur Philosophie* (Munich: Kösel, 1962).

or: Evolution and Revolution." This book was supposed to appear in the publishing house of Eugen Diederichs. Buber never completed the work. But the title shows something typical for Buber in this early period. The concept of "creating," which he shared with many of his contemporaries interested in philosophical, aesthetic and cultural issues, was taken from the realm of the philosophy of Nietzsche, who made a deep and great impression on him and all thinkers in these early years of the twentieth century. People were supposed to become "makers," "creators"—as with Nietzsche and all his friends in the time thereafter—creating a new world and new conditions in the world.

In 1906 Buber, in a letter to Gustav Landauer, addressed the issue in question something like this; he had invited Gustav Landauer to author a book about the problem of revolution:

> Understandably *the publisher* is interested in publishing soon a volume about the interesting and timely theme, "The Revolution." And *I* cannot help still holding that you are the one called to treat this topic. Do you think I am wrong, and can you with a clear conscience give me just *one* other name? The psychological problem of the revolutionary and of those experiencing the revolution is today more covered up with journalistic phrases than any other social-psychological issue. To whom else can I entrust its restoration? The pre-conditions are: an individual self-experience in an unblemished liveliness, a nevertheless already firmly grounded superiority possessing and mastering what is experienced internally and externally, and an *absolute* honesty—I mean that which is an arch-enemy of what is merely relative. And this as well: not only the publisher, but I, too, from my point of view, consider it most highly to be wished that in this time of paradoxical revolution as this one is, which we are allowed to experience, an essential word be said about revolution considered as an intellectual process. And you do not feel any inner necessity to such a task as this?

he asks Landauer.

We can take from this letter of 1906 the fact that Buber understood these first years of the twentieth century as a time of "paradoxical revolution." In 1905 the first Russian Revolution had taken place, which had its effects on the intelligentsia of western Europe, too. The theme "revolution" became an important topic for the intellectuals of western Europe—to be sure in a most unusual and strangely apolitical and actually only figurative sense. For the revolution about which Buber here is questioning Landauer is the revolution in an internal sense, an experience of the soul, which therefore requires a mental decision. There is nothing external, nothing immediately political about this concept of revolution. Gustav Landauer answered Buber in 1907, when he sent him the requested manuscript about revolution: "Now, after the somewhat complicated foundation, I am prepared to have march up 'The Revolution' from all sides, and what is for your purposes the most important thing: it will proceed from the constitution of the human soul and from human relations." The revolution resulting from the constitution of the human soul and from human relations with one another, from the societal connections, as an intellectual event—it is this, which Landauer, at this time completely in agreement with Buber, developed as the concept of revolution.

This is a little prelude, which yet has nothing to do really with socialism. It sketches merely a certain form of language, of self-understanding and terminology, which can have an effect later and will have an effect in Buber's works. The year 1914, with the outbreak of war, and the four years of World War I became a critical date for all of Europe's socialists: the date of failure or rather of the victory of a socialist party and of socialist thinking in general in the arena of European politics and society. How did Martin Buber and his narrower circle of friends experience and interpret the year 1914? Is there something in the way they experienced that period that can already contribute to an understanding of Buber's socialism?

In a letter of October 16, 1914, Buber says something extremely unsocialistic, something that could lead no one to the idea that here an already mature or developing socialist was speaking: "I see in the heart of this war the ignition of a great conversion, about which I cannot yet speak today." Thus, he values the event of war in any case positively. He uses the great concept of *teshuvah*, conversion, to describe what according to his recognition is taking place in the setting out of the European nations for war. He has the feeling that with the outbreak of war a great conversion, a *teshuvah*, is being "ignited." But at the same time he has the feeling that "today," in October 1914, he is not yet able to speak of it, that is, about the content of that conversion. He has a feeling rather than a concept for the events taking place.

We learn something more from a letter to Hans Kohn, who later became Buber's biographer. In 1914 Buber lived in Berlin-Zehlendorf, and here he writes to Kohn—who had been drafted as a soldier and, like other students and friends, provided Buber with reports from the soldiers' life from the front and back lines—on September 30: "What you report about the mood (that is, the bad mood) somewhat disappointed me. Here (in Berlin-Zehlendorf) it is quite different: Never has the concept 'people' [*Volk*] become such a reality to me as in these weeks. Among the Jews, too, there is something like a serious great emotion." And then he continues: "For everyone who seeks to spare himself in this time, the word of the gospel of John holds true, 'Whoever loves his life will lose it.' ... If we Jews would only feel it, feel it through and through, what this means for us: that we no longer need our old label, 'not by might, but by spirit,' since might and spirit shall now become one. *Incipit vita nova* [a new life begins]." What is that moving content that could awaken for Buber the thought of a great conversion in the summer and fall of 1914? "Never has the concept of 'people' become such a reality to me as in these weeks." It is for all of the later Buber (and already also for the early Buber) a very, very important concept: the concept of people— but now, in 1914, not a concept of the experience of the Jewish people, but a concept of the experience of the German people. For the Jews, whom Buber can observe here in Berlin, participate fully in the experience of the new beginning [*Aufbruch*] of the German people "with a serious great emotion." No one, including the Jews, should seek "to spare himself" from this. "If we Jews would only feel it, what this means!" And now comes a further step: In the book of the prophet Zachariah (4:6) there is an ancient Jewish saying, "Not by might, but by spirit," a pacifistic motto, and Buber has the feeling (and expresses it in this letter): We no longer need this old Jewish, prophetic motto, since might and spirit are no longer in opposition to one another but shall become one. And again he concludes with the feeling of a huge new beginning, when he quotes from Dante, *Incipit vita nova*, a new life begins. A people sets off. The nation people [*Volkstum*], in which all are a part and no one spares him/herself, is stepping out into reality, moving out into the light and revealing itself. Might and spirit, the great opposites of the past, are now merging; a new life is beginning.

Let us note: In 1914 Martin Buber apparently had at first a positive experience of war. He shares this experience with many of his friends.

On that same September 30, 1914, Ludwig Strauss, his young friend and later son-in-law, writes to him:

> For me it was totally new and surprising that the feeling of being part of a state could be as passionate as I now experience it. My feeling has nothing to do with the national—I feel myself as distant from German nationalism [*Volkstum*] as ever. It is this bright, great, well-ordered *Reich* with its thousands of starting points for a future perfection that has become so alive in me that dying in its service seems to be an easy thing to do. I believe that after this war, in the victorious outcome of which I am firmly believing, it will be a great and blessed thing to be a German citizen. A close connection between Germany and Austria will create an invincible confederation of states that will determine the fate of the earth.

In contrast to Buber, who experiences the emergence of the people, Ludwig Strauss has the experience of a feeling of the state. He experiences the state as an organization of future perfection, the German *Reich* as a bright, great order, which will benefit and protect everyone who belongs to it. And he sees in a closer connection of this German *Reich* with Austria "an invincible confederation of states that will determine the fate of the earth"—and Ludwig Strauss' opinion is of course: to determine it for the better.

This mood did not last long with Strauss. Half a year later, on June 8, 1915, after being trained at the troop training facility in Döberitz, he writes to Buber:

> My time in Döberitz . . . had ended with a total failure . . . My faith in the political mission of the German people has become more uncertain, that is, closer to reality. I know . . . that the future *Reich* for which I am fighting is far from winning, even in those who are to create it . . . In the week-long close living together with a representative selection of educated German youth I have learned a great deal about the present condition of the Germans. The student community, which was formerly energetic and pushing ahead, has become lethargic, spinelessly accepting. For very few the war itself is a great, pure, moral experience. Injustice against the foreign or servility before the stranger do not allow the upright, dignified and humble self-assertion to appear pure at all. Will this people wake up early enough to turn the course of history into the right path, when the deciding power is given to it? Will this *Reich*, possessing

such wonderful organizational power for the new ordering of the world, have also the spirit and the will to do it? Can the pure state emerge here, the open, all protecting, all encompassing shelter for the nations [*Völker*]? I still hope for it, but with a deeply overshadowed hope.

This is devastating to see: A Jew only has to come into close physical contact with other Germans to become disillusioned in his idealism and in the intellectual flight of his intellectual-political expectation.

For a completely opposite picture: Buber's friend, Hugo Bergmann, who has in the meantime also become a soldier, writes to him on May 11, 1915: "This war will be a huge blessing for mankind, for it will have shown what really is, what is there in reality. The collapse of all international relations demonstrated that they really were not there, just as the meanness of warfare revealed what humankind was, under the whitewash of the daily printed and spoken forms of speech, even before the war." This shows that among Buber's friends and students there were different kinds of reactions to the events of 1914.

But in regard of Buber's attitude the answer he gave concerning the reservation and critique and disillusionment of Hugo Bergmann's in a letter of November 25, 1915, is important and interesting. Buber chides Bergmann that he has allowed the immediate experiences of the meanness of the war to such an effect in him, and he recommends that he remain rather with the spirit than to depend too much on the impressions of the [present] reality. Buber says:

> True idealism is the reality of the coming generations, and it is this because it does not "get in touch" with the [present] reality, but copes with it. It does not let itself be instructed by its undigested pieces, by the raw, penetrating event, but grasps its totality and from that coins the law of its essence and creates [against the present reality] the law of a new "ought." Idealism that "gets in touch" with reality, that is, that takes it into account rather than coping with it, is just as false and without future as the one that does not recognize the [present] reality and indulges itself in exalted phrases. The one avoids the task, the other betrays it; the one proceeds to phrases, the other to compromises. You say that only now you have come to know more closely the powers that truly drive events and the people who stand behind them. I think you are mistaken. Those "who stand behind them," behind the events of these times, are dead; dead idealists who did not just "get in touch" with the reality of their time, but rather placed

against it the law of a new "ought,"—the law that educated the nations [*Völker*] since then to the immense doing and enduring, which we see today. For the genuine idealism of our time it is the same task as it was for their idealism: it must create the law and the reality of future generations. To do so, it must of course fully recognize the law and the reality of the present generation, but

—now a parable and a fine one—

it must recognize it like Odysseus did, tied to the mast of his idea, while the unbound crewmen have to stop their ears with wax, so as not to fall victim to the powerful song.

That is a rebuke to Hugo Bergmann, who allows himself to be impacted by the impression of the immediately experienced reality, and the advice to him is to fasten himself, as Odysseus did, firmly to the mast of the idea, which is stronger than any contemporary reality, in order not to be overcome by the powerful siren song of the war's miserable reality.

This priority of the idea reaching into the future over the reality is a basic form of what will also shape Martin Buber's socialism. It is a socialism of the idea seeking on the one hand not to be alien to reality, but unable on the other hand to allow itself to be impressed and shaped by reality—an idea, which does not "get in touch" with reality, but penetrates and copes with reality. The idea is to overcome reality—this is a basic formulation of Buber's philosophy, a basic formulation of Buber's religion, and a basic formulation of Buber's socialism when it comes into being.

II

The next important date that has the meaning of a test, a touchstone, in the history of socialism is the year 1917, the year of revolutions, the Spring Revolution and the October Revolution in Russia, the great overthrow, which had an enormous effect on all the intellectuals of Europe. What do we see reflected in Martin Buber from this event?

One exciting observation that is very revealing for an understanding of what socialism could mean to Buber: I at least know of not one word of Buber's out of this time saying anything about the events happening in Russia.

Behind this is the following: Great events were taking place in history that—probably for a majority of Jews, at least those in western Europe—were more important than the revolution in Russia, events in Jewish history that could mean a setting of the course for the whole Jewish future. There are actually three moments that are to be emphasized, because they made the year 1917 important for Jews. Firstly, with the advance of the Austrian and German troops into the eastern regions of Galicia and Russia it is possible for the Jewish soldiers in these armies, often for the first time, to have a living encounter with the Jews of the east. These events—the acquaintance of western Jews with eastern Jews through the advance of the Austrian-German armies into the east— occupy the whole receptivity to experiences of the young Jews in this year. Already in September of 1914 Martin Buber reacts to these possibilities newly opening through the war, organizing—in agreement with Jewish socialists—a great Zionist action in Poland. Not that the Zionist idea was not already established for a long time among eastern Jews, but it is important now for Zionists just to bring together the strengths of east and west, and we see here at this time one of the first activities of Buber joined with socialists. Secondly, the year 1917 is the year of the Balfour Declaration, which for Jewish self-understanding and the whole situation of Jewish history is of greater importance than all the revolutionary events in the emerging Soviet Union taken together. And for Martin Buber, too, this is *the* most important date of the year. Then there is the third: The Russian revolution proclaims, already in May of 1917, the emancipation of the Jews as a national group, which can claim the rights of a minority in the new society. That is a further great event in Jewish history: the inner liberation of eastern Jews through the socialist revolution in Russia, a date that for Jews is much more important than the revolution itself, which here can be seen as only the cause of a much greater effect.

There were of course a number of Jews, who actually did not regard the Jewish events of this year 1917 but just the socialist events in Russia as more important than was the case for Buber and many of his friends. Again for example Gustav Landauer, writing on February 5, 1918, to Martin Buber in view of that which now, with the Balfour Declaration, has become possible as a new Jewish history:

> The more Germany and Turkey on the one hand and England, America and the political Zionists on the other are interested in

Palestine, the cooler I am toward this region, towards which my heart has never drawn me and which to me is not necessarily the local condition of a Jewish community. The real event that is meaningful and perhaps decisive for us Jews is only the liberation of Russia. What takes place now and in the near future in and around Palestine are merely fictional affairs in the area of the political angle of sight, and there will hardly be more to come of it than from the Albanian kingdom of the Prince of Wied . . . I do not know yet what to think about the task of the Jews, once humankind will be through this fire [of the revolution]. In the meantime I agree, in spite of everything, that what is important is that Bronstein is not professor at the university of Jaffa, but rather he is Trotsky in Russia.

Similarly Viktor Jacobsen writes on May 14, 1917, to Buber: "I am, to put it *mildly, not* satisfied with the manner in which *Der Jude* [The Jew]"—that is the journal *Der Jude*, which Martin Buber published— "reacted to the Jewish resurrection to freedom in Russia. Really I am terribly sad that *you, Buber,* could not find anything more than to issue a '*testimonium maturitatis*' [testimony of maturity, i.e. graduation certificate] to the Russians and the Jews . . . *We* needed to show compassion and sympathy, a shared experience, understanding, hope, and a *shared joy*. That was missing in *Der Jude*, and because *Der Jude*"—again the journal is meant here—"is a historical document, so is also this mistake—a historical document. And that is why I am sad." It is the fact that Buber in his journal, *Der Jude*, simply said nothing about the Russian events, rather than expressing a shared joy, a shared understanding and a shared hope, just on the part of the Jews, that is here experienced as sorrow.

Buber on the other hand and others of his friends, e.g. Arnold Zweig, are stimulated by the new possibilities of the political situation— the Balfour Declaration and the Jewish liberation in Russia—to great and energetic activity. The Zionist question becomes once again acute for Palestine. The Paris peace conference is imminent, at which not only European conflicts at the end of World War I are to be settled, but also questions of humanity as a whole are to be discussed—and so the Palestine question, too. Therefore Buber is convinced that it is now more than ever crucial to work out the contours of a Zionism with good reputation, which proves worthwile and realizable, in the meaning of Buber's "realization" [*Bewährung*], in Palestine. Arnold Zweig writes from Berlin-Schlachtensee on April 3, 1919, to Buber:

> The sooner we register our claims and outlines before the forum of humanity [that is, the Paris peace conference], the sooner we show loudly and clearly that we are not nationalists, that the nationalism of the Jews is and remains a socialist one, the sooner we will be able to represent what matters to us there where it must be represented. For the time being the communist is no wiser than the capitalist: he [the communist] divides and equalizes like a donkey. We must hammer home to the people the fact that we are not working in a reactionary-nationalist manner, but in a *revolutionary* manner in that we give the Jews a soil.

Here the theme of a socialist Zionism is touched upon in the mouth of Arnold Zweig, and he asks Buber to join him in this direction, to combat a primitive, dreadful nationalism that may emerge in the Zionist organization.

Buber writes to Hugo Bergmann with a similar concern:

> A few days ago I had a conversation with Dr. Jacobson about what ought to take place in Palestine, after which I was close to despair. "We have to gain a majority in the land as soon as possible, that is by all means"—an argument that makes one's heart stand still; and what can one answer on *this* level? We ought not deceive ourselves that most of the leading Zionists (and most of those who are led) today are completely unscrupulous nationalists (according to the European pattern), imperialists, unconscious mercantilists and worshippers of success. They say rebirth and mean enterprise. If we are not able to create an authoritative countervailing power to this, the soul of the movement will be lost, perhaps for ever.

This is a letter of February 3/4, 1918, and in the same way he argues in a letter of February 4 to his student Franz Oppenheimer: "I am planning an anthology against the penetration of imperialism, mercantilism and other evil spirits into Palestine, which is not actually to have a polemic character, but rather to point to the threatening danger and at the same time to offer a picture of the community that we mean and intend." And he writes also on January 28, 1918, to Elijahu Rappeport: "The other concerns an anthology against the threatening penetration of the European evil spirit (mercantilism, imperialism, etc., in a word, greed) into an emerging Jewish Palestine: an anthology that is not merely negative, but would give a picture of a community worthy of humankind, worthy of God, in the land of Israel." Buber now feels himself called to this task in reaction to the possibilities opened by the Balfour Declaration and by the liberation of Russian Jews for self-determination: It is a fight for Zionism, a fight that in the Jewish settlement of Palestine it will not be European imperialism and European economics that will hold the scepter. But Buber does not at all want to be merely negative, merely to say no. He wants to say yes, and the work of the next decade serves the purpose of elaborating how a *good* Judaism in Palestine might look. Buber therefore prepares a meeting of German socialist Zionists, together with Nachum Goldmann, with Landauer, with Arnold Zweig, with Robert Weltsch, Bernfeld, Kohn and others. Goldmann draws up the design for the agenda for this meeting, Buber and Landauer issue the invitations. But the meeting never takes place.

In connection with this effort, Buber now joins the socialist organization, to which he would be loyal for decades, the group Hapoël Hatzair [the Young Worker], the People's Socialists. This group was founded in 1905 in Peta(c)h Tikva, and gathered around Aaron David Gordon, the great Kibbutznik of Degania. It is a socialist movement, although not a Marxist one, and many years later it formed, together with a Marxist group, the Mapai Party [abbreviation for Mifleget Poalei Eretz Yisraël, i.e. Workers' Party of the Land of Israel].

III

One of Buber's most important activities in connection with Hapoël Hatzair is his participation in a conference of young Zionist workers in Prague. He gives a speech there, the substance of which then becoming part of the speech at the famous Twelfth Zionist Congress, which took place the next year, September 1–14, 1921, in Karlsbad. With much give and take, he achieves that in the declaration of this Zionist Congress something is said about the question of the Arabs. It will be the only declaration of a Zionist Congress to make a statement on the Arab question. Here we have evidence of the meaning that Buber's socialist convictions concretely have in the context of Zionism. I quote from the declaration proposed by Buber at the end of his Karlsbad speech:

> Our return to *Eretz Yisraël* [the land of Israel], which must take
> place in the form of a steadily increasing immigration, is not

aimed at restricting the rights of others. In a just covenant with the Arab people we want to make our common home into a blooming economic and cultural community, the consolidation of which guarantees each of its national members an undisturbed autonomous development. Our colonization, which is solely dedicated to the salvation and renewal of our nation [*Volkstum*], does not have as its goal the capitalist exploitation of a region and does not serve any imperialistic purposes. Its intention is the creative work of free people on a communal piece of the earth. In this social character of our national ideal lies the powerful assurance of our confidence that a deep and abiding solidarity of the real interests will be revealed between us and the working Arab people, which must overcome all the contradictions produced by the confusions of the moment.

This remained a solitary document in the Zionist history. Buber recounted, toward the end of his life, what a shattering experience it was for him, as, in the preparatory discussion of the manifest of this Karlsbad Congress, one sentence after another and one phrase after another was deleted from his manuscript, so that he no longer could recognize his own text and the sharpness of his own statement. For him this was a deep disappointment determining his further relationship to the official Zionist organizations. But he nevertheless could not refuse his yes even to this watered-down declaration, because it was important to him that at least something be said from the side of the Jewish Zionists to the Arab question. The text quoted above shows how his socialist convictions led him to this fight for the Arab question.

IV

There is, however, a very different story to relate in this connection. Buber's friendship with Gustav Landauer lasted for many years. It was one of the deepest and most intimate friendships of Buber's, who had a wealth of friends. He observed with reserve, but with great passion, Landauer's participation in the Munich Soviet Republic [*Räterepublik*] of 1918/19. He writes about this on February 2, 1919, to Ludwig Strauss:

I found your letter waiting for me upon my return from Munich, where I spent a very moving week in continuous communication with the leaders of the revolution, a week that found its awfully natural end in the news about the assassination of Eisner.

[Buber left Munich on the day of the murder and did not find out about the assassination until his return to Heppenheim; and after that he was anxious about Gustav Landauer, who was also murdered a few months later.—F.-W. M.] The deepest human problems of the revolution were brought up without reservation. I brought my questions and thoughts into that event, and there were late night hours of an apocalyptic heaviness, when in the middle of a discussion silence became telling and the future clearer than the present. For the most of them this was only a new bustle, but I felt myself to be something like Cassandra among them. I saw into the demonic side of Eisner's divided Jewish soul, the terrible disaster to come flowed out of his smoothness; he was a marked man. Landauer kept faith with him, with the most extreme straining of his soul, and covered for him, a shield bearer of shattering self-denial. The whole thing is a nameless Jewish tragedy.

It seems that Buber had no feeling for the Munich way of carrying out the idea. He poses his questions into the event, he throws his answers into the event, but he cannot assume more of a role than that of a Cassandra.

Two months later he relates in a letter of April 28, 1919, to Sigmund Kaznelson: "Shortly before the assassination of Eisner I talked one whole night to the leaders in Munich about the inadmissibility of terror and about the disastrous impact that the use of violence would have on the idea—with little success; but Landauer at least completely agreed with me." So here we see what the night-long conversations in Munich were all about: about "the inadmissibility of terror and about the disastrous impact that the use of violence would have on the idea." This, too, says something about the characterization of what socialism might mean to Martin Buber. It is an indication that in any case a violent revolution was out of question for him, and his understanding of socialism differs in principle from this possibility of other socialists.

V

I see that I have taken on much too much for the evening. Therefore I am now just going to add a last part referring to a lecture that Buber gave in Berlin in December of 1928 on the occasion of the founding of the Liga für das arbeitende Palästina [League of Working Palestine].

Martin Buber gave a lecture for this titled, "Warum muß der Aufbau Palästinas ein sozialistischer sein?" [Why must the upbuilding of Palestine be a socialist one?]. In this lecture we have a first summary of what socialism might mean for Buber. But first I must say something about the situation in which this lecture was given: Since the spring of 1924 the so-called "new" Jewish immigrants were coming to Palestine, made up above all of manual workers, small merchants, and former business owners. Until 1926 there were 62,000 immigrants of this sort who settled for the most part in the cities of Palestine, half of them in Tel Aviv. This led to the question for all Jewish socialists of whether the socialist pioneer character of Jewish settlements in Palestine could be maintained, and what attitude one should take to the new, non-socialist immigrants in Palestine. That is obviously one of the backgrounds for Buber's question, "Why must the upbuilding of Palestine be a socialist one?" Buber names three pragmatic tasks presenting themselves for the Zionist settlement:

1. There must be a rapid increase of the amount of land in Jewish possession, so that it does not come to a situation of land speculation in Palestine.

2. In the Jewish population of Palestine the social value criterion must in any case be established and maintained, that is, a human being's own production must be recognized to have the highest value among all Jews, so that the sons of the fathers who settle there will want to stay on in the settlements. (Evidently already in the first generation of settlers developments had taken place, where in the social acknowledgment of the Jewish settlements one's own production as the highest value had been suppressed. Buber insists that this social value criterion be placed again at the head of the list.)

3. The social appeal of the communal life must be maintained in order to encourage an influx of new Jewish immigrants.

This represents the basic problem of this gathering of the "League of Working Palestine," and it was the inner theme of Buber's lecture on the nature of the *kvutza* [Kibbutz]. Buber speaks to the socialist situation: the people's initiative, that is, the people's socialism of Hapoël Hatzair, in fact, contrasts with the individual initiative of new Jewish immigrants.

How should one judge this individual initiative? Must one simply look askance at those who do not come as socialists and view them as people who merely want to indulge in their avarice? Must one, as a socialist, be totally opposed to them? Buber answers this question with a no. The Jewish entrepreneur also stands in a common context with our Jewish will to colonialization, and he has and therefore must have a national interest. But this has necessarily social results as well. Such a nationally interested entrepreneur is, under the Palestinian conditions, especially concerned to maintain the biological quality and the human substance of the worker and not to oppress him by exploitation and impoverishment. The Jewish entrepreneur wants to build up this land precisely on the biological quality and human substance of the worker. He therefore can have no interest in exploitation or at least in wild forms of exploitation. In addition, the Jewish entrepreneur must be and will be interested in not allowing social tensions in Palestine to reach a boiling point that would endanger the whole project of the upbuilding of Palestine. In maintaining a concern for profitability the entrepreneur would, in Buber's words, make "concessions" to socialism reaching beyond mere opportunity into the realm of a basic decision. This was at least Buber's conviction, from which he draws the conclusion "that we are not married, but unavoidably associated to the Jewish bourgeoisie." For without money, as many young Jewish idealists believe, there would not be any upbuilding of Palestine.

Then Buber asks: What is the way we as socialists must take? Answer: not the way of reform, not the way of class conflict, not the way of revolution, but we must risk "the experiment of community," the realization of what is possible in our Jewish settlement here and now. Every form of illusory realization of socialism must be prevented, as has, according to Buber, taken place for example in Soviet Russia, where it has only come to an illusory socialist reality.

Further, what is our position within the international socialist movement? There are three answers to this:

1. The world market develops today through the speed of industrialization in the receiving countries to the limits of growth. The moment has almost arrived when the agony of the world market will begin, Buber says in December 1928. In this situation the order of agriculture and the intensification of land use and the organizational forms of a new farming will be of

utmost importance. The Jewish settlement should concentrate on this. Of course it must be a matter of co-operative economy. More precisely, the relationship between the state of technical development and the life of each co-operative, of each Kibbutz, must be worked out and established in every individual case. The Jewish settlements in Palestine are experimental pioneers for the whole of humanity preparing for the moment of agony of the world market.

2. The relationship between human beings and the world of highly industrialized labor has not been discussed, either by the capitalists or by the majority of the socialists. One is silent about this issue even there, where socialism, as Buber puts it, has become a "ruler" [*Herrscher*]. He asks the question: "How is work being done there?"—under the conditions where socialism in the meantime has become the ruling system. "Is the human being just a continuation of the machine or is he/she a living body?" More precisely, he asks: Is not there, too, where socialism has prevailed, life torn into two parts, into the hell of the world of labor on the one hand, organized in a wholly inhumane way, and into the world of leisure on the other, infected throughout by the nature of this labor and not at all able to be a really effective contrast to this dreadful world of labor? Buber formulates—I am quoting: "We should not be fighting against rationalization of the economy, but for humanizing of the *ratio*. The reality of the living working people must have an influence on and participate in the tasks assigned to technology." And to this, too, Buber says: The Jewish settlements must take on the task here within the whole socialist movement of being social pioneers. The key word of "participation" of human beings in their place of work was one of the main demands of Buber's socialism.

3. Buber comments on the theme that has become the decisive one in his confrontation with Marxist socialism, the problem of centralization and decentralization. Buber says: A centralized organization of society and a decentralized organization of society are not at all to be treated simply as alternatives. The demarcation line between the two must always be drawn anew in the sense of true communality [*Gemeinschaftlichkeit*]. Buber

names limits in order to determine this line of demarcation, for example: "A centralistic socialism is no socialism at all. A socialism in which the balance of power has been changed to the benefit of the workers, without changing the relationships of the people to one another is no socialism at all." That is the negative boundary line for socialism. On the other side: "What everyone means in his heart, when he/she says 'socialism,' is real community between people, immediate relationships of life between I and Thou, genuine *societas*, genuine companionship [*Genossentum*]. We must have therefore a genuine autonomy of communities." Socialism is not only democracy *from* below, but essentially democracy below. And also in this question of centralization and decentralization the Kibbutz movement has a pioneering meaning for the whole of humanity facing the same problems. A Jewish socialist should say to the rest of the socialists of the world: We have the same basic convictions as you have, but we are realizing something of these convictions that is not yet being realized anywhere else.

Then Buber discusses the geo-political position of the Jewish socialists between Moscow and fascist Rome. "In Moscow," he says literally in this lecture, "the living idea is replaced by the principle. The living idea is always an image, a picture of what can and should be realized from certain possibilities of certain people and groups of people; the principle is a distortion [*Entbildung*] of the idea. The concrete persons and groups, defined by their nationality, culture and fate, are replaced by the abstraction of 'the' person, 'the' citizen, 'the' proletarian, the living body is replaced by the skeleton, the search for the path with its real decisions is replaced by the prescribed route. Moscow represents the rule of the principle, softened by the resistance of reality." On the other hand, there is fascist Rome: There prevails no idea, but one lives fully out of the contemplation of reality; but out of the contemplation developed a fully restricted, cynical knowledge of reality, that is, a knowledge of human desire for power, greed for power, enjoyment of power and anxiety about power. One views the state (in fascism) as stratification of having and wanting power, and that is bound up with an irreverent actualism, which gives every desire for power its due.

Now the concluding question that concerns Buber here:

> The great question that arises again and again in my heart, when I—depressed and stirred up by the massive existence of these two unfruitful giants [Moscow and Rome]—think of the near future of humankind, is: Is there a Jerusalem? Is there a third way, something not yet in existence, something coming into being—beyond these two? Is there aside from these two clay faces to be perceived everywhere a third, a hidden one, one of flesh and blood, with a bright forehead, loving eyes and a mouth able to sing, a *human* face?

Buber raised this question again and again in these years, and he concludes: "I believe in 'Jerusalem,' . . . for in the events taking place today in Palestine spirit and reality are encountering one another."

Buber repeated this again in the year 1945 in his great final account of the whole Marxist problematic, in *Pfade in Utopia* [*Paths in Utopia*]. There he calls Moscow the representative of a socialist unitarianism and says, "In spite of everything I dare to call the other pole Jerusalem." By this he understands a socialism from below, a socialism emerging from the already existing community.

Back then, in December 1928, young people in Berlin had asked him: Why do you, as a socialist, insist so much on the spirit? Is that not a contradiction to the materialism that is a part of every socialism? Is life not enough? Why do you not just leave to life what is going to happen? Why do you, Martin Buber, burden us with the spiritual problematic? And to this Buber answered, devastating in the choice of words: "A Zionism that believes it can rely on 'life,' fascist Zionism, is not merely distorted in its idea, but, seen just from the point of view of reality, nonsense and without any future." And he continues in this discussion: It is true, something must be realized; therefore the only Zionism that can succeed is one with a communal ideal [*Gemeinschaftsideal*], socialist Zionism. "The idea must be preserved just there where it is the most difficult, in its mixing. True purity does not mean to remain untouched. The real tests of life do not occur outside somewhere, but precisely in the mix [*Gewühl*]—there, where it touches, where it takes one's breath away, and where one nevertheless can prove oneself."

I am simply going to stop here. I have been able to show you a few main themes of Buber's socialism with these examples. In 1945, in his great concluding work about the socialist problematic, *Pfade in Utopia*, Buber expressly declared his support for that utopian socialism that Marx, Engels, Lenin, Stalin and many others had rejected. It was a socialism "seen from its goal" and without that analysis which Marx had called the scientific analysis of society, the analysis of the law of values, a socialism without concern for the class problematic, without concern for the existing proletariat. The subject of Buber's socialism was the Jewish people and not just some oppressed class. Buber could name and practice the utopian socialism in wholly other ways as well. He joined the movement of religious socialism, which above all emerged in the Christian church, especially in the Protestant church in Switzerland in the 1920s. He published articles in the journal of these Swiss religious socialists and was friends with the leader of the religious socialist movement in Switzerland, Leonhard Ragaz. He planned to found a federation of Jewish religious socialists in order to be able to create a socialist identity, which he—according to his intellectual insight—could represent and for which he could take responsibility.

When I think about it: Was socialism in the work and action of Martin Buber a necessity? Was it unavoidable for him to become and remain a socialist?—I would say this: As a socialist Martin Buber was above all a Jew. But as a Jew he did by no means mainly have to become a socialist. The socialism, Buber's socialist choice or his socialist decision is, as I see it, founded in three possibilities of his existence: first and above all in the large number of socialist friends, with whom he lived in close community, as for example Arnold Zweig or Gustav Landauer, so that the socialist question was pressed upon him—which he gladly accepted on the basis of that communication; secondly, in the compulsion to be able to practice his convictions and to do this in connection with a really existing socialist movement. In his case that was of course the Jewish socialist movement, though not its Marxist wing but what was called the Jewish people's socialism. A third motif was grounded in his biblical insight, in his religious socialism, in his thought about the kingdom of God, theocracy. This background and context led, as Gershom Scholem rightly recognized early on, to a basically anarchist attitude that was probably characteristic and typical of all forms of religious socialism, including those in Christian history. According to Martin Buber the most exclusive binding to the lordship of God does not mean enslavement of humankind, but rather to the lordship of God corresponds an unconditional and complete freedom of the human personality, the human individual. Here is the basis for the friendship with the anarchist Gustav Landauer, deeply rooted in the religious sphere, indivisible from the religious, just as on the other hand the religious is indivisible from Buber's socialism.

Has time passed this socialist Martin Buber by? In the world outside Israel, the world of Europe, Latin America, the world of Asia and Africa, where there are socialist movements today, there is apparently no possibility left of an utopian socialism, a religious socialism; or at least such a new possibility has not yet been able to establish itself. Similarly Buber failed in Israel and with the problems of Israel in getting the two prongs of his socialism through. The Arab question could not be solved in the socialist fashion, as was crucial for Buber. Likewise the settlements in Israel got into one crisis after another and had to hold out in a setting of social developments and social orders, where it happened that conditions of war and capitalism necessarily attracted each other, so that a socialist Israel did not come into being. Does that mean that the development in Israel has already moved past Martin Buber's socialist Zionism? I see only one single point where I could say that there is hope for anyone who would discover something worth considering in this socialism of Martin Buber's and who would wish this ideal truly to be realized: The society of the state of Israel still has one task ahead of it that has not yet been started, let alone completed, that is the cultural revolution, the internal conflict among Jews about the meaning and significance of being a Jew there in their land—and about the spiritual dimension, about the role that religion might play or no longer can play in this connection. It might well be that in connection with the unavoidable cultural revolution that is still ahead for this people the bell might toll again for the socialist Zionism of Martin Buber.

4

Why the Talmud Interests Me as a Christian

I

"Thereupon Jesus addressed the crowd of people and his disciples and said: 'The scribes and the Pharisees sit in the chair of Moses. Everything now they tell you, do and obey!'" (Matt 23:1–3). This is one of the sayings of Jesus of which we are perhaps least conscious, and still less have Christians obeyed it. The very names "scribes and Pharisees" have called forth all kinds of instinctive defensive reactions among Christians. One believes to remember that these are the bitterest enemies of Jesus, and, at the end, the driving forces behind his death. The solidity of this view is, to be sure, seriously called into question by such a saying as this one, and therefore preaching and theology and Christian consciousness have simply suppressed it. Nevertheless, it is in our New Testament, in the first gospel, and first of all we ought to think about it.

The "chair of Moses" is a teaching chair in a synagogue. It is said that God built a lectern for Moses on Mount Sinai, so that Moses could teach the people from there the lessons he had received on the mountain heights. Rabbinic Judaism traces its lineage as an immediate succession from this teaching of Moses in the following chain: "Moses received the Torah from Sinai and delivered it to Joshua, Joshua passed it on to the elders, the elders to the prophets, and the prophets passed it on to the men of the Great Synagogue (the *knesset ha gedolah*)" (*Avot* 1:1). And in their schools and teachings the Mishna came into being, the basic text of the Talmud. And this was discussed and commented upon in the two Talmudim and passed on from generation to generation. The institution of "chairs of Moses" in the rooms of synagogues makes this chain of teaching perceptible. While one reads from the Bible *standing*, exposition and teaching are performed *sitting down*, from the teaching chair.

Now Jesus says, scribes and Pharisees sit in the "chair of Moses." He says this without any overtones, just stating the fact: this is right and proper, this is where they belong; since the times of Ezra (which was, at the time of Jesus, more than 400 years earlier) they belong there. They are the ones who protect the oral teachings of Moses, pass them on and—develop them further, so that they might continue to be fresh and new in every generation, associated with contemporary questions, and as a living oral tradition.

[By the way, this is also how Martin Luther viewed the relationship between scripture and proclamation; not the written letters of the Bible, but the spirit of the *viva vox evangelii*, the living voice of the gospel— that is truly the word of God. And Luther had determined that it was also the relationship between the New and the Old Testament. Actually, he claimed that the Old Testament alone was the Bible; that it was basically a misunderstanding to add a written New Testament to it, for the message that we today have in the New Testament scriptures is actually to be understood only as an "oral cry," "good news." And this should properly be sung and spoken and cried out, but not really become scripture. Here Luther shares, though it is seldom noted and thought about, the Jewish rabbinic point of view: The Tanakh is Scripture—everything else is essentially to be passed on orally. Only so, from mouth to mouth, does it continue to be relevant, does it continue to be "new."][1]

Jesus speaks "to the crowd of people and to his disciples" about this oral teaching of Moses. Only in one other place in the New Testament, in the account of the Sermon on the Mount (cf. Matt 5:1), do we have this combination, "the crowd of people and his disciples." To both Jesus addresses the Sermon on the Mount and this saying with which we are concerned here. We might think: Well, Jesus says to the crowd of people: hold fast to the Jewish tradition, it is something with which you have long been familiar, keep it! And we think: But he surely would not have counseled that to his disciples and followers: remain Jews and keep yourselves in the Jewish tradition! But this is exactly what Jesus advised both the crowd and his closest friends: "Everything now they tell you,

---

1. This paragraph was part of an earlier presentation in December 1992. It was omitted in the later *Kirchentag* version (1993), which Marquardt authorized for publication.—Ed.

do and obey!" That is, Jesus asks his followers to learn not only from the teachers of Scripture, but also from the teachers of the oral tradition, and to learn and live the Torah as it is also passed on and developed further in the teachings of the Mishna and the Talmud. Jesus does not want to pull his followers out of Judaism, but seeks to lead them into the very heart of the pharisaic and rabbinic Judaism of the day. (Whoever has ears to hear should hear!)

This puts Christians in a difficult position. It is precisely the opposite of what we think we have heard up to now from Paul and the other disciples of Jesus! How shall we deal with this?

Perhaps, one thought, this might be something from the "pre-Easter world," possibly something from the "historical Jesus," and nothing essential, something historically relative, replaced by the Easter events, through which Jesus has been elevated to a larger dimension of humanity, out of the narrow confines of Judaism. But, with the image of an "historical Jesus," that is not so simple. We cannot get around a lot of arbitrary decisions. And even if we were able to prove that here in Matthew 23:1–3 we are concerned "only" with something from the "historical Jesus," the question remains as to why the first evangelist saved this saying and wove it into the story of Jesus. The author of the first gospel possibly belongs to the second or third generations of Christians—why would he place his readers and hearers still under this old instruction of Jesus?

The commentators on Matthew's gospel suggest today that the first evangelist might have been influenced by a Christian community—perhaps somewhere in Syria—, still strongly influenced by Jewish thought, but possibly in a vehement dispute with the synagogue congregation in the vicinity about the right to claim the Jewish tradition as a Christian heritage as well and perhaps even to claim to be "the true Israel." In that way, this saying of Jesus would be explained in the context of Matthew's times as follows: Christians want to connect to Judaism and understand this connection as an instruction even of their risen Lord. But here, too, we cannot be sure: this is only a scholarly theory.

Then, however, we have to face the fact that one or two generations later the Christians who gathered and composed the New Testament from various writings did not manipulate this text but still gave it to the Christians of their own time as an instruction of Jesus. We are there already very much in the middle of the second century CE, in churches no longer stemming from the Jews, but from "the gentiles." And gentile Christians also are to give heed: "The scribes and the Pharisees sit in the chair of Moses. Everything now they tell you (also you gentile Christians), do and obey!" There is also a Christian line of tradition. Among the Jews, there is continuity from Moses on Mount Sinai to the teachers of the Great Synagogue and those of the Talmud. So also (perhaps) among the Christians, there is continuity from the historical Jesus through the Jesus awakened from the dead to the Jesus of the second or third generations of Christians to the world-wide church of the time in which the biblical canon was formed and a New Testament was gathered and added to the Old. Christians also formed their chains of tradition and sought in this way to keep their traditions fresh and new. If we would follow the way of the church today, then the instruction of Jesus reaches us also saying: Everything that you can learn from the teachers of the oral Torah of Israel, give attention to it and follow it. Jesus counsels you so.

II

Against this teaching an inveterate mistrust has prevailed through two thousand years of Christianity. I am deeply moved by the report of a Dutch colleague (W. Dekker), which he shared for the first time publicly not long ago. According to this report the great Dutch theologian K. H. Miskotte encouraged Karl Barth several times to read some of the works of [contemporary] Judaism, such as, for example, Franz Rosenzweig's *Star of Redemption*. Barth rejected the advice later just as he did in 1935, after Miskotte's important book *Het wezen der joodsche religie* [The essence of Jewish religion] was published: "contributions to the knowledge of Jewish spiritual life." At that time, Barth reacted to Miskotte's book with the following words: "What are you trying to prove then with this thick book? Do you think perhaps that we have to learn from Jews about how to read the Scriptures?" Thus it was also my teacher Karl Barth, who in resistance to National Socialism stood the test of the time and contributed to the saving of Jews more than other theologians, to find it unthinkable that a Christian theologian or preacher might learn anything from Jews for a better understanding of the Bible. Barth was still speaking with the voice of two thousand years of Christian thought: it was simply presupposed that there was nothing a Christian could learn from a Jew. My teacher from Basel was not aware of the fact that he thereby despised a commandment of Jesus.

The theological reasons for Barth's attitude were the following: The sufficient context for a proper understanding of the Bible was for two thousand years only the story of the incarnation of the eternal word of God in Jesus Christ, the narrative of his death and his resurrection from the dead for the salvation of all humankind. The Old Testament, too, could be read, was to be read, and should be read, only in this context, through the filter of the New Testament. The possibility that the existence and history of the whole Jewish people, from which Jesus stemmed, might form another context for both parts of the Christian Bible—the Tanakh of the so-called Old Testament and the Jesus writings of the so-called New Testament—, was set aside as theologically irrelevant. It seemed to be merely something superficial, which could have no meaning for a theological understanding, because God's reality is suprahistorical and not to be sought or found in historical and temporal comings and goings. Something like this was the attitude of Christian dogmaticians. And the theological historians and biblical scholars were not any better.

For generations they had the quirk that it would be better to explain the Bible from a pagan perspective than from Judaism, and that the New Testament, too, was easier to understand from pagan Gnosticism, from the philosophical school of the Stoa, and from other pagan concepts than from the Tanakh and from the teachings of the Jewish people. It is true, they did look at sources of Jewish teachings in order to understand the New Testament. But how was that done? They made use of—and continue to use today—a collection (very commendable at the time) of Jewish parallel sayings to almost all the sayings, sentences and thoughts of the New Testament: the five-volume collection by Strack-Billerbeck, *Aus Talmud und Midrasch* [From the Talmud and Midrash]. But the Jewish texts are chosen there according to the dictate of the New Testament texts, simply according to their "concepts" and order, without any regard for their own relationship to one another or their meaning in their own sources. The Jewish texts, mainly those from the Talmud, are used here only as a heap of fragments, gathered to suit a Christian purpose and need. There is nothing here to be gleaned from their internal Jewish connections and meanings. And so it is no surprise that the use Christian "scholars" made of the texts confused things all the more. For generations this collection of Jewish material, split as though by a nuclear fission, misled theologians to present the smallest units as something that could not be compared with the Christian material, rather than as something comparable. After the Jewish material had been broken out of its own context, it was easy to claim a spiritual and religious "superiority" of the New Testament, compared with materials from the Mishna, Talmud and Midrash. Among theological historians as well as among Christian dogmaticians, Judaism was used merely as a negative foil against which one could more easily bring the higher heights or deeper spiritual depths of Christian thinking into the spotlight. This eclectic and arbitrary manner of considering Judaism was and is still today: methodical anti-Judaism in academic theology. It shows very clearly that Karl Barth was not alone in his question to Miskotte: "Do you think we have anything to learn from the Jews about how Scripture is to be read?"

III

Jewish instruction was rejected, because for a long time one had no longer seen any theological meaning in the existence and history of the Jewish people. "Christ is the end of the law" (Rom 10:4), Paul had said, and for more than two thousand years Christianity stubbornly insisted on understanding the text like this: Until the coming and activity of Jesus of Nazareth, the Torah from the Sinai was God's good gift to humankind; the Jewish people sought in good faith and some unfaith to live out of this gift and to lift it up among humankind. But then came the One who with combined divine and human power fulfilled the law, and God accepted that on behalf of all human beings, Jews and non-Jews. As a result of the fulfillment of the requirements of the law by this One, God decided no longer to require the fulfillment of the law by any human being, any single woman or any single man. God declared his readiness to love and praise humankind without any works of the law. It would be sufficient for God's benevolence, if they would use Jesus and his obedience as an excuse, reminding God of Jesus and his achievements on humankind's behalf. With this, of course, the Jewish people had already fulfilled its duty. Even if they continued to exist, the loss of the Jewish state, the destruction of the temple in Jerusalem, and their dispersion among the nations sufficed as evidence that the

Jewish people had finished its role in the history of salvation. Christ was supposed to be "the end of the law," implying that he was at one and the same time the end of the history of Israel. And there are to this day important Christian theologians who see in this the end of history itself: Only in our inner, spiritual life can anything good develop any longer. In the external sphere, in social life and in world history there is nothing more to expect from God; nothing more concrete is commanded, except to behave in all things with love and especially to let love "carry" all that torments us and all that is lacking for us in the world. As a result a question emerges: How should we, after Christ, still have anything important to learn from the Jews who have now become "a people without a history"? They have, along with their lost identity in world-history, also lost their appearance as God's people, which they once enjoyed in the Bible. Therefore all the more: What is there still for us to learn from a group of people who have lost the biblical form they once had?

Is this view frightening or is it still familiar to you? I learned it after 1945 from the two greatest teachers of Protestant theology in our century, who concurred in this respect: Rudolf Bultmann and Karl Barth. It determines the horizons of consciousness for my generation. Today, I can repeat this view only with dismay, because the Jewish people has reported back to the stage of world history with a claim and conviction that the Bible speaks of their history and their obligation to God. So a Christian today, who truly holds to the Bible, can do nothing other than hold together and consider the connection between the self-witness of the Jewish people and the biblical witness of God about this people. And the task consists of—at least belatedly—recognizing and coming to terms with two thousand years of contempt of the Jewish people and of neglect of their life and their ways with God. We must do this in order to become contemporary with Jews today and to be able to live with our Jewish contemporaries today. The decisive task laid upon us today, after Auschwitz, is to live with Israel *now*, to understand *now*, and to intervene for the Jewish people *now*—*shalom* for Israel, *achshav*, now.

In order to do this, we must deconstruct two thousand years of concepts evoking religious enmity and of understandings of Judaism which have been only caricatures we Christians have built for ourselves with the help of biblical materials. We will never accomplish this with books and academic theology alone. Theology and scholarly research have always been corruptible by anti-Jewish prejudices. Therefore, if we are sincere we will have *to learn from Jewish self-understandings* and let our texts be corrected from that position, because we have written down much too much historical nonsense and theological untruth about the Jewish people into them.

The Judaism that we do not know has its focus in the Mishna and the Talmud. The conversation of the teachers in the Talmud held this people together spiritually and practically through the thousands of years of their dispersion. And the two Talmudim are today still the identity centers not only for orthodox Jews, but also for conservative and liberal, and in part also for secular Jews who know that they can connect to biblical Israel only when they pass on the oral Torah from mouth to mouth, from person to person, through the generations, and develop and live that understanding further.

I have consciously spoken first about the *task of contemporaneity*, the necessity that Christians today must become contemporaries of Jews, and therefore, for example, must have a catch-up course in the Talmud, but then also in the Kabbalah, Jewish philosophy, and Jewish Haskala [Enlightenment]. In a time when we, in Germany, are letting ourselves be driven back into an untimely national self-satisfaction, back also into the ghetto of our Christian identity, this is a most important instruction: Learn with all your might to enter into a world which appears to you to be alien. Expose yourself to the task of learning to adjust yourself spiritually, mentally, morally, politically and socially to the culture and religion of others—not in order to deny yourself by so doing, but in order to give yourself a chance to change, to remain alive in progressive transformation, flexible, and not locked into a narrow fundamentalism. Ben Bag Bag said: "Stir around in the Torah and stir in it, because everything (the whole world) is there; look deeply into it and become old and used up in it and do not retreat from it, because there is nothing better than the Torah" (*Avot* 5:25).

But now we must immediately add something more. *It is worth* listening to the Talmud, listening to the conversation of the teachers of Israel about the life of God's people living in constant danger from within and from without. It is valuable for us, for our understanding of the Bible and for our self-understanding as Christians, in short, for our Christian identity.

IV

We will come to know Jesus in a new way.—Up until now we have learned
to know him from God's side—as God's eternal son, in "one essence
with the father," pre-existent in the eternal majesty of God. This son
then humbled himself and came into our humanity, and as the time was
fulfilled, he raised the human being Jesus of Nazareth from the *Galil*
[Galilee] into the community of life and nature with himself, so that
this man from then on not only gave witness of God's word and will,
but also was God in person. In his superior understanding of God he
preached the kingdom of God; in the healing powers of God he healed
the sick; in the power of God which is mighty in the weak, he lived, suffered and died, totally obedient to God. And then God awakened him
from the dead, called him home into his high, and set him at his right
hand where he pleads and intercedes for us, in order to turn everything
with God to the best end. And God will give him the last judgment and
complete all things, natural and historical, in him. That is how we know
and confess Jesus as the only begotten, uniquely from God.

But is that really the picture that the New Testament paints of him?
Is that the *whole* picture? Is not a great deal of the New Testament set
aside in such a picture? Is it the *right* picture? For centuries doubts have
been expressed. Some gave in their doubts and began a search for "the
historical Jesus," who was supposed to be just the opposite of the man
who came from God, a human being only according to the measure of
what we know to be genuinely human, quite apart from all things divine, which cannot be grasped historically and the essence of which can
only be seen with the eyes of personal faith. We still find ourselves in the
midst of this movement: We project one picture after the other onto the
man Jesus, today: a person in solidarity with the poor, the "new man,"
the outsider, the post-modern exotic, the pacifist, and who knows which
Jesus will be next in our midst; certainly there will be one after another.
Perhaps this human Jesus is less satisfying than the divine Jesus of our
traditional theologies of faith has been. Personally I can no longer, with
good conscience, follow the one or the other, since I have begun to get
to know Jesus the Jew.

As a *Jew* he is not exchangeable, and he balks at any further projections of ours; for there he stands in the midst of his people, which,
today, thank God, is no longer available for whatever pagan fantasies we

might concoct of what a "true Jew" might be, or what "true Israel" might be either—something terrible or something very great. I am seriously of the opinion that contemporary Judaism, so conscious of its own identity, protects Jesus from being made again and again into a target of whatever the latest human pious fantasies might make of him, even the most noble or socially important. Conversely, Jesus the Jew needs no other form of nearness to God than that which the Jewish people live in their survival and in their daily wrestling with the hearing and doing of God's will. Jesus is as much the "son of God," as God has spoken of the whole people of Israel as "God's son," making them certain of his eternal loyalty and fellowship. Jesus does not need to be perceived differently from any woman, any man, any child of his people. He is the "light of the world" precisely as, and in the same significance as, God has called the whole Jewish people to be *or goyim*, a light to the nations. This One lives out, perhaps in a concentrated form, the life of his people, but he does so in the commission of his people. For this reason Paul has called him "the fulfillment of the law" (Rom 10:4).

If this is so (and these are not our fantasies, but biblical proclamations), if Jesus is from God for us what his whole people is from God for us, then we very much need to let ourselves be taught by this people, from the wellsprings of their knowledge about God, their *daat Elohim*. Doing this, we will learn to know Jesus with other eyes and discover in the New Testament things that up until now have not seemed so important to us.

Paul said that Jesus was "born of a woman and made subject to the law" (Gal 4:4). Only those who know their way around the Talmud know that with these two designations Jesus is designated a Jew through and through. For according to the law of Jewish religion a Jew is defined by his/her Jewish mother (simply because in doubtful cases it is easier to prove maternity than paternity). Jesus' father in the New Testament clearly has to step back behind his mother Mary, and *one* of the reasons is the fact that it is his mother who gives him his Jewish identity. Lastly this was also very important in the Nazi era, when "German Christian" theologians sought to make Jesus into a Galilean Aryan and non-Jew, taking their mother-cult from Mary. And yet it was precisely his mother who was the guarantee of his Jewishness—being "born of a (Jewish) woman," in Bethlehem, in the land of Judea. He was born a Jew; and educated as a Jew—that is the meaning of "made subject to the law," i.e.

instructed in the Torah, and that was the source of his life and his prayers until his very last breath. But not only his parents, God also made him subject to the Torah. This is what Paul knew and said of him.

Appropriately, Jesus was *circumcised* like every Jewish male child and thus received on his body the sign of the covenant—as commanded by the law (Luke 2:21ff.). Then, according to good Jewish order, he became *bar mitzvah*, "son of the commandment," and was called upon for the first time in the synagogue service to read from the Torah and to enter the company of Jewish adults. The story of the twelve-year-old Jesus in the temple in Jerusalem records this. Still today, when possible *bar mitzvah* is celebrated at the foot of the western wall [of the temple]. From that moment on, Jesus could complete the *minyan*, the number of Jewish men necessary to be assembled before the worship service can begin. I experienced Yehoshua Amir once on a Sabbath evening, as the time for the service of worship had come, walking around worried, trying to get the men to come out of their houses for his synagogue Emet ve Emuna. Since that time I know how good it is that also with Jesus a Jewish service of worship could begin. He became and remained an adult Jew. He "fulfilled the law!" (Matt 5:17).

In the *first place* (and we cannot impress that firmly enough into our consciousness): He *prayed the Shema Yisrael* along with everyone of his people (Mark 12:29). He too, as with all Jews until the present day, considered it to be the most important commandment (Mark 12:31). It is, it seems, really questionable that we are right in naming the "Our Father" the "Lord's Prayer." At least the *Shema Yisrael* is it as well. Jesus also wore the *appropriate clothing for a Jewish service of worship*. We know this from the story about his healing the woman with the flow of blood. The text says, she touched "the hem of his garment." That is really the *tzitzit*, the blue-white tassels on the four corners of the *arba kanfot*, the small prayer garment belonging to the everyday clothing of every practicing orthodox Jew.

According to John's gospel, Jesus was a passionate *pilgrim* to Jerusalem where, according to the instructions of the Torah, a Jew should appear three times a year—for *Pesach* [Passover], *Shavuot* [Pentecost], and *Sukkot* [Feast of Booths or Tabernacles]. John has him in Jerusalem five times, and above all, of course, at Passover, the memorial feast of the liberation of his people from Egyptian slavery. He celebrated it with wine and bread and a sacrificial lamb.

He *learned and learned*—and thereby forgot his family. And when he taught later, he referred first of all, in proper Jewish teaching form, to what is written in Scripture, then to what the elders had heard from it, and then he added his own insight. The pattern of the Sermon on the Mount (Matt 5:21) is exactly that of Jewish teaching: "You have heard" (this and that biblical quotation), then that which you have heard from "the elders," and now I, Jesus, say to you teaching this and that. Precisely in the Sermon on the Mount, where Jesus allegedly distinguishes himself so radically from Judaism, he observed, like any good Pharisee, the teachings of the *knesset ha gedolah* and erected *a fence around the Torah* (*Avot* 1:1). Moses set the Torah before the Jewish people for life or death (Deut 30:15ff.), but he intended for the people to receive life from the Torah, not death. (That is why it was even commanded to break the Sabbath when life was threatened; it would have been foolish to follow the commandments for life come hell or high water, and thereby bring someone into life-threatening circumstances. This thought was *not* something new or original with Jesus; it was a rabbinic teaching that humankind was not made for the sake of the Sabbath, but the Sabbath was made for the sake of humankind [Mark 2:27–28; cf. b. *Yoma* 85b].) But in order to prevent humans even from approaching the death zone of the Torah, both rabbinic Judaism *and* Jesus created an anteroom before the really dangerous wording of the Torah. Already there one can keep the commandment, in order that one might not even come into the danger of transgressing it. So that you do not even come into the danger zone of the fifth commandment, "Thou shalt not kill," I say to you that you ought to get along better with your brother *already in advance*, even if he is your enemy. So that you do not even come close to committing adultery, I give you advice for your heart and your eye *already in advance*. So that you do not come close to the danger of false oaths, I create an anteroom for you—do not swear at all. And so forth. The Jesus of the Sermon on the Mount is not teaching anything originally Jesus-like, rather he teaches as a good rabbi.

In hundreds of details we learn today that Jesus drew completely from the currents which already have begun to gather in the Mishna and are further discussed in the two Talmudim. Jesus belongs to this conversation.

But decisive in our context is this: with eyes sharpened by the Talmud, we observe Jesus throughout his life living according to the instructions of the Torah alive in his people. He lives his life as a member of his people which God has called to sanctify God and to be sanctified; to complete all the movements of life, inwardly and outwardly, as a service of worship to God, allowing God to come near and to come near to God. Or, expressed in a Jewish manner, to become "one" with God over and over again and to become one with oneself. All of life is to become at-one with God: This is a picture of Jesus' reality which in any case tells me more than some christological determination about a unity of two natures—one human, one divine—in Jesus. Jesus' unity with God is the eternal history of Israel in him. It reveals how God and his people, his people and God try again and again to be practically unified. That is how Jesus lives, that is how Jesus helps. When he heals the sick and forgives sin, he does this always with the intention that they may once again be able to be a part of the worshipping assembly: "Go and show yourself to the priest!" (Matt 8:4).

V

We also learn to know ourselves in a new way. The portrait of humankind into which we are educated as Christians teaches us what sin is. Martin Luther said that it is the first thing the gospel does with us: it makes us sinners so that we have no illusions about ourselves and desire the help of Jesus. And adult Christians have to learn to understand themselves as beings of two worlds; somehow they must cope with their being before God, "both a sinner and justified." And above all, they must learn that they cannot help themselves. How differently the Mishna and the Talmud perceive humanity before God! While we Christians are always taught to look beyond ourselves to God and to see and judge ourselves through the eyes of God, rabbinic Judaism teaches humankind to live according to God's will in their human relationships. Humankind does not need to look up to God, because God looks down into their situations.

Let us look quickly through the six orders, *sedarim*, of the Mishna and the Talmud. According to the first order, *Serayim*, "Seeds," *a human being belongs to the land.* Humans are farmers, tillers of the fields, of the trees, vineyards, herbs. The poor also live from the produce of the fields; producers are obligated to care for the poor, to leave something in the corners of the fields for the poor to harvest. And for the priests and

Levites something must be offered. In this way agriculture takes on a quality of service to God, worship—not because the earth has anything originally mythical or divine about it, but because it is the land that God has promised and given to his people. It is no wonder that Zionism could emerge in modern Judaism. This is the first determination of humankind in talmudic tradition: human beings are regarded as living on the surface of the field (and, therefore, in the face of God), they are people of the land of Israel.

According to the second order of Mishna and Talmud, *Moëd*, "Festivals," a human being is essentially human in his or her *experience of times*. A human being's experience of time is not primarily determined by the dates at the edge of life, by the secrets of birth and the puzzles and anxieties of death, but rather by the middle of life, by the feasts of life. The first experience of time is the *Sabbath*. Then, for the people there is the most important experience, *Pesach* [Passover], the feast of the liberation of Israel. Then there is *Yom Kippur*, the day on which humankind appears before God and in the midst of the congregation as a sinner. Then there is the Feast of Booths or Tabernacles [*Sukkot*], a remembrance of the fact that the people are on a journey, on the way; and then *Rosh Hashanah*, the remembrance of a new beginning. There are, of course, times of fasting as well including a prayer that God might send rain upon the thirsty land; the ecological question is a question of time. There are times of pilgrimage that separate human life into sections: the journey to Jerusalem—not a children's game [German children play, "We are traveling to Jerusalem!"—Trans.], but a goal in life.

Then we are considered as *women and men* in the third *seder*, *Nashim*, "Women." A man is to marry his sister-in-law when her husband dies, so that no name is lost in Israel. Husband and wife are to be bound in legal covenant to each other, for marriages that are only based on romantic love or attraction cannot last. Above all, women are to have legal rights, and men should know what awaits them when they forcibly rape women. Vows and promises are also legally binding. Adultery is a bad thing. To be sure, there are divorces and they are to be regulated. However, the most important thing is the betrothal, *Kidduschin*: how husbands and wives come together, whether through payments of money, letters of betrothal, sleeping together, etc.

Human beings are *citizens*, usually in sensitive frictions with other citizens. The concept of "the neighbor" is hardly something ideal. The fourth *seder* [order] is *Nezikin*, "Damages," which characterizes us as citizens. There we are hurtful to each other, and therefore, we would do well to relate to one another through laws. All the things we can do to one another are recognized here in advance—what we can steal, how we can defraud one another, what we can destroy, how we can take somebody for a ride, beat one another up, do one another bodily harm. But also there is thought for how we do business with one another, how we set prices and wages, make house and land deals, bear witness for one another. For this reason the *Sanhedrin* is so important, the court of judgment, and a well-developed sense of all human beings that rights and laws are crucially important for life together. There is no room anymore for anarchistic strands and impulses which Martin Buber saw at work in very early Israel, where God alone should be king. Norms of justice and punishment belong to humanity. Beatings are more humane than extinction and expulsion out of the fellowship. The problem of the oath plays a role questioning our reliability in relationship to one another. And then also the *avodah zarah*, idolatry, belongs here. It is a civil problem, because idols call into question the identity of Israel.

Then, in the fifth *seder*, *Kodashim*, "Holy Things," a human being *worships and serves God*. This deals with what and how offerings are to be made and on what occasions—after births and transgressions—and how priests are to behave. It is something concerning everyone, the priests have no secrets. It also deals with the times for temple observance—morning, evening, night—and how they fit together. The service of God, worship, is as important for humanity as the civil responsibility. There is nothing of a "two kingdoms" distinction.

And, finally, sixth, the human being *keeps purity*, sanctifies him/herself: *seder Tohorot*, "[ritual] Purifications." This is related also to the service of worship. Not just anyone can enter there and participate. For whoever has touched something dead cannot enter, since the world of God is the world of life, and whoever touches death is foreign to God. Also whatever has to do with bodily fluids, which actually serve life, but without serving hang on us—for example, the semen of the man, menstrual blood of the woman—, causes one to need purification. Purity of body, clothing, things, furniture, walls have to do with hygiene. But hygiene serves not only health; it is also theology. God desires to see in the services of worship his image in integrity, and purity laws can be understood as instructions in the symbolism of the divine image. Human beings are to appear before God, in both the literal and symbolic sense, washed and with clean hands (*Yadayim*).

People of the land, people in their different time periods, but above all people of the festivals; people as citizen, people as worshippers; people who are fit for the presence of God: this is the concrete way in which the rabbis portray us as God's humanity.

Much of this can be gleaned from the life of Jesus, but unfortunately much of it comes to us without touching or obligating us. We have removed ourselves theologically from Jesus' concrete understanding of humanity and thereby from the practical smartness of human life in general. What we *think* about God, the world, and other human beings is more important to us than how we are to live as human beings before God. The Talmud interests me because of the 613 *mitzvot* [commandments] it contains, but it is still of more interest to me because it speaks of what it really means to exist as a human being, and to be a human being in co-existence with God.

VI

Now, finally, one very last item: *We get to know God more closely, more in God's own humanity.* God reigns, judges, and loves in many more forms than are outlined in the New Testament. In the Talmud God can cry from pain and anguish, roar like a lion, make self-accusations, admit to being wrong, and give human beings credit for being right; God can rejoice over being bested in debate, and ask for blessing from human beings. There is a treatise in the Talmud about the laughter of God (b. *Avoda zara* 3b). God even prays that divine love might overcome divine justice. God can and wants to be saved, redeemed along with Israel from the power of the *goyim*, and therefore he is a God who needs salvation. Christians often smirk at such *haggadot* [narratives]. However, I am always moved that *we* speak about God taking on human form, yet in the Talmud God appears much more human than we can possibly imagine theologically.

And I confess, last of all, that the Talmud interests me because it makes me consider what corresponds more to God—our Christian language about God taking on human form or the Jewish knowledge about the humanity of God.

"The scribes and Pharisees sit in the chair of Moses. Everything now they tell you, do and obey!"

And now I hear Jesus going on: "But do not do according to what they do, for they say it but do not do it" (Matt 23:3b). Is Jesus thus negating what he has just taught us? Is he now still denigrating the Pharisees and warning us about them? Unfortunately that is what most of the Christian theologians think to this day, and many members of Christian congregations think they can hereby save themselves from Jesus' Jewish demands that are so disconcerting to us.

But no, this is *not* what Jesus means. He says we need to learn the Torah as the Jews have done, along with the Pharisees. Every Jew knows from earliest times: learning alone is not enough; we must do what we have learned. There has been a continuing controversy among the rabbinic teachers: what is more important, learning or doing? One says one thing, and another says the other. There is no one in Judaism who can make this decision, no Pope, no global catechism, no synod and no church administration. Jesus holds the scale in his hand. First he says, "Learn, learn, learn!" Then he says, "Do, do, do!" And thereby do it better than many of the Pharisees—if you could, if only you could!

5

When Will You Restore the Kingdom for Israel?

ON EASTER EVENING TWO DISCIPLES OF JESUS WERE WALKING FROM
Jerusalem down the sixty stadia of the road to Emmaus. They had
turned their backs on Jerusalem, the place of their hopes and of their
last meeting with Jesus, disappointed from the futility of the path they
had gone together with him. His death was also the end for them. And
from the strange message of the angels, brought to them from the grave
by two women they knew, they had grasped only the first part: "He is
not here!" (Luke 24:6). They had not been able to do anything with the
"He has been raised!" The "He is not here!" confirmed for them the
reason for their resignation, which they suffered as deep sorrow, more
precisely, as *skythrōpoi*—people with a darkened, down-cast look (Luke
24:17). In this condition they did not notice that the stranger, who ap-
proached them and who brought them immediately into conversation,
was *kai autos Iēsous*—He, Jesus himself. They simply did not have an eye
for him any more (Luke 24:15). "What are you talking about?" he asked
them. And one of them, Cleopas, answered, "Are you the only citizen of
Jerusalem who does not know all that has happened here today . . . , the
things concerning Jesus of Nazareth?" And they instructed him briefly:
This was "a prophet, proved through word and deed before God and
all the people" (Luke 24:18–19). The high priests and Roman authorities condemned him to death and crucified him. And this was a hard
blow for us, because "we had hoped he would be the one, who was to
come and set Israel free, *lytrousthai*—to redeem" from the hands of the
Romans (Luke 24:21).

This is a *political* expectation of the Messiah, that is, the integral,
unadulterated Jewish hope of the Messiah, not distorted, even altered or
disguised by spiritualization, in such a purity as we rarely see otherwise
in the writings about Jesus. Perhaps it was effective only in a concealed

way in the expectations of the disciples at the time Jesus lived. Perhaps it is only hidden for *our* eyes, so that we no longer can recognize it accurately in the traditions, which the evangelists deliver to us. Or perhaps our eyes are not *yet* open for its possibility, which has revealed itself to us only since 1948 [the founding of the state of Israel] as a real, in any case discussible possibility for the first time in the history of Christianity. But even if this expectation might have slumbered in the disciples of Jesus, it broke down along with the collapse of all the hopes, which had rested on Jesus. And that shows, how closely the disciples had attached these expectations to Jesus. It is, according to the report in Luke 24, the first explanation these disciples could give of *what* had been lost for them with Jesus. The Zionist hope was for them a first expression of their hopes in Jesus: the liberation of their people from Roman domination. But of course it is characteristic of the hopes of Israel for a Messiah up to now, that they find their sharpest actuality not in fulfillment, but in failure. However that might be: conversely it is a challenge for our theology to make clear for ourselves that it is precisely the death of Jesus that allows the political hope of Israel to find expression in the mouths of several of his disciples—only in the form of disappointment, but nevertheless to find expression. It should be, in any case, more than merely a piece of collateral historical remembrance about the time of the "historical" Jesus. It should have its place in the proclamation of faith, and first of all in the kerygma about the crucified Jesus. This Zionist hope is buried together with him. This is an unheard of perspective: *Jesus—important for the political future of Israel!*

Luke has now disclosed the kerygmatic intention of this motif and removed every doubt from it by repeating it right at the beginning of the book of Acts. Here we find ourselves in the midst of the forty days of Eastertide, when Jesus revealed himself in many ways to be alive after his passion (Acts 1:3). These life signs of Jesus had set his disciples into a new expectation unknown to them up to that point: the expectation of the promised Spirit of God. They now looked forward to this in eager expectation. And now Luke must choose, here too, the Zionist hope as the first form in which the disciples can express their expectation: "Lord, will you in these days restore the kingdom for Israel?" (Acts 1:6), *apokathistaneis tēn basileian tōi Israēl?*—Will you give Israel back its state?

Of course, with *basileia* [kingdom] the theo-political concept of biblical language is meant, and not our secular state of today. But also in today's state of Israel secularity has by no means won through against its opposite, theo-political possibility. And the Bible does not yet know anything about these modern distinctions.

It is exciting: Jesus does not reject this political question, does not defend himself against these allegedly false, flesh and blood concepts of Messiah, as so many Christian theologians later and up to the present day seem to do. He makes no attempt to criticize the content of these expectations, let alone to correct them. He just sets the question of the "when" straight: I can know as little about that as you; the Father, God, determines that according to his own order, *taxis*. God alone has it in his power to know when the time is right to bring the state of Israel into being again. That is a good Jewish and proper correction, but it is the only one. Jesus does not manipulate this hope of Israel, he does not reinterpret it, he only gives the dimension of the "when" back to God, as is right and proper.

Let us then bring together, what this means:

1) Luke *closes* his Gospel with the Zionist motif, and *opens* his Acts of the Apostles with it. This expression of hope forms a bond between the two writings, and certainly Luke consciously wanted it to do so.

2) But it is surely more than a literary device. It is the way of God's own activity, that in the Gospel it is the *death* of Jesus, which wrings out from the disciples the word of their disappointed hope, and in the book of Acts it is Jesus *raised* from death, who awakens for them new hope. The fact that the hope, dashed at the death of Jesus, awakened along with and renewed in the activity of Jesus raised from death, has the same Zionist content the first time and the second time, shows that Luke means both to have faith-historical importance. Both the death and the resurrection of Jesus have something to do with the re-establishment of the kingdom for Israel, and thus the re-establishing of the kingdom should be a matter of concern for all of those who draw hope from the death and resurrection of Jesus of Nazareth.

But *what* do these two have to do with one another, and *how* does it concern those who know and confess the name of Jesus?

3) Let us get clear as to the signs under which the Zionist motif appears. First, in view of the death of Jesus, it appears in the *manner of disappointment*. Then, as regards his resurrection, it appears not simply in the way of a certainty, which could remove the disappointment, but rather in the form of a question, which is directed to Jesus, that is, under the *sign of questionability*. To be sure, the fact that Jesus does not correct the question gives an indirect certainty to what is inquired. It is a question, which *can* be directed at Jesus, which he does *not* have to set straight, so as to correct it as a question. He is a proper addressee especially for this question. But it remains a question, and an open question, in so far as Jesus is not the one who can answer it; only God can and should. But the question is one that Jesus—as such, as a question—awakens. Jesus awakens the question in the same way in which he earlier had awakened the question of John the Baptist, "Are you the one who is to come, or should we wait for another?" (Luke 7:19). *Jesus* himself awakened this question by his activity. The Zionist question on the other hand is awakened by God *with respect to* the death and resurrection of Jesus, that is, *through* Jesus. So it becomes—as, in this sense, open—a *question of the future* (and it belongs to that sphere where we reflect on the future: eschatology).

As a *question*, it prevents us for instance from forming the ideology of a Christian Zionism. But as a question *awakened* by God with respect to Jesus, it urges us not to allow Jewish Zionism—that is, the hope of the Jewish people to win back their state—to be something theologically unimportant to us. Rather: the question drives us to ask whether and for what purpose the name of Jesus engages Christians in relationship to the Zionist expectation of Israel, which is justified before God and also before Jesus.

First, let us bring together some evidence from the language of Luke:

4) In their Zionist question, the disciples of Jesus use the verb *apokathistanō*, to set something or someone back into their old condition, to restore, *restituere*. They relate this to the *basileia tōi Israēl*, the kingdom for Israel. From this verb derives the noun *apokatastasis*. Luke uses this in Acts 3:21 and relates it to the coming times, *kairoi* and *chronoi*, which he in Acts 3:20 names *kairoi anapsyxeōs*, the times of refreshment, in the sense of relaxation, renewal, relief from the hot pressures

of history. In Acts 3:21 he calls them the *chronoi apokatastaseōs pantōn*, times in which everything will be brought back into its proper order, as God had announced it from eternity through the mouths of the prophets of Israel. From this text a concept was taken that in the history of Christian eschatology has played such a large, and to be sure, much fought about roll: that of the *apokatastasis pantōn*, the doctrine of the restoration of all things. In the context in which Peter uses this word in Acts it has two possible meanings, one from the closest and one from a near-by context. The "restoration" of all that, which the prophets had announced from eternity, could mean what Peter in the Bible quotation of Acts 3:22–23 first suggests from Deuteronomy 18:15: God will cause a prophet like Moses to arise for Israel from among the brothers, and all should listen to him. No doubt he refers here to Jesus; he would be in person the *apokatastasis pantōn* to be awaited in the future, the restoration work of God. But Luke immediately added to Peter's speech another quotation, which he, however, changed from its original wording (in Lev 23:29) for his own purposes. There is in Leviticus the instruction: "Every soul that does not fast on this day [that is, *Yom Kippur*, the day of atonement], shall be cut off from among his people." Luke says, however: "Every soul that does not listen to this prophet, will be cut off from among his people" (Acts 3:23). That is, short and sweet: Whoever does not listen to Jesus, will be cut off from among the people of God. The association with the revision of the Leviticus text goes something like this: A prophet like Moses—that is Jesus; *Yom Kippur*, the day of atonement, the day of liberation from the pressures of history—that is the day of Jesus. The fast commanded on *Yom Kippur* is the turning again to Jesus—"that your sins may be wiped out . . ." (Acts 3:19). Luke may have understood the day of Jesus as a new *Yom Kippur*, which for every Jew is a day of prayer for forgiveness of sins and so for renewal and new beginning; and it is also a day of restoration, of *apokatastasis*, in so far, for example, as soon after *Yom Kippur* the reading of the Bible begins in the services of worship from the beginning, that is with Genesis 1:1. But whoever does not follow this, steps out of the cycle of the word about the history of Israel, separates him/herself thereby from his/her people and is thus cut off from his/her people. In this close connection the word about the *apokatastasis pantōn* could thus be speaking about the new *Yom Kippur* to be expected in the person of Jesus.

But Luke allows Peter to continue preaching. The *apokatastasis* is referred to additional prophetic texts apart from the two already mentioned. There is not only the critical prophecy of Moses and the restoration of the law. There is also a genuine prophetic prophecy, which Luke means to find with all the prophets, "from Samuel onwards" (Acts 3:24). Samuel, the prophet who anointed Saul to be king (1 Samuel 9). And as Moses with his Torah pointed toward a day of restoration, so Samuel and the prophets who came after him likewise pointed toward the same days as those to which the Torah points. But from the perspective of Samuel these days receive a different accent than that which Moses gave them. While Moses points to those "souls," who will be cut off from the people if they do not fast, do not fast themselves "into Jesus," Samuel points to "the sons of the prophets and of the covenant, which God made with your fathers" (Acts 3:25). And the content of this covenant is the blessing of Abraham (Gen 12:3): "Through your descendants will all the tribes of the earth be blessed." Thus Samuel, the king-maker, points toward the relationship of Israel with the nations, the mission, which Israel has toward them: to be a blessing for them. But far from holding onto the critical note against Israel, which is sounded in the perspective of Moses, and accusing Israel for having neglected the Abraham mission, Peter according to Luke forms from the promises to Abraham a very different kerygma and proclaims the servant Jesus as a blessing to the Jews, by which God blesses *them*. Those who are called to be a blessing for the nations are blessed by the servant Jesus. This is for them another *chronos apokatastaseōs pantōn*, the day of the prophecy of Samuel: God will bless Israel anew. *Jesus will become a blessing for Israel.* And the blessing will take place in the field Samuel stands for: the kingdom for Israel in the midst of the nations.

It makes therefore sense internally to relate the words *apokathistanai* and *apokatastasis* to one another, to hear in one word the other, the verb of chapter 1 in the noun of chapter 3: to hear in the restoration of the Torah of Moses and in the double-sided relationship of the blessing between Israel and the nations a contribution to the restoration of the kingdom for Israel.

But what would that actually mean?

5) There is, during the Jerusalem council of the apostles, a moment, when James, the brother of Jesus, seizes the word (Acts 15:13ff.). He re-

fers to the remarks of a Simon (perhaps none other than Simon Peter), who had just explained that God now for the first time—*prōton*—had chosen for Godself a *laos*, that is, a people of God—from the *goyim* [the gentiles, nations]. With this James circumscribes one of the missionary reports exchanged at this conference. The formation of purely gentile congregations has taken place. James says that this corresponds—so embarrassing as it must be for a Jew—with the Scriptures, and he quotes from the Septuagint translation of Amos 9:11: "After this I will return and I will rebuild the fallen booth of David. I will rebuild its ruins, and I will restore it"—with the goal that *hoi kataloipoi tōn anthropōn* (Amos 9:12)—the remnant of humanity, those left over, the survivors—ask about the Lord, may seek him, and all the *goyim* as well, says God, "over whom my name has been called." And this "says the Lord who does all these things, as has been known from eternity" (Acts 15:16 18). Thus the James of Luke reads in this quotation a connection between the Zionist hope of a re-building of the house of David, the Davidic state, from the ruins in which it now lies, and the new possibility "to seek the Lord" and to "inquire" about him, which is given therein for the survivors of Israel, but also for a large number of gentiles, who in the meantime have become familiar with the name of God. The restoration of the state, the religious restitution of the Jewish survivors and the religious participation of many gentiles form here a connection. More precisely, the restoration of the state is the presupposition for the no longer futile seeking of both Jews and *goyim* for God. These thoughts are theologically framed at the beginning with a self-encouragement of God: *anastrepsō*, I will return, turn again about-face. At the end there is the formula, "thus says the Lord . . ." who not only wants it and says it but actually does it, as it has been known *ap' aiōnos*, "from eternity." To the self-encouragement of God, "I will return . . ." corresponds the content of that which God does, when he "returns": re-building, reconstruction, restoration, setting up again the old order—as Zionism is, in fact, a movement of historical restoration, that is what *apokatastasis* means. The word, however, that the Lord really *does* this, as has been known from eternity, says that this is already in process. Without a doubt this refers to the winning of many *goyim* to the name of the Lord, and James is convinced that therefore the Christian mission to the gentiles—with all its embarrassment—still belongs to the way of the history of God expected for ages. *The Jewish state and the mission to the gentiles* have beneath the surface something to do with one another. But what?

Let us be clear about the citation from Amos: James quotes it in Jerusalem as it is found in the Septuagint. The exposition we have given to it is not something found especially by Christians, but it is a recognition from the Jewish diaspora. It is not first of all Christian preachers who link the Jewish state together with the mission to the gentiles: this is a complex Jewish experience from the *gola* [diaspora, exile]. James, in Luke's interpretation, simply used this factual connection with regard to the Christian mission to the nations. Simon says that God for the first time has chosen for Godself a *laos*, a people of God (Acts 15:14), and James adds two things to this: First, this is nothing really new; it has "been known from eternity" (Acts 15:18) that the Lord does so. Second, though—and this is what is uniquely James' contribution in this context—: The mission to the gentiles and God's will for the restoration of the kingdom of David belong together. For this reason one should for heaven's sake make no great difficulties for the gentiles imposing all too rigid and strict requirements of the Torah on them (Acts 15:19). The Noahitic *mitzvot* are fully sufficient for them (Acts 15:20). These practical consequences, to which James comes on the basis of the quotation from the Greek translation of Amos, show that he suggests a proper relationship in accordance with the Torah between the *goyim* and the house of David to be rebuilt. But this theological depth has already been a vision of the *Jewish* diaspora, presupposing the state of Israel as a condition for a new seeking and asking after God on the part of surviving Jews and non-Jews touched by the name of God. The state is that which is objective in the God of Israel, which can stand for the hope that the seeking after God, asking and inquiring about God will not spill out into nothingness. It is as though Luke allowed his James to speak to "us today." The *hopōs*, the "so that" or "in order that"—so that those who survived and *kol hagoyim* [all the nations] might seek the Lord—by which verse 17 follows verse 16, is one of the most contemporary words of the Bible. It connects restoration and future, the state of David and the world's religion.

6) What is it, really, that makes us so sure of the fact that, with the *basileia tōi Israēl*, which has become so disappointingly questionable for the friends of Jesus in the face of his death, and in the time of Jesus's resur-

rection appearances once again has become so insistently *worth* questioning, we really have a political, a "Zionist" motif? We are conscious of the fact that only very few commentators on the text have up till now said this. Most of them think rather of something exclusively theological, something that has to do with the "purely" eschatological reign of God, depicted more likely as equipped with the signs of the coming eon than with those of the old kingdom in Israel. We have already indicated what brings us to our alternative view: the actual rebirth of a state of Israel in the land of the fathers in 1948, the self-identification of its Jewish residents with the "ancient," biblical "state" of Israel lost in the years between 70 and 135 CE. This makes our generation the first Christian generation of all that can think about what was unthinkable for 2000 years of Christianity. We see the year 1948 as an hermeneutical event, an event that facilitates understanding. That does not yet mean that we in fact hit upon such moments of reality in the Jesus writings, which have become plausible for *us* today. We know that we first of all can undertake only some attempts at interpreting in the direction of what has become thinkable. For that reason we have consciously emphasized the form of the question and the character of questionability, in which the motif first meets us in the book of Acts (Acts 1:6). This is a questionability that concerns us, too. But we sense precisely in the questioning nature shaping the motif in Luke *something that can be grasped historically.* There the state of Israel is not something theologically questionable, as has been quickly explained in the Christian exegesis. Luke offers with the form of the question possibly a more exact indication of the historical-political situation, in which he tells his story. To be sure, Jerusalem, at the time of his writing, is probably already in ruins. But still there are forces at work in the Jewish people, which not only hold to a rebuilding of the destroyed city of David, but are prepared to fight for it in a "secular," even bellicose way; and we know about Jewish uprisings in the diaspora, and above all about the Second Jewish War, the Bar Kochba War, which not long after the time when Luke probably wrote actually broke out. The idea of a Jewish state was in this generation not only alive as a memory, but also as an achievable future. So it must not be historically beside the point, to see reflected, especially in the tension in Luke between the disappointment at the end of his Gospel and the revival of hope at the beginning of the book of Acts, the structure of a genuine historical situation.

Luke himself presents this with great clarity: in the vote that he has the pharisee Gamliel give during the interrogation of Peter and John before the *Sanhedrin*.

First: we have here within the Jesus writings the unique case, where a historically important figure of rabbinic Judaism encounters us by name and so opens for us historical Judaism contemporary with the beginnings of the church. It is Gamliel *ha-zaqen*, the elder, that is Gamliel I. We do not know much for certain about him. He is supposedly the son of a Simeon, who was the son of the famous school master Hillel. Nothing of this is certain, but this much probably that Gamliel I belonged to the first generation of the Tannaites, and there probably to the school of Hillel, which—with regard to the keeping above all of food laws, but also of other *mitzvot*—tended more toward an easing of the commandments, in contrast to the school of Shammai, which as a rule made more stringent decisions. Something of this liberal style of argumentation can be seen in the vote of Gamliel as Luke presents it, so that, as regards structure, Luke demonstrates a good historical knowledge of contemporary Judaism.

Luke calls the pharisee Gamliel a "teacher of the law, who was honored by all the people," a *moreh ha-tora*, a *nomodidaskalos* (Acts 5:34). He probably takes over from the high priest at this moment the chair of the proceedings of the Sanhedrin and orders as his first act that the two accused, Peter and John, be excluded from the rest of the proceedings, above all from the speech that he himself now holds (Acts 5:34). He does not want the accused to hear what he has to say, because he does not want to disavow the members of the court in their obstinate stance in the presence of the two. Now he gives his vote: "Consider carefully what you intend to do to these men." It could be the case that there is something to the proclamation of these men about Jesus of Nazareth. What then? Gamliel draws a historical parallel between what he has heard about Jesus and the memory about two others who claimed to be the Messiah: Judas the Galilean, who according to the report of Flavius Josephus in about the year 6 CE—Luke says, "in the days of the census"—had raised and led a zealots' uprising against the Romans; and a certain Theudas, who—again according to Flavius Josephus—at the time of the Roman governor Cuspius Fadus, who was in office between 44 and 46 BCE, likewise appeared as Messiah, and promised his followers a repetition of the miracle of the Sea of Reeds and of Joshua:

He would lead the people through the Jordan with dry feet, as Joshua did when he led the people into the promised land, and as Moses had done when he led the people through the Sea of Reeds out of bondage. Gamliel thought it possible that Jesus might be "one like these." Just like these, there was a movement among the people, which had started at him, as one could see in the two accused. To be sure both of these movements were relatively quickly struck down and destroyed and their leaders had thus turned out to be false Messiahs. That *might* also be the case with Jesus and his followers. But—and now Gamliel, the student of Hillel, speaks—we cannot tell in advance on the basis of any messianic appearance, "whether he is the One or not." The capability of being disappointed belongs to the essence of the messianic in Judaism. On the other hand, it is from the outset always a new and *open possibility*, that is, the sum total of the experience and the "subject matter," the way it is, with the Messiah. In any case a Messiah is to be taken seriously, for Israel and for those who share Israel's hope: every time it is perhaps a new beginning by God. Gamliel therefore reasons concerning the treatment of the followers of Jesus: "Leave them alone! Let them go!" Give this time and room; we will see whether there is something to it or not. "For if their purpose or activity—*to ergon touto*—is of human origin, it will fall. But if it is from God, you will not be able to stop these men, dissolve—*katalysai*—them, turn them aside." I advise you urgently not to do anything to these men, ". . . you will only find yourselves fighting against God," as *theomachoi* (Acts 5:38–39).

With this, Gamliel finds, as Luke tells it, the agreement of the court. They call in the accused, have them flogged as a deterrent, and let them go on condition that they stop their activities in the name of Jesus—which the two naturally do not obey (Acts 5:40–42).

What is important to us is the *clarity with which Jesus here—from the perspective of the Jewish, rabbinic side—is rated as a political Messiah!* Of course the possibility is seen that this could be an error, just as in the other two cases that were mentioned. But Luke wants to hold the *possibility* open; that is why he relates the opinion of Gamliel. And that demonstrates to us that a political messiahship of Jesus was a possibility to be raised for Luke, and therefore could be discussed. The little bits and indications that we have accumulated so far receive a firm basis and connection in the opinion of Gamliel. As we have said: the openness, the disappointable, and the questionable all belong to the concept. But the subject matter as such can be discussed for Luke—and not merely "historically," but also *theologically*.

We have already named a few pieces and indications that allow the possibility of theological discussion of the Zionist motif: in the form of the hope for *apokatastasis*, in the acceptance of the Jewish diaspora thought about an inner connection between the re-building work in Israel and the relationship of the nations to that, not last also with the interpretation of Jesus as a new *Yom Kippur*, a new turning point and event of renewal.

We want to consolidate exactly this last viewpoint by quoting a piece from the Mussaf—that is, the additional prayer for *Yom Kippur*—from the Siddur, the prayer book, which outlines the order of Jewish worship. It shows that and how the *Yom Kippur* worship service is also a cry for restoration—not only of the temple in Jerusalem, but also of the kingdom for Israel, the gathering of all the dispersed in Zion: that is, the Zionist motif.

> On account of our sins we were driven from our land, so that we are not able to fulfill our obligations in the house that you have chosen, in the great and holy house over which your name is named; on account of the hand that was stretched out against your holy ones. It is your will, o eternal One, our God and the God of our fathers, merciful king, to have mercy upon us, and in your great goodness over your holy ones, to build it up again quickly and to elevate its honor.

This is the prayer for the rapid rebuilding of the temple. But the prayer verses following immediately at this point prove that this is not only a prayer for a *religious* restoration, but for a restoration of the whole, that is thus a theo-political prayer:

> Our Father, our king, reveal the honor of your kingdom, the *kavod malkutkha*, soon over us, illuminate and elevate yourself over us *in the eyes of all living beings, le ene kol chay*, bring near those of us who are dispersed from the midst of the nations. Gather our scattered ones from the ends of the earth and bring us to Zion, your city, in exultation, and to Jerusalem, to your holy house, in eternal joy . . .

In this bit of prayer, too, the plea for renewal of the kingdom is combined with humanity, with "all living beings." The connection between the kingdom and the world of the nations is nothing specifically

Christian, but genuinely Jewish. Only the application that Luke gives to this connection in the book of Acts is specifically Christian. In the *Yom Kippur* prayer, the concern is for the eyes of the nations who are engaged as spectators. God is supposed to undertake the theo-political rebuilding of Israel so clearly that it becomes an incontestable fact in the publicity of the world. The witnesses to Jesus all together, on the other hand, think that Jesus, who has not done away with the relationship of the nations with Israel in its fundamental meaning, in the importance of Israel's election, has drawn them out of a mere spectator attitude with regard to Israel. The nations are to be participants in the restoration hopes of Israel *much more than merely spectators!*

But how?

Now I can only bring together a couple of splinters and stay with Luke. In his Gospel, Luke has seen the whole life of Jesus set under a double goal. In the canticle of Simeon it is expressed: My old eyes have seen the child Jesus and I foresee, he is "a light to illumine the gentiles, and for the glory of his people Israel" (Luke 2:32). He is, first of all, *or goyim* [light for the gentiles]; he is to bring the nations to the recognition of the God of Abraham, Isaac and Jacob, and open them for this God; and that is, secondly, to serve the purpose thereby that the people of Israel might be glorified, praised and celebrated by the nations. For when the nations are won for this *God*, that will also be good for the *people* of this God who has designated himself with the names of the fathers of this people from earliest times.

Luke therefore designated Jesus in Acts 13:23 as a descendent of David, and named him a *tōi Israēl sōtēra*, that is, in Hebrew, a *goël le Yisraël.* You know that word now: the *goël* is the near relative, who must "redeem" a family member who has gotten into difficulty, as the law commands.

And now Luke interpreted the Christian mission to the nations in the name of Jesus as this work. It serves the purpose of allowing Israel to be able to breathe freely finally in the midst of the nations, because the Christian mission wins them over for the God of Israel and along with this unavoidably for the people of this God. Luke knew it even more precisely. He heard Peter say (Acts 10:36): The word that God has now sent through Jesus "to the sons of Israel" is not intended to bring the Jews to believe in the Jesus of the Christians, rather it is the *davar* [word] that allows "*peace* to be proclaimed" to the Jews "through

Jesus Christ," *shalom*. Jesus serves Israel by making the nations ready for *shalom* with the children of Israel. That is the significance of Jesus and Christianity for Israel: It yokes the nations to the peace of Israel in their midst. If Jesus releases *that* among us Christians, *then* we can confess: Jesus is the Messiah.

Before Peter had finished speaking the Spirit fell on all those who had heard this explanation. And the greatest surprise was released among the Jews about the fact that the gift of the Holy Spirit was now poured out *even* on the non-Jews, "*even* on the gentiles" (Acts 10:45). Obviously it goes without saying that the Jews know the *ruach hakodesh* [spirit of holiness]. And the spirit of holiness poured out on the nations here means that they, too, will at last be won for peace with Israel.

That means: Jesus—a light to illumine the gentiles, and for the glory, benefit, profit, peace of his people Israel.

～

Now a leap into the apocalyptic. In the last book of the Christian Bible— Revelation, chapter 20—we hear of an angel coming from heaven, holding the keys to the abyss. The angel takes the dragon, the old serpent, the devil, and shuts him for a thousand years in the abyss, closes and seals the door, "to keep him from seducing the nations anymore" (Rev 20:3).

A thousand years of the nations not dominated by Satan! Just imagine what that could mean for Israel!

That is the vision of the thousand years' kingdom. A thousand years of peace for Israel over against the nations occupied by the devil. My Lutheran ancestors disapproved of the idea of the thousand years' kingdom. They thought that it was a *judaica opinio*, a Jewish opinion [cf. the *Augsburg Confession*, 1530]. It is certainly a Jewish *hope*. And we have seen how diabolic it was, when National Socialism, under the sign of the thousand years' kingdom, sought to win us and had won us over—not to peace with Israel, but to its eternal destruction!

That is all the more reason to fight for this millenial idea, and *not* to delete it from the Christian hope. A thousand years of peace for Israel, because Satan no longer has access to the nations.

It was Luke who reported that Satan, after Jesus had energetically rejected his temptations, "departed from him" (Luke 4:13). Luke portrayed the life of Jesus under the idea of the thousand years' kingdom, freed from Satan. The life of Jesus was to bring a time for Israel to breathe more easily. To be sure, after the thousand years, Satan was to have another opportunity to be "let loose" for a short time (Rev 20:3), as he appears once again briefly at the conclusion of the story of Jesus (Luke 22:3): "Then Satan entered into Judas called Iscariot, one of the twelve." Satan enters into the church! A thousand years are not an eternity, as we know also from our German history.

My teacher Karl Barth said: "Without at least a pinch of millenialism there can be no Christian eschatology." I agree and make my confession to this positive apocalypticism. No Christian hope for an end without a hope for a time when Israel can breathe easily, and phases where, through the activity of the friends of Jesus, the nations are won over *for* Israel, instead of always being diabolically put against it.

And, as for that "pinch of millenialism": I was in 1959 with the first group of German students in Israel. We spent the night in the youth hostel Poroyia above the Sea of Galilee. The director of the hostel had just immigrated from the United States. We got into a conversation and asked him, what sort of future he would give to the "experiment of a national rebirth" for Israel. He answered—something unforgettable for me up to this day—: "Oh, you know, even the splendor of Solomon's reign lasted for only fifty years."

I learn from that: All things, even great things, have their limits. But there is not only the sign of "apocalypse now," as it says in the film with the same title. There is also *eschatology now*.

Or better yet: hope now.

And [says Hillel]: If not now—when? *Im lo achshav—eimatai?*

PART TWO

Attempts at Understanding Karl Barth

6

First Report on Karl Barth's "Socialist Speeches"

I

IN THE UNPUBLISHED LITERARY ESTATE OF KARL BARTH TEXTS HAVE been found that Barth gave the handwritten title, "Socialist Speeches." These are forty-three manuscripts, some written on larger sheets (22 x 18 cm), some on smaller (18.5 x 11 cm). His handwriting is sometimes difficult to decipher since it varies between German and Latin styles of writing and contains its own abbreviations. Some of these manuscripts appear to have been written in haste. Apart from four exceptions, they are either thoroughly elaborated lecture texts or only outlines for lectures dashed off in shorthand. They date from October 15, 1911, to July 11, 1917, and later from February 11, 1919, to November 29, 1919.

These texts have a common "setting in life." They were meant to be lectures for the most diverse local groups and suborganizations of the Social Democratic Party of Aargau. Oftentimes Barth was invited to the so-called workers' associations, above all in Safenwil, but then also to various groups of the Gruetli Association. Historically, these two unions had emerged independently, partly from historically older organizations of originally diverse zeal and direction, which, when it came to the building of the Swiss Social Democratic Party (SPS) in 1870, gathered together under one roof of the new party. Occasionally they were officially recognized by the party as its local sections, while nevertheless leading relatively independent lives. In Safenwil, for example, the trade union was the local section of the party. The Gruetli Association formed the right wing of the party, and was often threatened by expulsion from the party, finally separating itself from the SPS. Nevertheless, this group politically strengthened the far-reaching socialist movement in Switzerland, among which also were included a line of anarchist groups and, above all, the religious socialist movement of Switzerland. It is remarkable that of the forty-three lectures in this group of unpublished works probably only one is intended for meetings of the religious socialists, the group that Barth is usually associated with at the time. All the others are documents of purely party activities.

As far as the content is concerned, four distinct groups of themes can be established, about which Barth reported many times under diverse titles.

1. A great complex of speeches is concerned with *inner problems of the Social Democratic Party*. They deal with questions of daily praxis, which kept all socialist party leaders from Engels to Lenin busy: problems of inner discipline, workers' education, exposure to the dangers of alcohol, the strengthening of marriage and family morals, contribution to the party, etc. In Safenwil Barth had extremely lively views on such problems of the party, which he saw from his own particular perspective. This will be outlined in detail later.

2. After 1914, naturally, the *war question* occupied a broad space. Barth frequently pronounced his disillusionment with his theological teachers, who had nearly all testified their loyalty to the Kaiser at the outbreak of the war, and he indicated this as the point of rupture in his theological thought. In the "Socialist Speeches," however, the war question also appears in other perspectives, that is, in connection with the socialist and internationalist discussions. Here Barth is not moved by a Christian pacifism. He has rather posed a question mark behind the rejection of the defense of the Swiss country by his party. Instead, we face him as he is occupied with the arguments around the question of the failure of the Second (Social Democratic) International and the formation of the Third (Communist) International between 1917 and 1919. Barth took part in these struggles closely and directly, as official party delegate in 1917, and as an eyewitness of the first post-war congress of the Second International in Bern in 1919.

3. In the decisive years of 1917 and 1919, Barth presented to his party many times reports on the *world political situation*: about the outlook for peace in 1917, about the Swiss general strike in 1918, and about

the course of the Bolshevik Revolution in 1919. On these occasions he lectured over a period of many weeks on the first Soviet constitution— "The Declaration on the Rights of the Working and Exploited People"— to the people of Safenwil. He went over the document paragraph by paragraph, interpreted it, commented on it, and confronted it with the bourgeois opposition to this revolution. Sometimes he analyzed and commented on a draft bill, e.g., for a new Swiss factory law, in painstaking and legal detail. Sometimes he interpreted literature, e.g., under the heading "conscience" a Tolstoy drama, or under the heading "the higher law" a story from the party newspaper, which was written in the genre of light fiction but nevertheless interested Barth as history of the working milieu.

4. Especially striking is a series of lectures in which Barth dealt with the external and internal *relations of religion and socialism*, Christianity and socialism, and church and socialism, but also the gospel and even Jesus Christ and the social movement. Naturally he was questioned frequently here and there in bourgeois and socialist circles, about how he, as a practicing Protestant pastor, could at the same time be a practicing socialist. Some lectures deal with such questions and partly contain confessory statements. For example, he says the following in a lecture on "Religion and Socialism" on December 7, 1915:

> I have become a socialist in a very simple way, and I live socialism in a very simple way. Because I would like to believe in God and his kingdom, I place myself at the point where I see something of God's kingdom break through. You should not believe that thereby I have constructed an ideal picture of socialism for myself. I think I can see the mistakes of socialism and its proponents very clearly. But much more clearly I see in the grounding thought, in the essential endeavor of socialism, a revelation of God which I must recognize before all and about which I must be delighted. The new society, which is based on the foundation of community and justice, instead of capriciousness and the law of the jungle, the new order of work in the sense of common activity of all for all instead of in the sense of exploitation through egotism of the individual, the new connection of humans as humans over the barrier of class and nation, . . . finally the way to this goal: The simple brotherhood and solidarity [that appear] first among the poor and underprivileged of all countries—I must recognize all these new [features], which socialism brings

into political and economic life, as something new from God's side . . . Socialism—despite its imperfections, which people should discuss calmly and openly—is for me one of the most gratifying signs of the fact that God's kingdom does not stand still, that God is at work, and hence I may not and cannot stand against it indifferently.

Therefore, I must express an opinion concerning it.

From the sentiment of duty, that tells me: this is where you belong, if you take God in earnest. Through my membership in the Social Democratic Party I believe to confess a very important point in complete plainness to myself and to my parish that God must come to honor . . . People may cling to religion and still associate themselves with another party or remain without a party. If only religion were my concern, I would probably stand on the side of people without a party or perhaps also on the side of a liberal-conservative party. However, I cannot find the kingdom of God there, where people again and again make money more important than human beings, where possession is again and again the scale of all value, where people set the homeland over humanity in anxiety and small-mindedness, where people again and again believe more in the present than in the future.

The well-known difference between the gospel and religion is accordingly in its origin also a political, even a party-political difference.

Or, from "Evangelium und Sozialismus" [Gospel and Socialism] on February 1, 1914:

How have I come to combine the gospel with socialism? I was educated to judge human beings not according to their money value, and to take material misery of others as a serious problem. As a student I came to know the jaded indifference of bourgeois circles and the poverty in Geneva. At that time I still regarded social misery as a necessary fact of nature, to which faith just had to provide a strong but impractical hope.—Something new was brought to me by Calvin's idea of "God's city" on earth, and this led me to the fact that Jesus has portrayed the kingdom of God as a state of complete love of God and love among brothers.—Through S. I was acquainted with socialism and I was driven to more exact reflection and the study of the matter. Since that time, I have considered socialist demands an important part of the application of the gospel. Certainly, I also believe that they cannot be realized without the gospel.

That is the idealistic, bourgeois, religious-socialist genesis of a socialist, but Barth tried to objectify it beyond all individualities. "A real Christian must become socialist (if he will be in earnest about the reformation of Christianity!). A real socialist must be Christian if he is interested in the reformation of socialism" (from "War, Socialism, Christianity," February 14, 1915). What this should mean became a question which preoccupied Barth lastingly. At first he could only say it negatively, as he still did later in the famous Tambach lecture: no "religious-social intermingling," which would harm socialism no less than religion. "I hold the 'political pastor' in every form, in particular the socialist form, to be an aberration. But I place myself as a simple soldier, so to speak, there where I am able to see God's traces and that means exactly: I place myself as a human and as a citizen on the social-ist and also openly on the social-democratic side" (December 4, 1915: "Religion and Christianity").

Barth understood his lecture activity for the party as connected with his [pastoral] work. One indication of this connection is that he placed the manuscript of a funeral speech for the Safenwil worker, Arnold Hunziker, among his "Socialist Speeches." Party and parish work belonged together. On Monday, September 3, 1917, his sermon was published in the *Freier Aargauer* [Aargau Free Press], the "official publication organ of the Aargau Social Democratic Party and of the cartel of workers' union[s]." Its words are a peculiar example of how socialist freethinker circles of workers and petit-bourgeois understood death and resurrection. This understanding was accepted and applied by Barth here without objection: one lives on in one's matter—in the "worker's matter"—and in the end the mourning congregation is re-quested to "Take care that you understand and grasp the living that was in our dead comrade, and let go of the transitory, human, affair that lies now over there. Take care of it, you of his sons and daughters, you of his colleagues and comrades, all of you that have known him—and not known him! Then it does not go backwards from this grave into human sadness and desolation, but forward to new and greater victories of life." Barth portrayed Arnold Hunziker as an exemplary worker, i.e., as an unselfish socialist, not directed by egotistical interest, who understood "that one cannot live only for oneself and one's family, but that there is a higher duty, which nowadays commands especially the workers to stick together and to vouch for one another."

> It became clear to him that the worker must be a conscious and not a sleeping person, a fighter and not a coward . . . Hence he had to become a *Social Democrat*. I say: he *must* . . . In him there came to light and breakthrough precisely this, which also moves the great masses unconsciously and spinelessly in their innermost hearts: the realization of the deprivation of the people in their dependence upon capital, and the insight into the sole help, which must consist in solidarity, in the willing and unselfish and brave community of the dependent, and finally the hope and will: Things must change, if only human beings would come to themselves.

For Barth this "must" was the point of divine effectiveness in the life of the worker, Arnold Hunziker, and so also of all workers.

Two texts (without information as to the time of writing) supply data attesting the history of two important industrial plants, the firm C. F. Bally in Schönenward, and Sulzer Brothers in Winterthur. Both of these are known as great Swiss enterprises even today. Here Barth is interested in the family history of the firms' owners, the technological development of their businesses, the social conditions that rule their companies, and also the religious self-understanding of these industrial owners. It is not yet clear whether these texts are extracts from existing histories of the companies or Barth's independent data collection. Their purpose surely ought to be clear. Through the collection of information Barth investigated the life circumstances and conditions of his parish members and comrades. Because the two enterprises offer examples of the social conscience of capitalists, it is also conceivable that these texts could be materials for the great dossier, which will be discussed in the next section.

A separate slipcase contains a detailed manuscript of sixty-one large pages, to which Barth gave its own title page, "Arbeiterfrage" [Workers' Question]. This text is especially interesting because it documents a way of working, which Barth does not use anywhere else, namely *empirical analysis*. Barth works here with statistical material in hardly calculable superabundance, such as wage and price scales, the "household calculation of a starch worker," statistics of working hours, paragraphs of labor law in various countries, statistics of youth labor, statistics of profit and receipts, insurance, bank dividends, occupational disease (e.g., of tobacco workers), statistics of accidents, women in the labor force (differentiated according to cantons), money devaluation, cost of intermediate trade, age structure in the industrial businesses, housing situations, overcrowding in living space, vacation periods, etc.—So far it is not ascertainable where Barth acquired this corpus of data. Partly he glued into his text extracts from newspaper stories in the socialist press, from the *Trade Union Review*, and the like. From the comparison with other parts of the "Socialist Speeches" it follows that Barth read and partly used the writings of W. Sombart, H. Herkner, and P. Pflüger on the workers' question. In these texts statistical material is used as well, but none of the materials used here finds a place in Barth's manuscripts. Therefore, it is to be regarded as Barth's independent collection for the time being, and it is in some cases more detailed than the possible model of this literary type. After all, there can also be found some important discussions significant for Barth's general perspective of the whole issue, e.g., his critique of so-called scientific management, the Taylor system, by which nourishment, motion, and timing of the worker as a human machine should be regulated from the sole standpoint of economic efficiency. Barth concedes that the present labor conditions include enormous squandering of forces and that every concentration of labor is to be welcomed, because promotion of production is equivalent to progress for humanity in the given circumstances. However, the primary question for him was whether this system of economic efficiency betrayed the humanity of the worker, whether here the system does not replace "the personality," whether the ideal of a worker who has as few sources of irritation as possible does not in practice intensify the danger of nervousness, and therefore increase the possibility of accidents in business incalculably; and whether this is not all the quintessence and goal of a through-and-through materialistic world-view. To this Barth's answer was unequivocal: As long as the economic principle of efficiency serves solely "the system," i.e., capitalist production, rationalization does not serve general progress, but only the monetary gain of the shareholder, and at the same time the moral and political oppression of the worker, who above all loses consciousness of solidarity due to personal isolation and due to the loss of thought and feeling. That again means squashing the working class, the will for resistance, and the will to self-organization of the proletariat.

Another example: Barth's No to the so-called "yellow" workers' organizations, which the entrepreneurs promoted as a strike-breaking organization and which campaigned among the workers against the class struggle and for peaceful negotiation. In confrontation with these groups, Barth argued using the concepts of Marxist political economy and remarked also under the heading "in principle":

> Remember the socialists have not created *the class division*. It is the product of the present economic order: A "free" work contract due to private ownership of the means of production. Through this order a part of society is made dependent as a matter of principle and exploited practically. The *class struggle*, i.e., the fight for the power of the working class, aims at overcoming such antagonism, i.e., at peace. *There is no other peace but that of the new order of [social] conditions for the one, who is in earnest about the healing of the working class.*

Here Barth specifies the meaning of the worker: "'Worker' in a general sense is every well-behaved human. Herein is meant: *the worker who stands in service and in the employment of industrial enterprise*"—i.e., the wage worker. Barth defines the worker's special feature with the description of his working conditions:

> The worker is without possessions, i.e., he is dependent on the employer for subsistence, who through the labor contract with the worker acquires and pays for labor power. The employer is . . . qualified for this contract as the possessor of the *means* of production (factories, machines, raw material) and therefore of production *profit*. *Labor contract*: An obligation between two opponents with equal rights, seemingly very clear and fair, in reality a sequence of disadvantages follows *on the part of the worker*. (a) The worker is dependent upon the labor contract for his survival, while the employer can live on property, pension, or labor. (Marginal note: "On the one hand a question of life, on the other a business interest!") (b) The worker engages his person in the labor contract; the employer engages (and risks) only his belongings. (c) The worker cannot restrict his "production" (labor supply), without going into ruin, while every other production can be restricted. If the wage decreases, he must work longer and more intensively. These two things together ruin him or reduce his standard of living. Through this fact, perhaps balance is produced between supply and demand. (Marginal note: "Hoffstatt, the steel industry in Pittsburgh 1909, to workers demanding wage increase: 'demand and supply determine the wages here and elsewhere . . . We buy the labor on the cheapest market. If a man is not satisfied with his wage or the conditions

under which he works, he can leave. Against this nothing can be said."")

Barth comments: The ruling classes

> regard it as a matter of fact, that the *worker reconciles himself to a position determined by a "free" labor contract.* In a misunderstood interpretation of the Christian concept of subordination, one regards the superiority of the employer that is based on capital possession to be of the divine order while rebellion against it is "indignation," "overthrowing," etc. Typical here is therefore the resultant attitude of state and society toward strikes, i.e., "laziness," "disturbance of economic life," emergency laws. For the worker the bare necessities should be good enough, while one draws no limit to the enrichment of employers. *Welfare of industry* becomes one-sidedly identified with the profit of the employer (factory law). The risk of the employer is morally valued very dearly ("Viking"), while the well-being and the risk (crisis, accidents) of the worker are second rate at best.

From several places in the text one can infer that Barth has also re-worked this writing for oral presentation. It is uncertain whether he used it already in the winter of 1913/14 in Safenwil or in Aargau; in that case it would be already a year before his entrance to the party, which happened in the beginning of 1915, and Barth would have done socialist grass root activism before he joined party.

Until now we only know for sure from his letter exchange with Thurneysen that he has "made full" use of this dossier "with local workers" "every Tuesday" at the end of 1915. "I make it without enthusiasm, simply because it is necessary," reads the letter of January 1, 1916.

II

The "Socialist Speeches" make it possible to clarify phases in Barth's understanding of socialism and that immediately means also to clarify his practical relation to socialism, to the Social Democratic Party of Switzerland, and to the Socialist International, and therefore to indicate the development of this relationship.

The first phase is to be designated between 1911 and the outbreak of war in 1914. Its point of ending is unambiguous, because the Yes of the Social Democratic Parties in Europe to the war changes Barth's relation to socialism in general—as we shall see. Harder to determine is the starting point of this first phase. The year 1911 is chosen at random, as it is the year in which Barth came to Safenwil and the year in which the "Socialist Speeches" began. But he had already encountered socialism itself earlier. We heard already about his Geneva experience as an assistant pastor. But we do not know yet who "S" is, who had brought him to socialism according to his self-testimony. Possibly Barth thinks here of his impression of Werner Sombart, whom he read as a student in Berlin. In Barth's bookshelves there is also found—clearly read, and annotated in pencil—Karl Vorländer's book, *Die neukantische Bewegung im Sozialismus* [The neo-Kantian movement in socialism] (Berlin, 1902) with the inscription: "Karl Barth. Cand. Theol. Berlin WS 1906/07." Perhaps one may see this date as at least ideologically the first indication of Barth's way into and within socialism. In that case, starting from the Kantian/neo-Kantian context of practical reason, which he had encountered in Marburg, he would later have been introduced to the more strict realm of socialist analysis. In any case, he underlined especially this sentence in Vorländer's book: "The crucial issue is not whether Kant somehow already had socialist ideas, but whether his ethics can really be the starting point for a socialist ethics." Documents of this neo-Kantian socialism were published anew in 1970 under the title *Marxismus und Ethik* [Marxism and ethics] by Suhrkamp[1] as contributions *Zur Enstehung der Ideologie des demokratischen Sozialismus* [On the development of the ideology of democratic socialism]. Here K. Vorländer appears again. Aside from more radical phases, Barth had finally dedicated himself to this idea. Admittedly, we cannot yet maintain that this yields a canon for Barth's understanding of socialism. In the first phase Social Democracy, in which he was active, into which he entered, and with which and for which he fought, was still radical and socialist, not yet the revisionist Social Democracy of the Second International before the outbreak of the First World War and before the detachment of the communist left wing from this movement.

In any case, Barth repeatedly dealt critically with solely democratic liberties; he even regarded free democracy in general as a failure.

> Ruetli [is] a good symbol for the Swiss Social Democracy; through progress to freedom. The spirit of Ruetli is also necessary today. Or is everything achieved already? The national

1. Suhrkamp is a renowned German publishing house.—Ed.

freedom is achieved. Does nothing more need to be done than to defend it militarily and to celebrate it with the mug? Wrong. Long dark centuries followed the oath of Ruetli, in which the ordinary people were allowed to shed their blood, but otherwise had to obey the noble caste. Peasants are under town dwellers, citizens under noblemen, politically nearly or completely without rights. The revolution brought political freedom: the privilege of the [noble] class was abolished, democracy practiced. Is that enough? In Germany they would say: If only we were there already! We see clearly: political freedom is not enough. The revolution brought the freedom of the economically powerful. One aristocracy is angered against the other; money against birth. Which is better? The nineteenth century became the century of tyranny of possession, = of *capitalism*. In (various) forms: the entrepreneur, high finance, commerce, ground speculation, exploitation of the actually working people.

Barth describes the consequence of this system: So-called freedom "became the freedom of the possessor to earn still more. Do not let yourself be taken in by individual well-disposed representatives of this system. The principle of the freedom to make money is the enemy because it means that countless people have to live in bondage, discrimination, misery, it means continual war among people. Also women and child labor. Overproduction and crises, price increases of provisions." Barth demands (November 1, 1913): "Goal: the economic and social democracy must come to political democracy. Lassalle!"

At one point during the first pre-war phase Barth defines his political and theological position on the occasion of a critique of Friedrich Naumann (July 1914). He asks: Is, according to Naumann, "the idea still to fight? Is the existing or the ought-to-be important? Are the compromises grasped and treated as something provisional? Which is greater, the unrest, the desire for an absolute future, or the enjoyment of the relativities of the present? Is the idea the reality or reversed?!!" In Naumann at last the pleasure in the "aesthetically transfigured reality is greater than the pleasure of the idea. As a reality one tolerates in an unexamined manner: (a) the bourgeois-capitalist economic development, (b) the national state, (c) the war." Barth blames Naumann for the fact that he (Naumann) has abandoned completely the protest against this "reality" and instead had given the strongest weight to the proclamation of relative realities. Naumann now lacked enthusiasm and faith in overcoming the world, which he had pushed back quietly into personal feeling. Certainly the idea was still valid in Naumann, but he approved the endeavor of Social Democracy only inside the existing [order]. He regarded the social democratic final goal as being a slogan or utopia. Barth accused Naumann of not understanding "the religious purpose in social democratic radicalism." For Naumann capital, technology, the workers' movement, racial type, competition, and war are only phenomena instead of objects of moral will. In general he discusses only disconnected ethical demands, instead of dealing with the question of God; Barth calls it Naumann's "moralistic misunderstanding of Christianity."

"Not the practical questions, but the question of God. We expect more from God, place ourselves therefore more critically in face of the existing, and make the ideal therefore prevail in a more lively way."

This text stems from July 21, 1914. Radicalization against any socialism that wanted to work only within the existing order revealed itself already fourteen days before the outbreak of war.

The outbreak of war starts the *second phase in Barth's reception of socialism*: a radicalization of his concept of socialism. "Social democratic, but not religious socialist." His analysis of the reasons for war is repeated again and again: nationalism, militarism, capitalism, and an undemocratic way of governing. Already beforehand he had spoken again and again: Capitalism means war, not only internally but externally. Now it showed itself, and the socialist analysis was proven right.

But more importantly, disastrously and oppressively, the three spiritual powers proved themselves as failures: Christianity, science, and socialism. These all, out of their deepest presuppositions, should have been each in their own way obstacles to war, joining peoples together, encouraging all to resistance; but they were not strong enough. They succumbed to the pressure of the reality; much worse, they justified the nationalistic division of Europe. "Socialism became national-bourgeois, changed from a revolutionary party into one among other parties in national states. War socialism becomes profit socialism."

What consequences should one draw? Retreat out of the party? There are people who drew this conclusion, e.g., anarchists, and it is good, if there are again and again such radical consequences. More important is the radicalization of the whole. Radical, eschatological Christianity, which now finally took seriously the gospel of love, was exactly the commandment for the time as a new radical socialism, which lives "only by faith," i.e., by faith in a better world of the future, in a zeal for socialist goals, in "the glow of Marxist dogma." Politically, it meant: down with political maneuvers forever, dogmatic inconsistencies, acts of concession, and the quest for power in the state, through which one adjusted oneself only within the existing order. Down with jostling for position and for gullible voters. These all squandered our socialist energy and compromised the revolutionary effort. As one party among others, we sacrifice our best: the force of our utopia. We must learn anew to believe in the possibility of change and empower the will to change anew in us and among us. Therefore, the first task is the education of socialist personalities, expressed in a less bourgeois way: the creation of a new human being. "Free humans, personalities. These should become possible in the future state. Thus they must become the main issues already today."

Two remarks seem to be necessary here: (1) This education program is to be appreciated against a background of the banal averageness of socialist life-practice, which Barth denounced in a lecture: "What Does it Mean to be Socialist?" (August 16, 1915): "The sluggish members say: to pay dues, maintain the newspaper and go to the [party] meetings.—The chair person says: to go eagerly to the gatherings and to be ready to agitate, etc.—The enthusiastic socialists say: to be convinced of the truth of the program and act in accordance with it.—This is all true, but it is not enough. There were enough socialists of this kind in all countries on August 1, 1914"... But: "The socialists could do nothing against all this! The socialists had to follow! The socialists *wanted* to participate!—just like in Christianity. It shows itself suddenly: They are by no means so dangerous; basically they can be negotiated with." And Barth now desired that the socialists finally become dangerous: "We would like to become dangerous to the structures, otherwise we may pack up. Hence: socialist personalities." (2) Is, as Kautsky thinks, the idea of a socialist personality, that changes the conditions, a bourgeois ideology? Against this view, Barth writes: "Historical materialism in the sense of Marx does not have the form of *merely* economic course, but more so the emerging independence of the living human over against matter. Within the circumstances and transcending them, the human wants to rise up. The relation is that of interrelation. The ideals may be illusory bubbles of the economic development; but the human being is the most real and stands above economy. This has been overlooked and there was a lack of depth in socialist praxis (not by the founders of socialism, cf. Engels)." "Not: first better humans, then a better situation. Not: first better situations, then better humans. Both of them together and interwoven." We need human beings, "grasped by the transcendental power of socialist truth. Only the redeemed can redeem. The new human being must be created."

In the year 1916 the question about the sense of the war pressed heavier. "The will of God," Barth says, "is the overcoming of evil and the coming of the heavenly kingdom on earth through the new human being." "Evil" is not only the war, but the war as a part of capitalism, appetite for power, and violence. And now he says: "To follow the will of God, which [is] not reform, but revolution." And this was finally thought through in a Leninist way: The evil of capitalist war is the immediate cause for revolution!

And now the third phase, 1917–1919: Revolution and the Third International. In the year 1932, Barth presented a book with the dedication to Fritz Lieb: "To the representative of the 3rd International from a representative of the 2 1/2 International." This is not a bon mot. In connection with the struggle to set up a Communist International in the years after 1918, there emerged an international coalition of socialists, (the 2 1/2 International), which followed the Communist International in its critique of the majority socialism of the Social Democratic Parties in Europe, but had conversely rejected the centralism of Moscow, which was formulated in twenty-one points during the creation of the Third International. Every party that wanted to belong to the Third International would have to sign the twenty-one points. In Switzerland, for example, P. Graber and R. Grimm belonged to the 2 1/2 International. Generally, the initiative for this gathering can be traced to Switzerland; the first summons to this gathering was issued on December 7, 1920 in Bern. Obviously, Barth regarded himself being closest to the ideas of this group, even twelve years later.

Like the communists, the followers of the 2 1/2 International stood on the ideological grounds of the Zimmerwald Conference of 1915, which strongly opposed the revisionist softening of the revolutionary character of the socialist parties. "Social patriotism" was rejected by both groups. But, of course, against the Moscow centralism one reserves the right to decide when in countries outside the Soviet Union the situation was ripe for revolution and which strategy and tactics were to be used for the revolutionary fight.

Barth spoke in this connection about the problem of using violence. Basically, he said that anyone who justifies violence "is no longer a socialist. One can only do everything to overcome violence." "The current social order is based on violence. Basically, socialism cannot think of using the same old means (violence). Admittedly, politics is never pure; even socialist politics cannot be." For that reason Barth considered the possibility of accepting violence in the following cases: "(a) In the case of defense against an illegal enemy, (b) at the decisive moment of victory." This last criterion is revealing about Barth and characteristic for him. He set success as a norm, the effective power of accomplishment, revolutionary potency. And he set this against mere "revolutionary hot air," against mere "revolutionary pathos," which he combatted especially in the second edition of *The Epistle to the Romans.* There the "demonstration against the Red Brother" is not an anti-revolutionary attitude but a pragmatic criterion for whether a revolution is to be carried out or not. In the "Socialist Speeches" he stated critically: "Dry talk of revolution, not merely noise, but with it we make fools of ourselves. When radical intent and the times are ripe, will the force for it still be there?" "Not just feeling, but careful practical deliberation." "The decision will be based on the question of whether the proletariat trusts in their own will and power." . . . Under the same criterion Barth criticizes the Swiss General Strike of November 1918. It brought no decision. The conflict continued. "The Olten Committee had the will to overthrow.[2] Was going in this direction not a bad error of misjudging the situation? . . . A consequence of the many phrases? Captive to its own network? Victory or death?"

Like the Communists, the adherents of the 2 1/2 International affirmed also the dictatorship of the proletariat. Barth took part in this discussion, but deviated in the following decisive point from his like-minded comrades. On April 16, 1919, he spoke about this theme under the heading "Democracy or Dictatorship." "*No judgment* about the Russian party. Principal significance of its attempt, let alone its historical attainment. Imitation is something else." (This was the criterion of the rejection of Moscow centralism.)

---

2. The Olten Committee was a gathering of SPS and unions that started February 4, 1918, and became a leading organ of the worker's movement during the General Strike in Switzerland.—Ed.

How do we locate ourselves with respect to the deviation of our program in the Russian sense?—The Soviet constitution is another story, one to be considered seriously. Our democracy must be better adjusted to the realities of life. What is at stake is the issue of dictatorship, the character of minority rule, exclusivity, and violent overthrow [of the government]. Would we like to [follow the Soviet example] or not?—If it happens without us, it is not an unjust retaliation, and I speak as a person, who suffers together with the others: the bourgeois have misused their position. Democracy and church have not proven themselves worthwhile. Violence calls for violence, but the question is whether we want that to happen.

The principle of retaliation must be excluded as immature, unfruitful. Reverse the world, not only something here and there in the existing world order, otherwise it remains the old. Otherwise our previous protest and endeavor are untruthful. The power of socialism bases itself on the fact that socialists were earnest in their demands . . . (a) The violent overthrow. In that case the new society is established on an old foundation. Hence, success does not justify the means. It represents itself the hot air of a green house [*Treibhauskeller*]. History calls for such violent eruptions—the goal is not achieved—concessions to human weakness should not to be made into a principle.— Possibility for us?! (b) Minority rule. The acknowledged errors of democracy are not remedied by abolishing democracy. Who protects us from the errors of the workers' leaders . . . ? . . . The minority should rule through its intellect, i.e., become a majority. (c) The exclusivity of the working class . . . and the goal for the abolition of class? How about spiritual values? Thus: No, on the contrary make use of the present situation through political work, more of co-operative system, more social formation!

This is the opinion that Barth called "more than Leninism" in his first *Römerbrief* and that Lenin would have rejected as being anarchist. Barth would have acknowledged his position in these terms. He dealt with Kropotkin in detail and reported about him in Safenwil. His comment on the first post-war congress of the Second International, in which he took part as an observer, sounds obviously satisfied: "The International marches again, not in the direction of the social patriots, but in the direction of Eisner," i.e., in the direction toward the goals of the Munich Soviet Republic.[3] Clearly at this time, Barth was not orient-

---

3. The "Munich Soviet Republic" (*Münchner Räterepublik*) in 1919 was a short attempt to form a socialist state of Bavaria. "Workers' and Soldiers' Soviets" [= councils]

ed toward an anti-revolutionary principle. He supported at the time the view that the proletariat fights a "holy struggle" representatively for the rest of the human race and is the bringer of renewal. And he approved of the Soviet constitution of "the rights of working and exploited people" as "offensive measure for the sake of the previously under-privileged." So in this phase he is to be recognized as taking a stance during the first inner socialist conflict over the centralistic claims by Moscow.

III

Whether Karl Barth's socialist activities documented here have also a certain significance for his theologizing can be established only after the publication of all these texts. However, with high probability one can assume this already, because some of these speeches deal with the relation between Christianity and socialism. Possibly then the parallels between the development of his political ideas and the development of his theological ideas will be apparent.

In that case, e.g., the time between 1911 and 1914 would have been truly the religious-socialist phase in Barth's thinking. Above all, Kutter's tone resonates here with Barth's. That Arnold Hunziker *must* become a Social Democrat and that in him a more general reality revealed itself, is what Kutter described as "They must." That socialism brings a piece— but at least a piece—of God's order and brotherly love, which Jesus had proclaimed, and that this piece is a prerequisite for further pieces: this corresponds to Ragaz's determination of the relation between God's kingdom and the new society. Like Ragaz Barth was convinced that "the end goal of socialism is a preparation for the end goal of the gospel;" that "socialism had become one of the most important mirrors of the great basic and life fact" of God—a fact upon which the existence of the human race depends ("Religion and Socialism," December 7, 1915); he recognized "in the essential endeavors of socialism" a revelation of God, about which he had to be delighted. Barth committed himself to Social Democracy, because he is serious about God; yes, God is where the proletariat fights and works: this is already a Barthian radicalization

---

(*Arbeiter- und Soldatenräte*) were orginally groups to govern cities after the Monarchy ended. Participants were SPD (Social Democrat) and USPD (Independent [= left wing] Social Democrat) members, not communists. Eisner was the party leader of the USPD.—Ed.

of the idea of religious socialism and an indication of the fact that he could identify the God question with the question of human society. In the lecture "Jesus Christ and the Social Movement" on December 17, 1911, he confessed to the following statement of identity: "Jesus *is* the social movement, and the social movement is Jesus in the present." Because what Jesus Christ wanted, achieved, and lived, was completely "a *movement from below*, if seen from the human side." "The spirit, which is valid before God, is the social spirit. And social help is the way to eternal life." Jesus "and capitalism, the system of unlimited increase of private property," are incompatible. And Barth finds something of God's power in Jesus' blood shed, the risk of life for others, the "consciousness of solidarity, which considers others to be equal to yourself," "in the organizing idea of Social Democracy," as it was pronounced in the famous concluding sentence of the Communist Manifesto; Barth comments that he finds God's power "also elsewhere, but I find it here more obviously and more purely, and I find it here, as it must work in our time." "Jesus wanted what you want: he wanted to help the weak, he wanted to establish the kingdom of God on earth, he wanted to abolish self-centered property ownership, he wanted to make human beings comrades. Your endeavor is in line with that of Jesus, the right socialism is the *right* Christendom in our time." In other words, Barth says that in socialism we touch the hem of the clothes of the living God.

Possibly these problematic, bold, hardly tolerable, and un-Barthian sounding identifications belong to the earliest thought-forms of Karl Barth. But as the understanding of socialism became radicalized toward the idea of revolution, so the idea of God eschatologicizes itself in the second phase after 1914. One realizes this most quickly if one hears Barth speak of exclusively political connections in the biblical-eschatological language of "expectation," "desire," "better world," and "believing in the future." These are exemplary expressions within the political-social situation and for this situation. With the help of such language the pure socialist ideas, goals, and enthusiasm, "the glow of Marxist dogma," should be liberated from the contamination of the existing conditions. The demand conceals itself behind the fact that now socialism should be conceived in really radical, i.e., revolutionary terms. Here, in my opinion, belongs also the famous "wholly other." Whether the term comes from R. Otto (Barth has nothing to do with the religious phenomenology of R. Otto), "wholly other" is the coming world overthrowing over against the present capitalist world. And when "God" is called "the wholly other," then it is in this radical social sense.

The third phase, critical of revolution (in the well-understood positive sense), is documented in his literary estate with a lecture "Christian Life" on June 9, 1919. In form and content it is obviously the last piece before the famous Tambach lecture and is to be appreciated as a working-piece in preparation for the Tambach lecture. Here Barth speaks no longer of "identity," also no longer of *totaliter aliter*, but rather states: God is the *presupposition* for all our movements. These are no longer mirrors or projections, but analogies, parables.

> The kingdom of God is the kingdom of God. We cannot imag-
> ine radically enough the transition from analogy of the godly to
> the godly reality. The concept of development fails . . . The new
> Jerusalem has nothing to do with the new Switzerland or with
> the revolutionary future state, but it comes to earth by God's
> great freedom of choice, when the time is ready . . . Then the or-
> der of creation becomes completely rearranged. There is a bar-
> rier against the perfecting of the present conditions that only
> God himself can break.

Also, these assertions have their setting in life. Since these are words after the revolution, after the struggle, and after everything that happened, they must defend themselves against the suspicion that this "God himself, God only" might now again be a projection, a bad projection this time, a projection not of encouragement and empowerment to fight, to "redeem through the redeemed," but a projection of resignation and discouragement, as if "God himself" would be only a stopgap for the disillusioned revolution. Barth has clearly put a stop to it. "We do not need to fear that the view of this completely new turn in the history of God's deeds would take away from us the courage and the power for today and this earthly [life]." And now Barth forms all the more sharp new fighting identities: "The power of the other-world is the power of this-world. The hope of the future (*spes futurae vitae*) [is] the secret lever of all worldly progress and revolutions. Perhaps it serves as quieting or disquieting, when I tell you that I am all the more delighted to be a Social Democrat particularily in view of this last deliberation." And a further identity is inserted:

> We have enough pure cosmopolitans, we have also enough en-
> thusiastic fighters; we also have enough seekers after heaven,

which is in the light above. All are right in their own way. But we have too few people who realize that the kingdom of God is all of these at the same time and is one in the other: the kingdom of nature, the kingdom of grace, and the kingdom of glory. If we were such people and would stand in this central knowledge of God's ways, which is the right knowledge of life, if we were disciples of the resurrection of Jesus, then we would need no Christian ethics.

To this baffling, provocative sentence, Barth adds, "He who has ears to hear, listen."

7

The Secretary of the Church Administration

From Barth's Pastorate

ON MAY 1, 1911, THE CONGREGATION OF SAFENWIL [SWITZERLAND] resolved to call Karl Barth as their pastor. His predecessor gave the church administration as grounds for his leaving that it was "solely the prospect of a greater field of work and especially the preferred work with the children" that allowed him eventually to accept the call to Olten (whereas it was precisely the work with pre-confirmation and confirmation youth that would become a major emphasis of Barth's work there as pastor, at the same time, however, one of the most difficult conflict points with the local industry; these confrontations accompanied him as a matter of fact for all of the ten years of his activity in Safenwil).

The installation service for Barth took place on Sunday, July 9, 1911. One of the confirmation girls, born in 1896, who was part of the class in this year, remembered later: "It gave us a huge amount of respect that he came from Geneva to us in Safenwil, to our quiet little village, where most of the people were farmers or worked in the factory." Barth's father, Professor Fritz Barth, gave the sermon. He took as his text 2 Cor 4:1–2, going with his exegesis into the usual expectations that people directed to their new pastor: One thought especially about the sermons; another hoped for good work with the youth, while another wished for activities of the pastor that would benefit the community. Precisely in these directions lay then the main emphases of the new pastor. Father Barth commented on these wishes: "So many people, so many expectations, who is right? Is the pastor to be there for everything that anyone would want from him? Is he to be 'the man for everything'?" Karl Barth took up this motif from the sermon of his father's in 1916, about half-way through his time in Safenwil, in a sermon that became known in much wider circles than Safenwil, about "The pastor, who does what the people want."[1] Here he came to speak of "the different contradictions, which in the course of time grow up around the parsonage," and about the wishes for peace and harmony brought to him from the congregation. Barth explained the clearly present unrest in the congregation as finally an irresolvable disturbance caused by the gospel. "There can be 'peace' between the different personalities. Why not? But there can be no peace between the Spirit of God and the Spirit of Mammon." Apparently that expressed the content of the basic problem of the "unrest" in Safenwil. That is, that the activity of the pastor in behalf of the community, about which father Barth had spoken, awakened conflict. But instead of pursuing such a desirable Christian ideal of harmony and reconciliation, Barth turned the sword around and wished a decision and a vote from the divided congregation: either to resolutely reject the "Will of God" that Barth presented in sermon and activity or to allow themselves finally to be overturned by this "Will" and allow themselves to be taken captive.

What was going on in Safenwil?

The materials and the remnants of publications from the Barth's estate do not permit us an impression of the *complete* conduct of Barth's pastoral office. The activities that he took on in these ten years, together with their written records, show Pastor Barth though every bit as rich and broad in his development as we know of the later Professor Barth. We are missing the full knowledge of the more than five hundred sermons that he gave in Safenwil, the many years of materials he prepared for his confirmation classes, the knowledge of the "Socialist Speeches," the lectures for his Bible classes and his presentations to the Blue Cross, other in part longer presentations during this period, the many political and church magazine and journal articles, the many letters to friends, other than Eduard Thurneysen and Martin Rade. We are missing more precise examinations of his Christian-socialist and party activities from this time. Whoever is interested in Pastor Barth, in order perhaps to make clear from the practical life of the pastor something for the theology of the later professor, if only to know what the author of the *Church Dogmatics* brought from his own activity for the horizon of activity of

1. Karl Barth, "Der Pfarrer, der es den Leuten recht macht. Predigt über Hesekiel 13, 1–16" [The pastor, who does what the people want: Sermon on Ezekiel 13, 1–16], in *Predigt im Gespräch,* no. 3, ed. Rudolf Bohren und Hans-Georg Geyer (Neukirchen-Vluyn: Neukirchener Verlag des Erziehungsvereins, 1967).

the church, will apparently have to wait a long time, in order to be able to make a clear and comprehensive picture. What we have up till now are two years of sermons, from 1913 and 1914,[2] and a few individually published sermons from this time, plus the correspondence between Barth and Thurneysen[3] and Barth and Rade,[4] and, finally Eberhard Busch's portrayal[5] of Barth's refined autobiographical recollections, and of course the *Epistle to the Romans,*[6] the production of which, however, cost the congregation some loss of their pastor and his time. In what follows we will bring some materials about Barth's pastorate from "the minutes of the meetings of the church administration and the congregational meetings in Safenwil," which, for Barth's pastorate are found in the "Church Administration Minutes," pp. 254–382, plus some materials from the Aargau newspapers and some remembrances of members of the congregation.

On Thursday, July 27, 1911, the first *Kirchenpflege* meeting with Barth began at 8:30 p.m. *Kirchenpflege* is the Swiss term for what is known in Germany as *Presbyterium* [presbytery] or *Gemeindekirchenrat.* [It is translated here as "church administration."] In Safenwil, in addition to the pastor, there were six elected members, and the chair and vice-chair were not held by the pastor, but by one of the elected members. The chair called the meetings to order, usually every two months or so, at no regular time, and usually in different locations, as a rule in the parsonage, but also after worship in the church, as the situation required. The church administration was the place for the pastor to take his appeals and complaints, but it was on the other hand also the place where the appeals and complaints of the congregation were taken to the

---

2. Karl Barth, *Predigten 1913*, ed. Nelly Barth und Gerhard Sauter (Zürich: Theologischer Verlag 1976). K. Barth, *Predigten 1914*, ed. Ursula Fähler and Jochen Fähler (Zürich: Theologischer Verlag, 1974).

3. Karl Barth and Eduard Thurneysen, *Briefwechsel*, vol. 1, 1913–1921, ed. E. Thurneysen (Zürich: Theologischer Verlag 1973).

4. Karl Barth and Martin Rade, *Ein Briefwechsel*, ed. Christoph Schwöbel (Gütersloh: Gütersloher Verlagshaus, 1981).

5. Eberhard Busch, *Karl Barths Lebenslauf: Nach seinen Briefen und autobiographischen Texten* (Munich: Kaiser, 1975). English translation: E. Busch, *Karl Barth: His Life from Letters and Autobiographical Texts*, trans. John Bowden (Grand Rapids: Eerdmans, 1976).

6. Karl Barth, *Der Römerbrief* (Erste Fassung) 1919, ed. Hermann Schmidt (Zürich: Theologischer Verlag 1985).

pastor. The church administration had an institutional relationship to the "Congregational Meeting," which was to take place approximately every six months, to which the administration was accountable, and which served as the place where the election to the church administration took place. The administration was also responsible for the continued employment of the pastor, budget questions, such as the salary of the pastor, and also was an important (and likely also problematic) link between the congregation and the political community. We will see how the political "burden" of Barth's pastorate also derived from the fact that the administration, because of its institutional function, was often open to questions of political interests and determinations. A connection between the congregation and the political community was already in place (in a form unknown meanwhile in Germany after 1918, and not least of all as a consequence of the impact of the understandings of church and state that Barth later developed.) The political parties published, for example in 1913, a slate of officers that they proposed for the church administration, along with the community tax board, and the finance and accounting commission, and these elections took place on the same day. It was not totally incorrect that the church administration described itself as an authority [Behörde], and election to the church office could bring one into conflict with the general regulations for those who held government offices or were government employees (for example, with regard to familial relationships, the last president of the church administration during Barth's time, a socialist, was in 1919 challenged by the chairman of the Liberal [Freisinnigen] Party with reference to such laws, though without success). The political "municipal council" administered the church taxes and approved the church funds, while the next higher manifestation of church government, the Reformed Council of Aargau for example approved or denied the standing of the pastor for election to a pastorate, set the conditions for salaries (of the pastor, church secretaries, caretaker, and organist) and was responsible for all other church tasks beyond the local congregation. (I am confining myself with these observations only to those institutional relationships that came to have importance during the time of Barth's pastorate in Safenwil.) Naturally there were two representatives of the Safenwil congregation elected to the synod in Aargau, and in 1913 Pastor Barth was also elected to the synod, although we up to now have not enough material to be able to experience much about his activity there.

As Barth began his pastorate in Safenwil, Gustav Hüssy-Zuber was the chairman of the church administration. He was a member of what Barth called the "House of Hüssy," a factory dynasty in Safenwil, whose different family members in the area owned a weaving establishment, dyeing works and a saw mill. From this dynasty two members succeeded one another in the church administration under dramatic conditions, and a third member drew Barth early into a press campaign, which probably strongly determined the further internal developments between the parsonage and the church and political communities. The teacher J. Dambach served as vice-chairman. Others on the administration were: social worker Fritz Diriwächter; school administrator Jakob Schärer, who was a socialist; Jakob Lent and Rudolf Wilhelm-Niffenegger, who, with Diriwächter and Dambach, declared publicly in a newspaper announcement that he would not accept nomination for re-election in 1913.

At that first meeting the newly elected pastor was greeted by Gustav Hüssy. Barth on the one hand answered with a request for trust, and on the other with a request for "open and honest criticism on the part of the honorable church administration members."

The first decision of the administration consisted of the election of Barth, as was his predecessor, to the position of secretary of the administration. We are indebted to this decision for important notes from Barth's own hand for the process of his pastorate in Safenwil—at least for its official aspects. Barth held this office until the election in the year 1919, i.e. until he had an administration with a majority of socialists and then passed on the office of secretary to the haulier Arnold Scheurmann. So we have Barth's minutes from July 27, 1911, till February 20, 1919.

Barth at first understood his task as secretary only in the sense of preparation of minutes of resolutions passed, and otherwise only naming more precisely the objects of the agenda for each meeting—and in addition from time to time adding the carrying out of certain resolutions. To be sure, that no longer sufficed to the church administration members due to the intensification of inner controversies. After the first great crisis, on March 31, 1914, at the wish of the newly elected (second) Mr. Hüssy, "more complete reporting of the discussions that took place" was included in the minutes. This was in part also because the minutes of the church administration were read and examined by the municipal council—a further example of the close connection between the congregation and the community. In any case the political institution soon thereafter, at the wish of Mr. Hüssy, gave more emphasis to this request, which was also followed by Barth, so that in certain critical situations one can gain not only a view of the objects of the discussion, but also the course of the discussion as well. Here the different positions and the character of the Safenwil administration members can be recognized, and one can have both an objective and human picture of the administration at work.

The way Barth formulated the minutes always includes naturally a bit of interpretation of the events, and one also senses at the same time Barth's humor (for example, in the minutes of the first meeting, "Mr. President made the suggestion to hold the Sunday morning service some time or other in the forest, as is often done elsewhere [it was done successfully on the Sundays of August 6 and 20]"), as in other cases a biting irony and angry opposition show through. Alone in the "official language" that Barth uses in these minutes, one often can hear clearly the undertones of irony. More than once the church administration members complain about this and demand at the next meeting a revision of certain formulations of the secretary. This all gives us a living portrait, and so these minutes, apart from their historical value, also give an authentic picture of Barth's forms of expression.

I

We (unfortunately) cannot be concerned with all details. All the normal everyday cases of a church congregation are reflected here, which then as now belong to the orders of the day. Conversations over *church finances* took up the greatest part of the time in Safenwil, too. The congregation had, for instance, the right of determining the distribution of the collections to church and diaconal, Christian, and non-Christian causes and individuals. Other than as is the case with most of our congregations today, where the purposes of most of the collections are determined in advance by manifestations of the church beyond the local congregation (synodical, regional, denominational, etc.) the members of the church administration had to inform themselves about the different institutions and causes and decide: a clear task determined by the situation, if one not simply and normally wished to divide up the money, "as we've always done it." During the time of Barth's pastorate there were situations in which decisions were made on theological grounds and had to be determined by a majority vote (about which more will be said later). The collections were distributed annually, usually amounting to between 300 and 500 Swiss francs in Safenwil, and at the distribution amounts of between 5 and 10 francs were at that time a matter of contention.

Likewise there were always discussions about *the salaries*. On November 5, 1911, Barth's salary was raised from 2800 francs a year to 3000 francs. On January 17, 1918, from 3200 to 3600. At the church administration meeting of August 7, 1919, it was found out that within the Aargau synod, the pastoral salary level, which until the end of 1918 stood as it was at the fifty-first place, since the beginning of 1919 had fallen to the fifty-seventh place. Therefore, the church administration on May 31, 1919, was ready to increase the pastor's salary from 3600 to 4500 francs. But during the difficult conflicts of 1919 a resolution was brought to the church administration by the Liberal Party and the local Farmers' Party to set aside the church budget, especially that the pastor's salary, "because of the activities in which he was engaged as pastor," not be raised. By a congregational vote (153 to 99), the motion was defeated (with 7 empty ballots), but this shows that the pastorate in Switzerland at the time clearly had an economic nerve. According to church guidelines, Barth was entitled at the end of 1919 to an increase in his salary to a minimum of 5000 francs. But in his church administration, which by now had become socialist, Barth did not even let this point come up for consideration, but declined to take his minimum salary, which brought the congregation the next year, with the election of Barth's successor, into some difficulty, since it was to be expected that the successor would need to be offered at least such a minimum salary.

There were always repairs to be made to *the parsonage*, as well as *the organ*. The question of attaching a back-rest to the seat in the pulpit was carried over from Barth's predecessor, and Barth now demanded it (the Reformed preacher sits in many congregations in the pulpit through the entire worship service). Such *questions of seating* also led often to discussions in the church administration. One time the pastor's wife was told, according to the minutes, to take the place in the church set aside for her, and not to seek her seat elsewhere. At one of the high points of the political conflicts (after the election victory of the socialists in Safenwil in December 1917), Arthur Hüssy charged that Barth, "after the victory of the socialists, changed his seat in the church in a suspicious manner," an item in the minutes of December 18, 1917, whose gossip character only documents the high degree of tension within the congregation (and which we quote, because we are interested in this specific contribution in the specific character of the public nature of Barth's activity as a pastor). Nevertheless this challenged changing of the places could, as the refused increase in salary in 1919 have had a symbolic meaning (without our knowing it)—for the order and place of seating have, as the example of the place where the pastor's wife sat, a symbolic meaning that is understood by all. So the minutes from May 14, 1921, read, "A discussion developed because of the seating of members of the church administration, and it is resolved, from now on that administration members will sit facing in the same direction as the rest of the participants in worship, but on the second row from the front." That was the socialist church administration!

Church music was served by the teacher, Hans Jent. He later characterized himself as "the stopgap on the organ bench." He held the position since long before Barth's time, and in 1909, through the efforts of the pastor at the time, was replaced as organist. The grounds apparently were: playing too slowly. Jent said later that it did not go any better with his successor; he, too, was fired, and since then, "the pastor not only preached, but also played the organ." Shortly before Barth took the pastorate, Hans Jent was once again elected unanimously as organist, and had, at the urging of his mother, whom the new pastor had asked for help, already explained, "to begin on the first Sunday in May." So he began again at the same time as Barth assumed the pastorate. In the first church administration meeting with Barth it was confirmed that the singing in worship would be limited to two songs, and in the next topic on the agenda the members of the church administration noted "with satisfaction" the intention of "the organist" to "take an organ course in Zofingen"—no doubt in accordance with an agreement reached in advance with Barth. On December 29, 1911, the recommendation of the Aargau Organ Association for a raise in the salary of the organist was up for discussion. "The church administration, however, resolved to wait, in the hope that our organist would give us cause for rejoicing by improved performance on Sundays. So it is moved instead that the council of the church repay the organist half of the costs for the organ course in Zofingen." But apparently that didn't help much. The end of December, the president of the church administration was asked to have a conversation with Mr. Jent, "in order to express to him the general wish for a somewhat faster accompaniment of congregational singing." Later Hans Jent (who filled the vacancy on the organ bench until 1943, awaiting a better organist in Safenwil) remarked with gratitude: "Pastor Barth, this very capable preacher, contented himself with my organ playing," in marked contrast to Barth's predecessor. As a substitute for the organist, the "Music of the Evangelical Community" served from time to time in the worship services. And the sanctuary was available for concerts by the Working Men's Choir, whose conductor was also allowed to use the organ for rehearsals. That, and how Mrs. Barth made herself heard in regard to music in the church, will be reported in another context.

An important right of the church administration was also the *granting of vacation* for the pastor. We must make it clear: It was only in May of 1914 that the Aargau synod granted the pastor a two-week vacation per year. But to actually set this vacation was the determination of the church administration. We can see from the minutes how little Barth in these years took a vacation, though we can also determine during the time of Barth's work on the *Epistle to the Romans* exactly which Sundays Barth requested to have off for this work: for the winter of 1917/18 two times two Sundays free from preaching, which were granted him two in November 1917, then again in February 1918, "for urgent study purposes." A new application in August 1918, again two Sundays "over the Day of Repentance," however, met with resistance. The effects of a flu epidemic that affected all of Europe had led to cancellations of public worships, because of the fear of spreading the disease. Barth declared, on the one hand, "that a study leave and vacation are two different things," and on the other, that he, "during the so-called flu vacation, as throughout the whole summer, was involved with a great literary work, which would benefit the congregation. He was amazed that, with the usually such small numbers in attendance at worship, anyone could take offense at hearing the preacher from the neighboring community twice." "In view of the prevailing mood," Barth did not, however, take a second free Sunday. It was May 1921, before he sought once again, "for the purposes of a literary work," to get four or five Sundays free from his duties.

Often there was something concerning *the permission to use the Safenwil church* for purposes other than congregational purposes: for evangelism, mission presentations, work of the Salvation Army,

Alcoholics Anonymous meetings, and, even prior to Barth's time: for the consecration of the flags of the Workingmen's Choir, and later for their concerts.

An important right of the church administration was the *determination of the schedules* for church membership and confirmation classes. Disagreements over these items take up a great deal of space in the minutes.

Regularly the naming of *the persons to hold the chalice* for the coming communion services was listed in the minutes.

A point in the minutes from the meeting of December 19, 1912, also shows a problematic sense in which the church administration functioned during Barth's time as an "authority" in the community: "A letter should be written to the municipal council, to make them aware of the scandalous co-habitation of the painter Bollinger and Ms. Kaspar 'Auf der Hard' [on the street 'Hard'], and to occasion the council to intervene in this matter." Fortunately we are only aware of this one instance in the minutes of an example of such moral "observation." But it is enough to show the breadth of concerns in which a church administration was involved at the time (and also, by the way, to demonstrate something of the Calvinist discipline, in which the church laid claim on the civil government in matters of morals.)

On March 19, 1918, a point belonging to the realm of *instruction and pastoral care* was discussed and decided as a matter of church administration action: "The secretary reported on the difficulties accompanying the custom of having individual texts for each confirmand, as a result of the tendency, which we have not been able to overcome, of hearing from this text praise or condemnation of the child. The Bible is too good for such misuse, and this year the custom should be dispensed with completely, and every three to four children should be given the same text. The church administration is in agreement with this attempt." One of the confirmation youth remembered later the problem that was under discussion. "As a confirmation youth I was given as my text Isa 43:1–2, to accompany my life's way. I could not understand especially the second part. I often was angry: Why was I given this Word? Later I thanked Pastor Barth for it. For this Word did help see me through: 'When you pass through the waters, I will be with you, so that the streams do not overwhelm you.'"Nevertheless, Barth was seeking with his appeal to get past the "for me [alone!]" misuse of the Bible.

Regarding such practices as *baptisms and funerals* the following resolution from September 4, 1912, belongs: "The authority, after having a discussion, declares its agreement that the secretary may hold more comprehensive messages in funerals than heretofore had been the case. This is to be understood especially with regard to those who otherwise are seldom or never in church services, and who ought not to be allowed to go with merely a recited prayer and details of the deceased person's life." (Certainly an argument concerning the practice of the church, against which later Götz Harbsmeier raised justified objections in his writing *Was wir an den Gräbern sagen* [What we say at the graves].) Barth allowed the example of such a more comprehensive funeral sermon to be printed in the paper of the Social Democrats, the *Freier Aargauer* [Aargau Free Press], on September 3, 1917: "The message of the pastor at the burial of a working man"—a most peculiar text, insofar as the connection of the deceased working man, Arnold Hunziker, to the working man's cause, in its selflessness, and constant unrest was honored as an expression of a higher "Must." The Easter hope of resurrection was seen therein, so that the family, colleagues and comrades of the deceased "grasped and were grasped by the living spirit, present in our deceased." The Party journalists would have valued this sermon as a document of a humanistic socialism. In any case Barth would have sought to elevate a life given to work into the light of a higher Common Realm and take it out of the bare realm and cynicism of mere "personal information." This is the content of Barth's motion to the church administration. One can understand this immediately, when one walks along the graves and monuments in the Safenwil Cemetery of, on the one hand, the "House of Hüssy" in its many branches, and on the other hand the graves, which bear the names of many persons familiar from the administration minutes, and so often have the inscription "From Work to Rest" on the stones. Here one can detect still today a piece of Safenwil social and mental history.

Here also belongs the following minutes entry from September 8, 1914:

> The gardener Ritschard expresses the complaint that is raised in certain circles concerning the funeral service for Oskar Zuller, died on July 18. It is charged that personal information about the deceased had been omitted and that the prayer prescribed in the liturgy for suicides had been used. The secretary answered

that no personal details about the life of the deceased had been given to him from the master and mistress in whose service Zuller had been employed, and that he, the pastor, had used the prayer in other situations already, without having complaints raised about it. So the case is considered closed.

One whose life had been left anonymous by "his master and mistress" should not be branded liturgically and sent thus to the fringes.

We hear nothing in the minutes about questions of baptism or weddings.

II

Half of Barth's time in the Safenwil pastorate was a time of *war and revolution*. How is that reflected in the administration minutes? No one would expect to find evidence of the deep meaning that the outbreak of World War I had for Barth in these texts. But there are even at this practical level a few signs that accompany what took place much more comprehensively in the sermons, "Socialist Speeches" and letters in this regard.

On September 8, 1914, a "municipal council letter," "re: the position of the pastors and the church administration concerning the economic conditions that have arisen through the war," was apparently at first only received. It did not come immediately to any decision regarding a new and corresponding determination of the purposes for which the gifts and offerings would be given. In his correspondence with Thurneysen Barth came several times to speak of this circular extremely critically.[7]

Their status of neutrality required the Swiss already in World War I (as even more in World War II) to develop a high degree of military defense readiness. So we note during war time that one or another of the church administration members were absent because of military service. Members of the congregation recalled later that Barth, at the mobilization of the Swiss army early September 1914, "was at the Safenwil railway station every morning, in order to give his good wishes to those who were being called to duty. He said to me," one remarked, "that he wished he were coming along." (So Ernst Widmer-Wilhelm, who was president of the church administration from June 1916 on. He was, as we shall see later, of another mind politically than Barth, but he

7. Cf. K. Barth and E. Thurneysen *Briefwechsel*, vol. 1, 19.

praised Barth's *practical* position regarding the Army greatly to me in an interview.)

The change-over to the business of war brought, for example, a shrinking of the railroad traffic, which affected Barth's ability to travel outside Safenwil for evening lectures. So he had to try to organize some kind of carriage, for autos also were not permitted to be used. Once there was such an evening undertaking in the city church in Aarau. A carriage proved to be too expensive. So it was decided that Barth should travel at 7 p.m. with the train to Aarau, "and then two or three members of church administration would pick him up after the lecture at the church in Aarau and accompany him on his pilgrimage home 'on shank's mare' [on foot]. We were introduced to a Pastor Grob (in Aarau) as one of those who would accompany Pastor Barth on his way home, and were therefore praised, but also asked, if we would not be afraid of walking home so late at night in the dark and through the forest? Us afraid? We stalwart Home Guard soldiers? And with a pastor along? Besides, it was not as far as from Safenwil to Leutwil and back!" (E. Widmer.—Leutwil, the village where Eduard Thurneysen was pastor, was several hours by foot from Safenwil, and the congregation there knew about Barth's frequent visits on foot and bicycle.)

On September 11, 1914, Barth received permission from the church administration to turn a room in the parsonage into a reading room for soldiers of the Seventy-third Battalion stationed there—apparently a fairly common custom in Switzerland, for in 1915, a collection for the purpose of supporting such "reading rooms" was recommended and collected by the church council. A similar arrangement was made as the Eighty-third Battalion moved into Safenwil in the summer of 1915. Such things belonged to the cultural functions of such a congregation at the time. There was, for instance, then no public library in Safenwil. It was founded during the period of Barth's pastorate, and there was a collection also in the church for helping furnish the library.

On these two occasions there was also talk about worship services in the field. "On June 13 (1915), the sermon and church school classes were omitted, in the expectation that most of the congregation would take part in the services held in the field. But the interest did not seem to be all that great." Once before already, in December 1914, the church was "requisitioned for a lecture held by Military Chaplain Wegemann on the theme of Hannibal (!!)."

It came to a conflict within the church administration, as, in March 1915, a request was made for financial support for a military newspaper, published by an evangelical church organization, "A Good Defense and Weapon." The president of the church administration moved to approve a sum of ten francs from the budget, and the motion was supported by Misters Hüssy and Ritschard, "while the secretary took the position that the maintenance of such a patriotic-military Christianity, as that which the named paper had as its purpose, should be left to the army staff and the military chaplains, while we *as church congregation* stood on another foundation than these circles." Here there is reflected in the matter of a practical decision Barth's essential position with regard to war, in a very definite form: A church congregation, as such, was to stand "on another foundation" than the military chaplaincy. For the church there could be no question of a "patriotic-military Christianity," and this was the case not only for the Germans and the French prosecuting the war, but also for the neutral Swiss. "Hüssy holds, on the contrary, that one needs to put himself in the position of the soldier and from that vantage point will gladly have such material created for him." After some pro and contra it was moved to table the motion, but the motion was defeated by vote. "In the vote the recommendation is passed by a vote of four to three. The motion is passed for approval by the municipal council."

In the next minutes we hear then that the municipal council refused the proposed support of the newspaper from the budget and requested that it be supported with funds from the offering with the notation: "This amount can be used at least as well in this cause as in other purposes for which sums from the church offerings have been used." The secretary noted this decision with irony as "a very dear writing." "The church administration moves to receive this compliment and to proceed in the manner indicated." Barth took a narrow defeat in this question, but remained on guard, as regards the question of financial support for conservative church activities. We hear a year and a half later, on the occasion of the distribution of the collection in December 1915 of his motion: "The mission contribution this year is again to be given to the Basel Mission, with regard to the very strongly expressed national-political orientation" of the general Evangelical-Protestant missions work, which had been supported in the past. "This motion was passed." It was a question of an amount of twenty francs. (In the same year there was a special offering taken for the support of war refugees, which brought in the exceptional amount of 202.31 Swiss francs.)

As a result of the war one can also count the extraordinarily dangerous flu epidemic, which from late summer until December 1918 took 21,500 lives in Switzerland.[8] Its danger was intensified because of the food shortages and the economic condition in which the war plunged the mass of the Swiss people. It was surely also a result of the fact that Switzerland was cut off from much of the imports from abroad, but it was also related to the social injustice, because so many of the working class families, whose men were drafted into military service, were left without sufficient support. The threat of this epidemic was so great that, on the one hand the socialist Olten Committee, which organized a revolutionary movement throughout the entire year 1918 (in the middle of November it came to a three-day general strike throughout Switzerland), saw itself hindered because of the health conditions of the working class, and on the other hand the government hesitated to pull together too many military units to combat this unrest. In general there was a prohibition against assemblies, which also affected the holding of services of worship. We already had heard that Barth applied for two Sundays free in August; we know that during this time he was working feverishly on the conclusion of the *Epistle to the Romans*. But the church administration also noted "the involuntary interruption of the services of worship on account of the flu." "Mr. Hüssy declared," in this regard, "that he had heard our pastor preaching here only one time this summer. One time in addition, he made things comfortable for himself by exchanging with Pastor Thurneysen in Leutwil." There seem to have been preaching occasions again in September and into the second half of October, as we read on November 15, "Worship services were cancelled on account of the flu the past three Sundays," and Barth raised the question, "if the worship would take place again on the coming Sunday, November 17. The president of the church administration," it says, "is against holding worship because of new outbreaks of the flu." (Today we have the month by month statistics of this epidemic: Throughout the whole of Switzerland there were in September 1918 41,672 flu cases registered; in October 238,399, in November still 155,422, and in December 104,612.)[9] Still Mr. Ritschard is "in favor of reopening the

8. Cf. Willi Gautschi, *Der Landesstreik 1918* (Zürich: Benziger, 1968) 204.
9. Ibid.

church, with certain precautions, as they are taken elsewhere." Because of internal political grounds, about which we will report later, Barth voted, contrary to his own motion, against the reopening of worship services, which was then accepted (these internal grounds have to do with a difficult crisis, connected with Barth's position to the nation-wide general strike). On November 20 it was decided: "The service of worship will be begun again." This was again discussed on December 20 "whether the two communion services, on Advent 4 and Christmas Day shall take place, despite the flu. The president is in favor of doing whatever possible to prevent further danger of spreading the germs, and therefore proposes celebrating communion only on Christmas Day." Mr. Ritschard is against communion on that day, too. Here Barth: "The secretary warns about the tendency of always making the school and the church the objects of such precautionary measures, as though precisely the spiritual values were easiest to do without, while work in the factories and life in the taverns continue their way undisturbed. As church authorities we ought not accept this understanding so easily. If we confess faithfully our belief in communion, it will certainly not be a danger for us." A *strong* theological statement! The church administration voted for the compromise: Communion only on Christmas Day.— Apparently this position of Barth's thought and the holding of worship during this time occasioned outraged reaction in the bourgeois press. It was asked that the authorities immediately prohibit this "gathering of people." In a "letter to the editor" from Safenwil Barth's affirmation of the services of worship was politically attacked.

> The actions of our pastor in regard to the flu epidemic is inex-plicable to us. While he regularly sounds off in social welfare questions, and is always there in the middle of state, village and private undertakings, to combat the capitalistic economic sys-tem, here he seems not to be touched at all by the people's good, but continues calmly to conduct his confirmation classes, re-gardless of the danger of spreading the flu germs. If a bourgeois citizen claimed the right to make such exceptions, he would soon hear it about how little understanding he had for the social welfare. We don't want to use the classical caricatures here, with which the Authorities would again be labeled, if they, to put it mildly, were to be accused of such presumption. *Sapienti sat*!

(This appeared in the bourgeois *Zofinger Tagblatt* [Zofingen Daily News]).

As testimony to the war as noted in the Safenwil church administration minutes, both as conclusion and summary, there is a statement that confirms sufficiently what the sermons, "Socialist Speeches" and letters of this time express. As it came, in February 1919, to the resignation of four presbyters from the church administration, because of Barth's position with regard to the general strike in Switzerland, Barth asked each of them in the final meeting in which they were all present once more about the reasons for their resignation. While three of them pointed to Barth's social and socialist position and activities, which made any further cooperation of theirs with him impossible, the gardener Ritschard gave as his reason "the anti-militarism of the pastor."

III

According to the minutes, Barth introduced a few *innovations* in Safenwil: a weekly Bible study, a "weekly evening for the confirmed youth, alternatively for young men and young women" (October 10, 1912). In addition, from January 1915 on, there was an annual lecture series in the church.

All three innovations sought to take seriously biblical, life issues, and concerns for church-theological education—as all of Barth's pastoral activities, also in the realm of the Blue Cross, and in the Party, demonstrating a strong pedagogical accent, which certainly had to do with the cultural and social conditions in his village, but also with the impetus of his understanding of the pastoral office. In any case he could not limit himself to the classical ecclesiological functions and sought always to expand the possibilities of his activity in the village, by creating them for himself, in contrast to his predecessor, who only lamented their lack. One can speak of a socially creative pastorate of Barth's, by not least pointing also to the three labor unions founded in Safenwil, to which Barth later looked back with satisfaction.[10]

The *introduction of the bible study* might have had something to do with a criticism about Barth's sermons, registered early in the congregation. At his installation, Barth had asked for "open criticism"—signs of his own internal openness at a time in which there was not yet a need for self-criticism, as it is today a psychological and social syndrome. After something more than a year in Safenwil we read already, "The preaching

10. Cf. E. Busch, *Karl Barths Lebenslauf,* 116.

style of the secretary has given occasion in the course of the summer for various complaints and also to an article in the *Zofinger Tagblatt*. He is admonished on the one hand to be careful, and on the other side, however, encouraged in his effort to be open and clear, and he should seek if possible to combine these two [care and clarity]." (This is clearly marked with humor.) Here again we run into the bourgeois *Zofinger Tagblatt*, which already six months earlier had initially launched a serious affair in regard to Barth's conduct of his pastorate, and until his departure in 1921 sought again and again to intervene in his work through various campaigns.

It is therefore clear that a public newspaper brought complaints about Barth's sermons into the discussions of the church administration, because this body was sensitive to such defamations by the press, and because that, as mentioned, in the short time since Barth had started came already to be said a second time. This newspaper, in its edition of July 15, 1912, under the title, "Pfarrherrliche Hetzereien" [Pastoral Agitation] attacked "a sermon held this past Sunday in a congregation in our district" as an example of the pleasure of "certain pastors" to "seek to bring to life once again the times of the religious upheavals, even though in a modern, social-political dress."

> Did the pastor think about what the results of his words, in our area and throughout our nation, might be? We don't think so. Does he really think that a community can do better with sharpened political conditions than when peace reigns among its citizens? Fortunately—and this a word of real comfort for us—the conflict between the two parties in our community is not conducted with such bitterness. Those employed in skilled trades and labor, after working all day, have built something for themselves, and have more useful things to do than to grovel about in the unrest of our times. Finally, we would like to ask whether the church is the proper place for the pastor to express his political views? The great majority of our church-goers, Liberals [*Freisinnige*] alongside the Social Democrats, do not wish to have even those who disagree with them insulted on Sundays in church. They seek on this day, with more reason than their shepherd demonstrates, an hour of edification and meditation. *That* is true worship, Dear Pastor, and not what you dare to offer us!

From a reply to this article we can see what was really going on in this sermon, for the attack of the *Zofinger Tagblatt* found an echo in a second newspaper, the *Aargauer Volksblatt* [Aargau People's Paper], close to the Catholic-conservative People's Party, where, under the title, "Ein fürchterliches Verbrechen" [A Terrible Crime], in the edition of July 16, 1912, the following was to be read: "In the district of Zofingen a reformed pastor gave a sermon last Sunday, in which he, referring to the Sunday gospel of the Reformed Lectionary, (Matt 5, about the self-righteousness of the Pharisees) somewhat castigated the Pharisaism in political life, and illustrated the hollowness, half-heartedness and inconsequentiality of certain people, whose greatest lie is their claim that they are 'Liberals.'" The *Aargauer* defended the pastor against the "liberal" attack, and offered "to the reformed, genuine and consequent liberal theologian, whom the *Zofinger Tagblatt* treated so badly, their full sympathy. A free word in a free land, freedom of speech also from the pulpit, whether catholic or reformed!" The courage on the part of the church administration to call the pastor into account because of his preaching, is probably to be traced back to such public pressure, which placed the church administration members in what was for them an uncomfortable position. The resignation affair of 1919 had, finally, also its reason in the fact that the presbyters showed themselves not equal to the diverse forms of public pressure against Barth's pastoral activities. A very different kind of sermon was no doubt behind a note in the minutes from September 9, 1915: "Mr. Schärer introduced a lively conversation through a question about the most recent sermon."

Schärer was a man from the Workers Association. Unfortunately we do not know the sermon in question and therefore are not able to draw conclusions about its content. Barth apparently found this conversation especially good, for he recorded: "The secretary requests a repeating of such questions and discussions." In a letter to Thurneysen from September 10, 1915, we read: "We had yesterday evening an interesting church administration meeting with a long discussion about God and God's position with regard to the people of Safenwil especially, in connection with the sermon of last Sunday. This time there was only talk around the edges about new tiles on the parsonage roof and such things, and it was voted to have such *objective* meetings more often!"[11]

---

11. K. Barth and E. Thurneysen, *Briefwechsel*, 80.

Clearly it was important for Barth to have conversations with the congregation about his sermons, and from the evidence of letters to Thurneysen this happened on several occasions at least within the circle of the members of the administration outside the regular meetings as well, with invitations to the parsonage. The question of how to bring people to an objective conversation about the sermon was one he placed several times to his friend in Leutwil, where he suspected a greater gift than was granted him (Barth). Therefore he published in 1916 the already mentioned "The pastor, who does what the people want," at first primarily as a special printing to be distributed to members of his congregation. And exactly a year later we find out that the sermon from February 18, 1917, was "to be distributed to every family in the congregation," and was therefore printed and a sum of two-thirds of the cost was approved from the church budget. It was most likely the sermon on Mark 10:32–34, Jesus' way to Jerusalem, with the title *Ueber die Grenze! Ein Wort an die Gemeinde Safenwil zur Passionszeit 1917* [Across the borders! A Word to the Congregation of Safenwil during Lent 1917], printed by the Ringier and Cie. Press, Zofingen. The theme: With Jesus God has become the great "Boundary crosser" into the so-called "real" life and no longer accepts the boundaries that humans have set to "reality" against the world of God. Such a God would be "a terrible lie," "whom anyone anywhere could show out the door: Here you have nothing to seek, nothing in the store, nothing in the factory, nothing in the school, nothing in the tavern, you have nothing to seek where serious people 'with life experience' talk about 'important things' and nothing to seek where people are having fun, nothing at the weddings and the funerals, nothing with the educated or the politicians and nothing where people have much to do, and oh yes, basically rather nothing in the church!" With the true God of Jesus, however, Barth wanted to call the people of Safenwil at last "over the border." That the church administration, with all its scarcity of funds, was prepared to cover so much of the costs of the printing shows that they did not want to remove themselves from Barth's sermons and considered their circulation worthwhile. Still Barth was very clear how much his sermons went over the heads of his congregation—partly because of their length, but also because of their content. Before the great theological crisis and turn of 1916 it was possibly also because of the one-sidedness in the practical consequences of his proclamation, after that then because of his "waiting and hurrying" with regard to the kingdom of God, which could hardly be adequately communicated—and at the same time there was his continuing criticism of individualistic forms of piety. The correspondence with Thurneysen demonstrates the fact, not yet sufficiently taken into consideration, that *the relation to practice* was regarded as the essential problem of the new theology—clearer with Barth than with Thurneysen. More than one member of the congregation reported decades later that they never did properly understand Barth at that time. "'Oh, this socialism!' sighed my mother, as she came home from worship. She said she didn't understand such sermons any more. That oppressed me, and as I spoke with Pastor Barth about it, he was of the opinion, 'If everyone were like your mother, there wouldn't be any socialists!'" (Barth meant, no doubt, that if everyone were so moved by questions and so ready to help others, there would be no *need* for socialists.) "The *rich* young man was commanded by Jesus to go and sell all that he had . . . Abraham on the other hand could keep all that he had." That's what one of the women from Barth's confirmation class remembered, probably reflecting very accurately Barth's understanding. And Hans Jent, the organist, declared later: "It was the same with me as with other listeners to his sermons: I didn't understand all of them completely. They were for our listeners something too elevated and too learned."—Exactly the opposite is remembered of Barth's confirmation classes. Ernst Widmer-Wilhelm remembers things in a more differentiated fashion: "The members of the church in Safenwil did not always get sweet morsels to hear from Barth's pulpit. Sometimes he really laid the ax to the wood: 'Now this needs to be said again.' After such a 'Sunday morning bouquet'—no one was allowed to say anything against it in the church—then there was often from Sunday afternoon into the evening a mighty battle of words about the church in the taverns, at which the church administration members were not left out, insofar as they still supported Pastor Barth." A sharp sensitivity for the problematic incontrovertible form of the sermon! And probably just on that account a transfer (probably no longer qualified) of the "talk back" about the sermon to the tavern. Probably it was from such a source that that "Eingesandt" [Letter to the Editor] to the *Zofinger Tagblatt* originated, and a connection: The pulpit-regulars at the tavern-press connection became a very strong feature of the specifically public nature of Barth's activity (whereby "style-critical" suggestions cannot exclude the possibility that all of the "letters to the editor" that accompanied the whole Barth decade might have come from the same pen; but it would be nice to be able to determine that more exactly).

This seems, in any case, to be the "situation" in which Barth decided in 1912 to institute a weekly Bible Study, probably as a place for instruction and conversation, which might also lead to a better hearing of the sermon. But it was not possible to remove its "church function" from the tavern. But apart from these relationships Safenwil no doubt needed a church counterbalance to a strong, pietistic and sectarian, popular Christianity in the village.

The innovation of a series of *lecture evenings* in the church belonged also to the educational task and the formation of an ecclesiastical consciousness in the congregation, to which only speakers from the outside were invited. The lectures were to have a certain style, framed by special music. This was the venue for Mrs. Pastor Barth with her violin playing. Barth taped into the minutes the newspaper announcements, which invited to such "Public Gatherings." In the first lecture evening, Sunday, January 31, 1915, Mrs. Barth played Handel's Sonata in D Major, accompanied by the organ prior to the lecture, and after it the Adagio from Bach's Violin Concerto in E Major. The lecture, however, had the rather uninspiring theme: "Wozu die Religion? Wozu die Kirche?" [Why religion? Why the church?] given by the attorney Dr. Widmer from Lenzburg. By the end of that year there were a whole series of lectures, "Vorträge über die christliche Hoffnung" [Lectures on Christian Hope], from November 21–24. It was especially pointed out that the introduction to the entire series was to be the Sunday morning sermon on November 21, most likely to be held by Pastor Barth. The lectures themselves took place in the old school house in Safenwil, with the first, on "Die Arbeit der Heilsarmee und die christliche Hoffnung" [The Salvation Army's work and Christian Hope] held by Barth's school comrade from Bern, Ernst von May, who had gone to the Salvation Army, and who was highly regarded by Barth. Then "Unser Vaterland und die christliche Hoffnung" [Our Country and the Christian Hope], next "Der Sozialismus und die christliche Hoffnung" [Socialism and Christian Hope], given by Barth's friend, Pastor Paul Schild from the neighboring village of Uerkheim, and finally Eduard Thurneysen, on "Unsere Kirche und die christliche Hoffnung" [Our church and Christian hope]. One sees a well-thought out progression in the whole series. Here Mrs. Barth did not provide the music, for the newspaper announcement read, "There will be singing from the church hymnal." The proceeds were designated for "the suffering Armenians," for whom sixty-one francs were collected. Already in February 1916, because of visible affirmation of what had taken place, a third public presentation was held (now again with violin and organ special music). Pastor Richard Preiswerk from Umiken spoke there at the express request of the members of the church administration to the theme: "Christentum und Bürgerpflichten" [Christianity and Civic Responsibility]. A parallel project for 1917 fell through in the following way. This time Barth proposed a woman as the speaker for a lecture with the theme: "Die Aufgaben der Frau in der Kirche" [The responsibilities of the woman in the church]. "Ms. R. Gutknecht, theological student in Zürich . . . Ms. G. will shortly be taking her theological examination, and would enjoy the chance to make a presentation here and there. Our lecture series would be an appropriate occasion." The form in which this notice is given no doubt reflects well the situation of women theologians at the time: They were allowed to study and take their exams, but then it was up to them to see how and where they might have an opportunity to speak in church. For the Safenwil church administration Barth's proposal was no doubt something quite novel. "In response to the question from Mr. Schärer the secretary declared that he had basically no reservations against the admission of women to pastoral functions, and that here, as in every case, the judgment must be made on the basis of the inherent merit of what is said." This statement apparently was not able to overcome the objections of the other members of the church administration, who covered themselves in the surprising manner as follows: "Mr. Widmer would prefer to allow Ms. G. to come to preach and then to form a picture about the possibility of her intentions." So it was decided. A woman in the pulpit seemed to be less questionable than in a public gathering. The logic of this opinion and decision might on the other hand lie rather in a consideration of the village public beyond the local congregation. A substitute speaker for the public gathering could not be found, so that the 1917 lecture did not take place, and we hear nothing more from later years about the continuation of the lecture series. We do hear that Ms. Gutknecht did accept the invitation to preach, but nothing more. Barth had explained to Thurneysen that he would have left the choice of themes for these lectures to the church administration. Nevertheless, we can no doubt assume that the two projects, concerning the Christian Hope and the Women's issue were suggested by Barth himself.

Innovations can also be expressed in *refusals*. The two cases documented in the minutes we could value as external evidence of the critical development of Barth's thought in these times.

The first case concerns an invitation in the summer of 1916 from the church administration of Zofingen to institute a district-wide church festival, i.e., a Christian gathering, somewhat along the lines of a small *Kirchentag*.[12] As reason for doing this, the Zofingers claimed: "Our state church lacks life and inner cohesion. The public takes no notice of the things that concern the church. Many circles are turning more and more to merely material interests. At the same time many are turning to the sects, and the educated members are leaving the church." Against this: "The secretary has serious objections to these means of confronting the evil conditions that have been mentioned. An improvement is only to be expected from within, and through the quiet work done in the congregations, not from such . . . special events.—Widmer points to the fact that such attempts have already been made earlier and not succeeded.—Hilfiker expects nevertheless some new impulses from such occasions.—Hüssy is of the opinion that the church needs to have her gatherings in a larger circle, as the gun club and political parties do." (!) "With all votes against that of the secretary, it was resolved to accept the invitation of the Zofingen church administration without objection." In the following year the discussion was repeated about the participation on the district church meeting, with the result that Barth refused to take part in it, while especially the bourgeois presbyters all voted to take part. There were reports following the meeting, which, however, also noted waning interest on the part of the general public. For the third district meeting, on September 1, 1918, in Rothrist, Barth said he would accompany Mr. Widmer "and bring his and our fundamental concerns in this matter to discussion." The result was neither Mr. Widmer nor any other church administration member found the time to participate—so that Barth also did not need to go. Barth's position in this matter was shaped by his increasingly sharp criticism of the church—the flip side of his theological concentration, which came just in the summer of 1916, in connection with his work with the *Epistle to the Romans*. It was not

12. Church congress, post–World War II nation-wide gathering of the Protestants in Germany.—Trans.

that the theological work forced a church-practical interest aside. The preceding examples show that Barth could begin new practical efforts, when they served the theological advancement of the congregation. But his theological concentration led also to the formation of criteria for developing practical priorities, which could set him against the majority of the members of the congregation.

The content of his concerns becomes even clearer with the second case documented of his refusal to participate. Only a few weeks after the first invitation from the Zofingen church administration the Aargau Church Council offered a brochure by Prof. Dr. Hadorn as preparation for the upcoming (1917) 400th anniversary of the Reformation, with the clear expectation that the congregations would treat the remembrance of the Reformation comprehensively. Here, too, Barth immediately took a principled position: "The secretary does not expect much from this effort. What should come from this, again and again to celebrate a great past at the cost of the present. The church once more is trying to glorify itself." "Mr. Widmer expects some success from this brochure against the agitation of the conservative church groups. The secretary would like to confront this agitation with nothing other than a certain seriousness within the church itself. On the motion of Mr. Widmer it was resolved to order fifty copies of the brochure."—And the congregation was to take in from the sale of each brochure ten Rappen. In August 1917 it had to be reported that only a few of the copies of Hadorn's brochure had been sold. "There does not seem to be much interest," and Mr. Widmer, who had been responsible for the purchase, now declared: "It is questionable whether in today's situation such a celebration is appropriate, and he proposed to leave the celebration with the ringing of the church bells on October 31, and the annual opportunity for the preaching on Reformation Sunday." "The secretary grounds his negative position to the Anniversary Celebration: The Reformation four hundred years ago was barely awakened, then stood still again. Our church lacks the reforming spirit. So we have no right to celebrate those men whose living word is totally foreign and frightening to us." The remainder of Hadorn's brochures were then later distributed to the confirmation youth—the profit that had been hoped for didn't come. But—in a very noteworthy decision—Administration President Widmer spoke, in three successive meetings of the administration in the spring of 1918, about Luther, Zwingli, and Calvin. To the presentation on Luther on March 8, it says: "Mr. Widmer gave a presentation on the life and meaning of Luther, following which a lively conversation took place, especially about the essence of religious experience, about the weakening of the reform movement, and the understanding of God that turned Luther away from political life."—Safenwil's contribution to the year of the Luther Renaissance! Where would we find such a church administration today? Barth noted in those minutes: "Meeting adjourned at 11:15 p.m.!" (the only time that the adjournment hour was noted).

IV

Finally we want to talk about the *political history* of Barth's pastorate, insofar as it is recorded in the minutes of the church administration, in polemic in the newspaper and in remembrances of members of the congregation. There is a whole chain of affairs, which arose either from the political views of Barth that became known, from political references in the sermons, or from connections with explicit political speeches and actions. These very differentiated forms of political expression and appearance are to be noted. Precisely because of their many different forms they awakened in Safenwil (and beyond, in the canton of Aargau) the impression of a stubbornness, and on the other hand enabled Barth to make a differentiated defense and ground for his political activity as pastor: one could not attack him with merely rough and general charges.

For an understanding of this part of Barth's pastorate, an orientation to his socialist development during this time would really be necessary. A number of years ago I deciphered, translated and commented on the "Socialist Speeches," but they still lie unpublished in the archives in Basel and, for reasons of copyright, I cannot really make use of them here, and must confine myself to the external mention of them. The "Socialist Speeches," however, accompany continuously almost the entire period of Barth's pastorate in Safenwil, and belong therefore to the understanding of Barth's practice of ministry and the history of the congregation, as much as the knowledge of the sermons, the confirmation lessons, the Blue Cross Bible studies and the correspondence.

Barth began his pastorate in Safenwil on May 1, 1911. Already on October 15, 1911, four and a half months after beginning his work there, he gave his first (later by him so named) "Socialist Speech" at the meeting of the Laborers' Society in Safenwil. The "Arbeiterverein" [Laborers' Society] was the official name of the local group of the Social Democratic Party of Switzerland. One needs to know the organizational history and internal development, especially in the pre-war, war and post-war years (the time of revolution) of this party somewhat more precisely, if one would understand and describe correctly Barth's political views and their changes during these years. But that is not our task here, and would require a much more detailed presentation, so we will confine ourselves here only to what is essential for the history of the congregation. Barth was, when he began his "Socialist Speeches," not yet a member of the party, and we know about his hesitancy to take this step from his correspondence with Thurneysen. That permits us to view the whole body of these "Socialist Speeches" as one of the many cultural educational means, with which he sought to cross the boundaries of a narrower and "proper" pastoral activity. To this also a "Lesson on Health" and an "Accounting Course" (both of which were kept in written documents) belong, which Barth presented in the house-keeping school in Safenwil, likewise in 1911. To this also belong "Lebensbilder aus der christlichen Religion" [Life Portraits from the Christian Religion] or a "Missionskunde" [Missionary Study], which he intended above all as a complement to that which he was not able to include in his confirmation classes, perhaps in the newly instituted evenings for confirmed youth. One might understand this as a practical cultural Protestantism and regard this with the best possible evaluation. But we note that the earliest "Socialist Speeches" were written out word for word, just as the sermons, and form long, comprehensive texts (in contrast to the later speeches and the lectures to the Blue Cross, which from the beginning were worked out only in key words and concepts). That allows us to conclude that Barth himself gave these speeches a certain weight—in the sense of the passion and precision of his proclamation.

The already mentioned first speech was to, according to the wish of the president of the society, deal with the question of the origin and meaning of the state. Barth, however, right at the start, said why he preferred to give his lecture a different title: "Menschenrechte und Bürgerpflicht" [Human Rights and Citizens' Responsibility]. He transformed thereby any temptation to create a metaphysical, divinely conception of the state order into an explication of the theme by using

social concepts and did not hide from a criticism of the concept of social class, which the socialists had elevated "in a conservative manner"
to a definitive social form—a criticism that could *only* be carried out
on the level of functional, social, but not theological-essential conceptualization. The second lecture took place already on February 4, 1912,
at the Laborers' Society, with the theme: "Religion und Wissenschaft"
[Religion and Science]—i.e. on the theme that was widely discussed in
the educational circles of the German workers' societies, and beyond,
about the problem of Darwinism and Haeckel's Monism. [Evolution
and Creationism]. Again two months later he spoke at the Textile-
Workers' Society in neighboring Fahrwangen in more detail on the
theme: "Verdienen, Arbeiten, Leben" [Earnings, Working, Life]—i.e. on
the question about the meaning of human life under the conditions of
the capitalistic ordering of labor.

All of this belongs indirectly to the pre-history of the first fierce
struggle noted in the minutes. We read in the minutes of February
13, 1912, nine months after Barth began his pastorate, that the church
administration had unofficially received the notice that "Mr. Gustav
Hüssy-Zuber tendered his resignation as president and member of this
authority. Preliminary notice is taken of this fact." Naturally the matter
triggered a discussion immediately in the meeting. Barth noted:

> This resignation is connected with a polemic that appeared in
> the *Zofinger Tagblatt* from February 3 to 12. Pastor Barth had
> given a lecture on December 17, 1911, in the local Laborers'
> Society on the theme: "Jesus und die soziale Bewegung" [Jesus
> and the Social Movement], which was extensively reprinted
> in the *Freier Aargauer* between Christmas and New Years. On
> February 3 Mr. Walter Hüssy published an "Open Letter" in
> the *Zofinger Tagblatt*—to which Pastor Barth responded on
> February 9. On February 12, two anonymous writers mixed ar-
> ticles into the discussion, of which at least one took a position
> with more roughness than understanding against Pastor Barth.
> A number of members of the church administration expressed
> the wish to reject this last article with a declaration of the ad-
> ministration. The secretary thanked them for their friendly in-
> tention, but asked them respectfully not to undertake this step,
> since he did not feel himself seriously burdened by this attack,
> and since every thoughtful reader would himself have drawn
> the moral from the story, while the thoughtless one was not to

be instructed anyway. Therefore there will be no declaration in the newspaper.

The speech in question, from the "Official Organ of the Laborers' Party of the Canton of Aargau," was published several times during the Student Movement period of the 1960s, and therefore does not need to be presented again in detail. It is still a classic example of a typical religious-social identification of the Laborers' movement with Jesus and Jesus with the aim of this movement. In comparison to the speeches that had gone before it was marked by its energetic Biblical content and claim. But that was apparently not what set off the furor. Even if we can assume that the three speeches that had preceded it gained the attention of the village and occasioned the corresponding divisive reactions, so that this fourth lecture clearly demonstrated a particular tenacity of the pastor along this line, probably what set off the scandal could be found in the fact that the socialist party newspaper printed the complete text of the speech. Its text was so long that it took three editions of the *Freier Argauer*, November 23, 26, and 28, 1911, to print the entire speech. The paper reported about the speech: "The lecture of Pastor Barth last Sunday here on the theme 'Jesus und die soziale Frage' [Jesus and the Social Question] given at the request of the local Laborers' Society, was well visited. The female sex was present, too. The theoretical treatment and the comparison with today can be found on page two of this number."

The "Open Letter" of Mr. Walter Hüssy, a nephew of the Safenwil church administration president, was printed on February 3 in the *Zofinger Tagblatt*. It declared Barth's lecture to be an "agitation speech, sprinkled with a huge mess of religious quotations," and heard from it the call: "There must be an end to private property!"—to which Barth defended himself with a letter, published in the same paper on February 9, that this was a fundamental misunderstanding. He sought to set the matter straight by quoting as a goal from the party program of the Social Democrats the abolition of private property in the "means of production" and the nationalization thereof. Both letters used a rough tone, which was characteristic for all further writings to the paper, and Barth declared expressly that he would carry on the fight with Mr. Hüssy "despite the prevailing coldness, not in an overcoat, but with his sleeves rolled up, and demand his due with all clarity." E.g., "You address me in my capacity as pastor that I should work 'in a mediating fashion.'

Oh yes, as you understand that, no? That would suit you just fine! But with your permission, I have in mind for myself another program, for which I owe you no accountability." It is interesting to note in the manner in which Barth responded that, on the same day he made his response, he wrote a letter to the father of the man, Mr. Hüssy-Juri in Safenwil, in which he announced his hard response and said to the father that this was not directed "personally" to either the father or the son. This feud in the press was not what he wished, and unpleasant for him. He was seeking to attack the system of capitalism, not its particular expressions, where he had no particular reason. He hoped, in the interest of the congregation that this would not cause any disturbance to the friendly relations that had existed between the pastorate of Safenwil and the "House of Hüssy." However, Barth objectively claimed that this only confirmed his position, as we can see from the fact that his official answer was one of the texts using Marxist argumentation most clearly that we have from Barth.

All of this turned really bad, however, through the aforementioned anonymous publication in the *Zofinger Tagblatt*, above all the first "Letter to the Editor," from February 12, under the heavy headline "Concerning the Red Danger in Safenwil." Here the writer sought, as he said, "to catch Barth in the fly of his pants," insulted him as "a red doctrinaire," a "Red Messiah," the "Messiah from Safenwil," "a combative little pope," as "Mr. Trade Pastor," as a dogmatic hiding himself behind books (a reaction to the Marxist form of argumentation), as "a wise man on the lectern," who secretly stirs things up for class struggle and then falls into a berserk rage, when from the side of the opposition (as through Walter Hüssy) the nonsensical fantasies are dragged into the sunlight. Similar, but more moderate in tone was the second anonymous letter on February 14. The editors of the Zofingen paper closed "the fruitless conflict" with these words to the readers:

> The open letters of the two Safenwil gentlemen have brought me great joy. In this way no one needs to lick any more envelopes to close them, and everyone can read the letters. I think the best thing would be for the pastor to become an industrialist. With his intelligence and good books, from which he thinks to derive his life experience, he would quickly have a learning experience behind him. Then he could share profit and loss with his workers and see whether they stay with such an arrangement or break away. To Mr. W. Hüssy, the nobleman, who knows

less of life's needs, we would recommend that he change and become pastor in Safenwil. The spiritual profession would not harm him. After a few years industrialist and pastor would have come closer together in their view. Yours sincerely.

We read about the end of this affair, the form and tone of which we have laid out in somewhat more detail, because they contain already at the beginning of Barth's activity something of the temperature and the way it occurred, something of the conditions and course of the events, in the minutes of March 25: "Mr. G. Hüssy, President, gave his resignation as a member of our administration to the district office, but he was turned away. He declared, however, most determinedly, not to be able to work any more with this administration and will no longer attend meetings. It was resolved, from now on to place the leadership of the administration in the hands of the vice-president." That was the teacher, J. Dambach. This resignation of Gustav Hüssy shows the whole thing to be a family feud with Barth, above all, however, the great importance that the press got for the pastoral office—whereby the quarrels in Safenwil were also carried in the newspapers of the different political parties with their own commentaries. The *Freier Aargauer* commented on February 20 on the events in Safenwil as Carnival fool's games. "But for Pastor Barth, it is as though he were a wanderer, passing at night through a strange village. Some biting dog begins to bark. At a sound from the wanderer he is surrounded by a raging mob and some yapper always steps forward." Barth had for his part also not been hesitant to use the most important medium of public communication of his time and placed it in the service of his concerns and his "wandering."

In the spring of 1913 the conflicts began with another of the "Great Ones" in Safenwil industry: with the owner of the textile firm Hochuli & Cie. Since this conflict from this point on accompanied the whole period of Barth's pastorate, I would like to report on this at the conclusion of the section.

At the end of 1913, according to the sole entry in the minutes in this regard, there were new elections to the church administration. The Misters Dambach, Jent, Diriwächter and Wilhelm declared publicly their resignation—no doubt as a result of the Hüssy affair from the spring of 1912, so that these events cost the church administration five of its six members. "Newly elected were the Misters Hans Hilfiker, wainwright, Ernst Widmer, Arthur Hüssy, Arnold Scheurmann, moving company

proprietor, and Ritschard, gardener. Mr. J. Schärer, school property administrator, was elected president."

This election was accompanied by powerful political movements,
as we can follow in the newspapers of the time. To the best of our knowledge, it began again with a "Letter to the Editor," to the *Zofinger Tagblatt*
of November 26, 1913. There Mrs. Barth was attacked in the most brutal
form—as "the no-less red-tinged spouse" of "Comrade Pastor," because
she, although she bought a load of manure from a farmer for her garden, didn't let the farmer deliver it, but had her maid bring it, because
she thought the delivery price of five francs too expensive. Under the
title, "Sozialismus in Theorie und Praxis" [Socialism in Theory and
Practice], the author of the letter ridiculed her. "What do our comrades
think would happen, if Mrs. Comrade Pastor were a factory owner?
Item: the upright farmer, out of genuine Christian love of neighbor,
would take pity on the pastor's maid and deliver the manure himself
to the hungry garden, for which the spouse of our pastor would reward
him with 20 Rappen?—Every laborer is worth his wages!" To this the
Freier Aargauer, the socialist paper, responded three days later:

> It is in the article of course not said, which Mrs. Pastor from the
> district of Zofingen was meant, but certain circles confidentially
> say it is clear enough, for whom the letter is meant. We know the
> pastor's wife in question. She is a young housewife who has lived
> up till now in one of Switzerland's biggest cities. We can there-
> fore understand that she perhaps is not used to all the customs
> of such a small country village, and has to get acquainted with
> them first. But, as concerns character and education, however,
> she surely stands head and shoulders above many of the well-
> known chatterboxes of a certain Zofingen village.

"It is bad enough," that the author of the letter, "has to attack
women, because he is afraid to take on men who might wield a mightier
pen." The medium of gossip, to which the press is open we will encounter again soon in a more serious connection. On the December 1, 1913,
once again in the bourgeois newspaper, there appeared a statement that
Paul Wilhelm, editor of this section, "completely distanced himself"
from the letter to the editor with the title "Theorie und Praxis."

This is the atmosphere in which it came, at the end of November
to an open outbreak of hostility. On the last Saturday of the month
some 50 residents of Safenwil met in the old schoolhouse to form a

local association—a political group beyond political parties. Barth, too, was present. Constitution and by-laws were discussed and adopted, a seven-member executive committee elected, whose president was the aforementioned Paul Wilhelm, and to which the teacher and organist Hans Jent also belonged. The *Zofinger Tagblatt* reported on December 2: "From the proposed representatives of the Workers' Association, not one received a majority of the votes. After the results were read, Mr. Pastor Barth asked present members of the Workers' Association and the Blue Cross Association to leave the tavern with him, which took place amidst whistling and cat calls. All these conditions contribute little to peace in the congregation. May all understand this!" So here, too: Barth is declared to be a political partisan and a divisive force. Corresponding to these events there appeared then on December 4 in the Schönenwarder local press two separate election appeals for the upcoming church election on December 7: one from the newly formed "Local Association," with the names of the candidates, who later won the majority, and the other worked out jointly by the Workers' Association and the Blue Cross Association. Pointing to the results of the spring of 1912 and what followed, men were proposed "with a conviction matured through experience and their own reflection, with a certain character, and with a serious intention of working together on church life and work." "Whoever is of the opinion that especially with the election the objective religious interest of the congregation must be the most important consideration we invite to support this list with us. No one can make the charge that any on this list have political party or personal interests at heart." In my opinion the text bears clearly Barth's handwriting. Three of the candidates proposed here—Schärer, Hilfiker and Scheurmann—also were on the list of the "Local Association." The combination of the Workers' Association and the Blue Cross brought an immediate angry reaction from the *Zofinger Tagblatt* (December 6, 1913):

> The church administration election seems to us to want to cause much higher waves than the political [municipal council] elections. We were unusually affected by an election slate with the signatures: The Workers' Association and the Blue Cross. Would it not have been simpler just to write: K. Barth, Pastor? These are his darlings, whom he would love to have around him, not because of their counsel, not by a long shot, but only so that he could push through his programs. From now on the pastor

rules. That's what he wants. Can and will we citizens of Safenwil accept so easily such impertinence? No! No, we will not allow our authorities to be dictated by the pastor and let ourselves be ruled by him. We want men in our church administration who are willing to stand up to the pastor when it is necessary and to tell him that our church is no place for socialist propaganda. Therefore we cast our votes on Sunday for the slate of officers proposed by the Local Association.

And so it was. Looking back on the election, the *Zofinger Tagblatt* reported on December 10, "thoughts of a layman" on "Die Pfarrer und die Kirchenpflegen" [The Pastors and the church administrations] (in general form), thus: "Since thirty years I cannot remember that the election of a church administration made such waves, or that the pastor himself took part in such a fashion orally and in written form." Critically, it went on:

> The sermon is often not an hour of edification. Generalities, village stories, electioneering do not belong on the pulpit. The Christian-socialist pastors use their shock words in every sermon, such as capitalism, elbow freedom, etc.—For the oppressed farmer they have no understanding. The manual worker lies off to one side and the employer is loathsome to them. The pastors have things more difficult today than ever. So they should do everything they can to win friends for themselves and the church. There are not only church administration members unsuited for their office. There are also pastors who lack understanding in many things.

In Safenwil it was not Arthur Hüssy or Ernst Widmer, the decided Liberals, but the three candidates nominated jointly by the Local Association and the Workers' Association, Hilfiker, Scheurmann and Schärer, who received the most votes, while in the election for President Jakob Schärer and Ernst Widmer each received 121 votes, and Schärer was named president through a drawing of lots.

Immediately in the first meeting of the new church administration on January 15, 1914, it says in the minutes: "There followed an open discussion about the activity and especially the form of the pastor's sermon," in this succession. We know from the collapse of this body in 1919 something about the self-understanding, in which a man like Ernst Widmer accepted his election. He understood his task as a call to a service of reconciliation in the divided congregation, which he did not achieve, and which, given the situation in Safenwil, could not succeed. A new representative of the "House of Hüssy," an Arthur Hüssy (but as far as we know not the same one as that newspaper opponent from 1912), now once again belonged to "the authority." He asked immediately—as noted above—a more detailed account in the minutes of the votes when they were taken. We will continue.

For the year 1915 we only hear about the comparative little opposition in the question of support for "A Good Defense and Weapon." In 1916 there was the Hochuli case, which we will discuss later. On June 24, 1917, there was the periodic re-election of Barth by the General Assembly of the congregation. With 277 votes cast, there were 189 yeas, 49 no's, 36 put empty ballots into the container, and 3 votes were invalid.

The end of 1917 the Socialists in Safenwil won the political municipal council election with one vote over the Liberals. This was not without its effects on the internal situation in the congregation. Socialism grew much stronger this year throughout the whole of Switzerland, not least on account of a rapidly worsening economic situation throughout the working classes on the one hand, and a clear war-profiteering situation on the other. In August there were general warning strikes and demonstrations against the rising inflation. In the middle of November, after the Bolshevik revolution in Russia was known, there were violent sympathy demonstrations, above all in Zürich, on which the left wing of the party did not take part, but representatives of pacifistic groups, and for example Willi Münzenberg did participate, and where four people were killed.[13] The Safenwil election results therefore were part of a much larger connection.

With the following consequence in the Safenwil minutes (in the meeting of December 18, 1917; in the meantime Ernst Widmer had become president, after Jakob Schärer in 1916 had taken another office, and there was a prohibition against one person holding too many offices.): "The president expressed the wish of the church administration members, Pastor Barth should place himself above the parties in community politics (village, not congregational politics was intended here)." "Mr. Hilfiker underscores this wish. The pastor should not belong to any party or attend any party gatherings. There should be no party participation at all. Mr. Ritschard: We have above all the interest

---

13. Cf. W. Gautschi, *Der Landesstreik 1918*, 69.

of getting more people to come to church. The participation of the pastor in the municipal council elections turned many people off." What did this participation consist of? Eberhard Busch reports[14] that Barth in this summer 1917 was involved in the formation of labor unions (about which we unfortunately don't know much in detail.) It came to "conflicts" in the village in this regard at the end of August, beginning of September, about which we also have no detailed reports. Barth appeared as one of the speakers at a demonstration. We hear from Administration Secretary Barth about all of this the following: "From all the claims about his involvement in the village elections, only that is true, which he shared himself with Mr. Widmer, that he one time in a meeting of the Workers' Association warned against using again the same failed election tactics that they had used four years earlier"—so a personal political suggestion. In the view of the liberal church administration members, however, it appeared to be quite different. While Mr. Scheurmann said he didn't know anything about the alleged cooperation of the pastor on the side of the Social Democratic Party, Arthur Hüssy on the other hand said for the minutes: "The Socialists would not have been successful without the help of the pastor. The pastor agitated for them. The result was the cohesion of the Liberal Party on their side"—which, according to that statement, had not been the case in the village of Safenwil before. Hüssy requested that the situation be discussed in the next congregational meeting and spread the news that a number of "bourgeois" would gather signatures for the purpose of leaving the state church and refusing to pay their church taxes. That was a real sharpening of the church conflict in Safenwil in 1917, the year of the Russian revolution. In further discussions, those who were of a mind with the Liberal Party brought out all manner of gossip arguments: e.g. "The pastor was observed during the election in a conversation with a group of workers," (!) or that already reported story of Barth's changing the location of his seat in the church on the afternoon of the election, or that he was present on the eve of the election at an election rally of the socialists (which he could prove wrong with evidence of his Blue Cross Bible Study taking place at the same time). Barth himself made two statements in the course of this meeting: (1) "The secretary is amazed as this need of neutrality on the part of the church administration for the benefit of the liberals, which in congregations with liberal pastors

14. E. Busch, *Karl Barths Lebenslauf*, 116.

is not at all the case for the benefit of the socialists. Why won't we let one another do what we wish to do? Fifty years from now people will wonder why there is so much concern about a socialist pastor and even a movement started to leave the church!" (2) (speaking generally on the political rights and responsibilities of the pastor:) "The church administration has a right to speak to the way I conduct my pastoral office; my participation in political life on the other hand is my personal affair, in which I can allow myself to get advice, but in no case can I accept binding rules." (3) "Finally I am convinced that the negative response and anger of the 'bourgeois' is not directed against that little bit of politics that I am now doing, but essentially against all of that which I am trying to represent as pastor and which apparently is new, alien and unpleasant, for the 'bourgeois' as well as for the socialists." This last sentence would need to be looked at critically. Something could be said along the lines of Barth's exclamation against Arthur Hüssy: You'd like that, wouldn't you, Pastor?—Attack on your politics to be perceived as attack on your gospel! What do you understand then by "essentially"? Do you mean: "essentially" you are concerned with something other than politics? Then why don't you let the politics go? Or does "essentially" mean for you: Your politics springs from "the essence" of your preaching, and so then any contradiction to your politics is at the same time a contradiction to the gospel that you expound? But then what do you say about the gospel, when you state: it is "in essence" this which releases the anger of "the bourgeois"? Do you mean by this: the gospel, as you claim to understand it, is indeed anti-"bourgeois"? Then why do you make the jump to humanity in general, and claim, "your" gospel is also "for the socialists new, alien and uncomfortable"? Why do you identify yourself then as both pastor and political being, so clearly for the political victory of the socialists and still more clearly against "the bourgeois"? And how then can you harmonize the differentiation between your pastoral persona and your private persona, which you want us to recognize? Are you practicing, despite your criticism of Luther's "unpolitical understanding of God"—nevertheless a "two kingdoms theology"?—I bring up these questions because the explanations of "essentially," according to which Barth allegedly represented an essentially intended gospel against a receding political criterion, do not seem to be so simple either historically or objectively. In any case what Administration President Widmer declared at the conclusion of the debate seems understandable to me: He said he would "not give in, before this matter was dealt with satisfactorily." The Thurneysen correspondence from this period shows quite clearly that for Barth himself the problem of this "essentially" (precisely in the form in which the matter on this evening was discussed) was in no way "dealt with satisfactorily" (other than for Thurneysen).

In addition, this crisis meeting, in which the intention was to politically neutralize the pastor, also had a last surprising turn: "The president would like, in view of today's discussion, that in the church administration some time a really objective conversation would become possible. The members should learn to read something, understand it and be able to express themselves about it. For this purpose then there will be some folders with reading material to be circulated, beginning with literature about the Reformation." Apparently this was to help to build a bridge over the gap between the knowledge and language of pastor and presbyters. In following minutes we hear that Widmer himself did not have sufficient knowledge of the literature for the collection of such folders, and that this task finally was taken over by the pastor: with the notation that the included material was not to be confused with his (the pastor's) own opinions.

What does "satisfactorily dealt with" mean? Eberhard Busch reports that in view of this meeting Barth refrained from political speeches some time.[15] Indeed the series of "Socialist Speeches" jumps over the year 1918 and begins again in 1919. 1918 was the year when pressure was on to complete the commentary on *Epistle to the Romans*. But that did not remove the political tensions in Safenwil. On May 15, Mr. Hüssy wished "that in the meetings there be no further discussion of politics, because this led to personally unpleasant things. It was noted that in any case a conversation in this regard had taken place *after* the last meeting and not in the meeting itself, and that it had not been so terrible. But he maintained steadfastly that in general, in contrast to before, a certain element of distrust had come into the group, which was a result of politics. The rest of the members took notice of these statements with amazement."

In November it became clear how right Hüssy was, as it came to the affair concerning Barth's position with regard to the general strike, one of the greatest revolutionary attempts in Swiss history. On November 15 President Widmer announced in a consciously indefinite

15. Ibid., 117.

form a special administration meeting to be held in the next week. He was not able to give any details about the content of the surprisingly announced meeting, because he was still gathering information about the object to be treated. There was "something unpleasant," which would probably force him to resign from the administration. Barth protested that it was once again probably a case of an "anonymous charge." To this Mr. Hilfiker gave the following statement: "As a result of the day's events" (i.e., the general strike, which had come to its high point in the period of November 11–14), "there was a gathering of the Liberals, out of which Safenwil now had a civil defense group" (a bourgeois self-defense group against the threatening revolutionary elements, such as had been formed in these days in many places throughout Switzerland).[16] "On this occasion Mr. Ernst Hüssy-Senn, architect, made the following revelations: One of the worst supporters of socialism was the pastor. He namely, in a private conversation in a family glorified the strike, saying that the Swiss government let poor children starve, and that the strike was necessary because of the hunger wages paid by the S.B.B. [Swiss National Railroad] to its workers. He further regretted, on account of the flu, not to be able to preach, because otherwise he would have a lot to say." An escalation of the price of milk, especially grave for child nutrition, played an important role in the history leading up to the strike, and the participation of the railroad workers on the nation-wide strike created one of the most difficult problems for the Olten Revolutionary Committee, since the opinions of the various railroad unions were wide apart, although the wage and personnel policies of the National Assembly since the beginning of the war made especially the railroad workers angry. In 1918 they were still working for an hourly wage of fifty-eight to sixty-eight Rappen.[17] At the height of the strike only a few trains, under military guard, could be maintained between the largest cities of the country.[18]

Five days after this announcement, on Wednesday, November 20, 1918, the announced special meeting took place in the parsonage. In a statement "to the agenda" Barth protested before entering the discussion that an utterance made privately be made the object before the

16. Cf. W. Gautschi, *Der Landesstreik 1918*, 316.

17. Cf. Paul Schmid-Amman, *Die Wahrheit über den Generalstreik von 1918: Seine Ursachen, sein Verlauf, seine Folgen* (Zürich: Morgarten 1968) 128.

18. Cf. W. Gautschi, *Der Landesstreik 1918*, 104a.

administration of an accusation and examination. He had refrained so far as possible after the municipal council elections of 1917 from political activity. "Now, however, the church administration has gone further, and seeks to prevent his freedom of thought and speech." Against this he had to raise a protest from the outset. It was said to him, however, that this was not a case of an "accusation" against him, but an attempt to find out "what was behind this latest excitement concerning the pastor," and how they should relate to it. The situation existing between the people of Safenwil and the pastor was becoming "increasingly untenable." There was "no confidence in the pastor; no confidence in the administration. There were accusations and attacks on both at every opportunity." The conversation in question took place in the family of the Hüssy-Kunz, from where it was reported through other Hüssy families to Mr. Hüssy-Senn, who passed it on in the well-known manner to the "Bürgerversammlung" [gathering of the citizens]. In the meantime Mr. Hüssy-Kunz discredited the related version as totally distorted, but claimed the fact that Barth's remarks could be (mis-)interpreted as they were was "a necessary consequence of the general situation and the ruling politics." So Mr. Hüssy considered the situation also untenable.— In the discussion doubt was expressed, as to whether things would be better with another pastor. "There are simply people, who seek an opportunity to attack." The pastor could not be simply subjugated to public opinion, and that needed to be said, even when one could not approve of the general strike. Barth noted the word from Mr. Hilfiker: "About the general strike there is nothing to discuss. I don't even need to think about it. The thing in itself is to be condemned." And Mr. Hüssy: "One ought to be allowed to hold his own views on a subject, but there are views that are from the outset impossible and no one can represent these. The matter is just that the pastor is angry at the failure of the general strike. There is, as the events in Olten demonstrate, no freedom with the socialists." (I can't tell what this last remark relates to.) Barth asked, in his contribution to the discussion, once again for the freedom "as pastor to be able to represent opinions, which may appear to be impossible in public opinion or a part thereof." About the condition of public opinion in Safenwil he claimed that it was, "for the most part, created by the *Zofinger Tagblatt*, which was the possession of a group of men and whose interests it represented." And so it was a tool of "dumb citizens," (this last expression Barth had to take back in the course of the discussion as "a bit too sharp.") But now:"To the thing itself it must be said that it is not a case of glorification of the general strike, but a calm comprehension of it. The use of violence is self-understood to be evil. But this determination does not justify the absolute condemnation of such an appearance. By the way, there is at least a question, which side started the threat or the use of violence. The freedom to express such thoughts, where they exist, cannot be denied the pastor either."

From the perspective of three months later, Barth gave a speech on February 18, 1919, in the Workers' Association on the general strike from November 1918 and sought to gather all the materials that were available to him at that time. He showed an amazing precision in detail, as one can see in comparison with the historical materials that have appeared concerning this subject in the last ten years. His summary was that on the one hand the bourgeois understood the danger that might result from the victimization of the workers in the society politically and economically, but that one would have to remain skeptical as to whether the bourgeois would draw from that the appropriate practical consequences. If, as the majority of the Swiss citizenry wanted, the authorities were to react to the general strike only with repressive force, "then they would bring about precisely that which they were trying to prevent," i.e., they would only stir up the desire for revolution in the lower classes. If there were to be a genuine and serious intention to improve things, then deeds would have to follow soon. More important to Barth was the question: "And what of us?" (i.e., he meant himself and the workers in Safenwil). Barth was of the opinion that the neck-breaking aspects of a radical Bolshevist position had become clearly apparent in the course of the strike. Now one stood before a great deal of work that needed to be done. Out of the "Socialist Speeches," which unfortunately cannot be used here, Barth's own political convictions come very clearly to the forefront. His own position within the Party, against Bolshevism but for a radicalized socialism is not annulled by the fact that we find him in 1919 as a member in a "Swiss Union for Reforms in the Transition Period"—according to Gautschi's judgment an "idealistic group, whose efforts formed a point of light in the darkness of the social relations of the time," but which did not proceed "beyond a certain beginning success, because personal tensions hindered fruitful work."[19]—Small wonder in a group, in which proven Swiss labor leaders such as Emil

19. Ibid., 372ff.

Klöti or Charles Naine were to sit down at the same table with Division Colonel Emil Sonderegger, who on November 10 gave the orders to fire on the demonstrators on the Münsterplatz in Zürich!

In that special meeting of the church administration from November 20, 1918, the President Ernst Widmer drew finally a facet of the church situation in Safenwil. The present church administration since 1913 was a result of a party conflict. At that time they set themselves the task, "of creating a different relationship between the opposing parts of the congregation and the pastor." This had succeeded within the administration itself.

> We took the part of the pastor. The opposition now turned their sword against the church administration and accused them of becoming dependent on the pastor. Again and again there was a fire in the roof. Now the bitterness of these circles is greater than ever. "Failed attempts at reconciliation turn into the most angry enmity." His decision to resign was irrevocable. He took this step without resentment. He names himself as co-responsible in the situation, in that he apparently was not the right man for the job to withstand such storms in this place. The shared guilt of the pastor in regard to these sharpened relationships consists in the fact that he was not always careful enough.

Barth regretted this decision, but added: "He never saw the reconciliation tactics of the church administration as filled with good prospects. The church can never seek reconciliation for its own sake, but rather the main goal must always be the representation of the truth, which according to its nature will call forth opposition. It is not necessary to resign on this account, and to do so would become dangerous." "Whereupon Mr. Hilfiker and Mr. Hüssy stated that, in the event Mr. Widmer held to his decision, they would join him in resigning." Therefore the same situation as in the spring of 1912!

Widmer stuck to his decision, and on Thursday, February 20, 1919, the last meeting of the administration in this configuration was held. In the meantime a fourth presbyter, the gardener Ritschard also tendered his resignation. Barth's concluding words: "The secretary thanks those who are leaving the administration and especially those members of the administration who are continuing for the measure of trust that they have shown the pastor as a whole, despite the confusions of the time. He regrets the step that those who are resigning have taken but can completely understand it. He, too, feels the pressure of the situation, but thinks for his part to continue to stand against it. However, he can understand it when others find themselves compelled to avoid it." One can see in Barth's formulations how hard Barth wants to remain "objective" and finally is not able to accept personal motives and sees them only as weakness. At the very end Hüssy asked the secretary, "whether he [Barth] was satisfied with the results of his activity up to this point, e.g. at the growth of the workers' movement. The secretary answered that he did not understand this question. The workers' movement would have happened without him, and the pastor did not concern himself with his success or failure, but only that he followed his way."

That was on February 20, 1919. On March 19, the election was held to replace the resigned members. Through this election only socialists were elected to the church administration. There were actions initiated by the now no longer represented Liberals, which testified to their base thinking and showed them to be sore losers. We have already reported above about the attempt to prevent the election of Gottlieb Jent as president because his brother Hans Jent was the president and a member of the municipal auditing commission. As this failed in the course of June and July 1919, it came to the already mentioned attempt by the Liberals and the Village Farmers' Party in the congregational meeting of August 10, to prevent a salary raise for the pastor. In a motion that the president of the Liberal Democratic Party, merchant Hans Widmer, read himself, it said: The pastor "glorifies Spartakism and Bolshevism, deals in socialist propaganda, writes inflammatory articles in Labor's newspapers, takes part in May Day marches, and on these accounts neglects his office as pastor." Then a counter came from another side: "One can see that this is a matter of party politics, and not something else."

> Pastor Barth defends himself calmly against the charges and accusations made about him. For two years the resentment against him has grown, and now it finally breaks loose. It is a lie to claim that the pastor glorifies Bolshevism and Spartakism; he has done precisely the opposite, warning the workers that this would not be the right way, and counseled them against it. He does not now nor has he ever dealt in socialist propaganda. The articles that he occasionally writes for the labor newspapers are not inflammatory, if one is able to understand them aright, but are calm and objective. As a socialist he has every right to participate in the May Day marches, since he takes the part of the

workers and is not ashamed of it. Now his enemies want to play their trump card against him by denying him a raise in his salary, in hopes that he might become discouraged and leave. But he will not leave on this account, and if his salary is not raised, he will leave when he is ready to do so, or if the congregation does not extend his contract for him at the next opportunity.

The newly elected secretary of the administration, Haulier Arnold Scheurmann, subsequently noted: "The rest of the mutual expressions that took place in the course of the discussion are not recorded in the minutes." The result of the vote, with 259 votes cast: 153 in favor and 99 against the increase in salary, with 7 abstentions.

All of these individual affairs that we have reported here were continually accompanied by a permanent political confrontation, which once again intervened quite differently in the specific responsibilities of Pastor Barth and at the same time in the statutory rights of the Safenwil church administration. The fact that the church administration, despite all the internal tensions, took the side of the pastor again and again, may well have been the result of the conflict to be reported below with the factory owner Hochuli in Safenwil, into which the administration was drawn as an institution. Against the threatening interference of Hochuli, the church administration, setting aside their own criticisms of the pastor, had to defend their ecclesiastical rights and responsibilities. The conflict had to do with the times and the length of the confirmation instruction.

On December 29, 1911, Barth was given "the competency" by the church administration to extend the confirmation instruction in the last three months, between New Years and Easter, from two hours to three hours a week. This was confirmed by the congregational meeting on February 18, 1912. In the confirmation classes that year there were forty-three in the first year and forty-seven in the second year class. That caused the pastor to get permission to divide the classes into two, boys and girls.

We read from February 6, 1913: "The firm of Hochuli & Cie. complains in a letter of January 28 about the scheduling of the confirmation classes in the last three months of the instruction year: three hours per week for boys and girls separated . . . The secretary is asked to give the firm of Hochuli & Cie. written information, with reference to § 44 of the Aargau church order, which prescribes for the summer two to three hours and for the winter three to four hours per week." Hochuli answered this information with the notice that he would no longer accept any more confirmation youth in his factory. On April 17, 1913, the minutes read: The firm "was successful insofar as there were voices raised in many circles within the congregation against the church administration." It was discussed whether the church administration should give in to these voices. Barth proposed, "for the sake of peace," to reduce the three hours per week during the final three months to one hour and a half a week twice, "as regrettable as it would be, and so little he was basically inclined, to encourage factory work for those just out of school." The administration therefore adopted the provision: from May to New Year's, twice a week an hour's class for all confirmation youth, then for the time from New Year's twice a week an hour and a half session, with boys and girls separated. The factory was notified of this regulation, whereupon the factory accepted all the confirmation youth in question into the firm, "except some who had already sought and found work in Aarburg and Suhr," who therefore had been frightened off by the unheard of threat of Hochuli.

In 1915 Hochuli inquired about the hour of the confirmation lesson and received this answer, as regards the summertime, 6:30 a.m. At the end of December we hear: "Without notice or reason all the confirmation youth working at Hochuli's factory came twice 15 minutes late to class. The pastor protests about this interference to the president and he was able in conversation with Mr. Hochuli to reach an agreement that in the future the hours on Wednesday and Friday would be kept at 5:15 a.m. In connection with this Mr. Widmer wished that the church administration now for once take the question of setting the hours for the confirmation classes in hand without any consideration for Mr. Hochuli," while Mr. Hüssy "desired that the confirmation classes also during the winter semester be given in the mornings."

On January 17, 1916, there was "a letter from factory owner Hochuli." "The occasion for it was the sermon of January 16, and an address to the confirmation youth two days earlier, in which the pastor took issue with a party put on by Mr. Hochuli. Mr. Hochuli considers the expressions used in the sermon and the address to be 'slanderous and discrediting,' and demands their retraction within three days, or threatens to file suit if the pastor refuses to do so." We learn more about the situation from a letter to Thurneysen of January 10. "Our factory owner

Hochuli hosted a drinking party for his 500 employees on the occasion of his daughter's wedding, and all of them, including my confirmation youth were totally drunk, and conducted themselves shamefully. So are our people kept as fools, with whips and sugar bread, and are at his beck and call."[20] (Interesting is the fully different commentary by Thurneysen to the situation, "When I observe the advertisements for entertainments in my local newspaper on Saturdays, I see the same picture. That Hochuli makes the offer in this case is in so far no basic difference, as the people will have their feast, and take it where they can get it. All of this can only strengthen you in your appeal to the little flock."[21] That is, Thurneysen, through his generalization and his refusal to consider the pastoral implications for the confirmation youth, downplays the political nature of the event, which is viewed by Barth as a political situation, pointing to the relationship of the ruling class and the people.)

The "slanderous and discrediting" expressions are presented to us through the following denial of the secretary: It is determined, "that he [Barth] did *not* characterize the textile works as hell, and Mr. Hochuli as the devil." The president moved for an invitation to have Mr. Hochuli attend the next meeting, but at the same time to register the protest of the church administration against serving wine to the confirmation youth.

Naturally this whole affair also was carried by the press, but this time it was the socialist paper that picked up the case. The paper reported from the most recent church administration meeting (in whose minutes, however, we don't find the corresponding information) that here Mr. Hochuli used the occasion to clear himself of the accusations that were made against him by the pastor and the church administration. "Through the hateful and dirty jostling, however, the clearing was not accomplished." "Every upright person is outraged at Hochuli's dumb remarks." "Hochuli knew very well that no one would dare to say something against him, other than members of the church administration who were defending themselves. Almost every working family is dependent on him, either working in his factory or having work they do for him at home. He has therefore the power and the will to use it." That was how Barth saw the situation. The announced consequences from the socialists: "But the Workers' Society should at last come out of their reserve; they are aware of many things, too." (The pastor's office

20. K. Barth and E. Thurneysen, *Briefwechsel,* 123–24.
21. Ibid., 124.

was therefore to become an advance troop for revealing the problems in the factory; the party should follow.) "The tireless Pastor Barth can be assured of the sympathy of the great majority of the population."

On November 13 Hochuli notified the secretary (Barth) that he (Hochuli) would henceforth only send the confirmation youth twice a week to their classes, and on December 6 he actually forbade the confirmation youth to participate in their class on December 7. That caused the church administration to instruct the young people about their rights, to that in this case Hochuli had to retract his orders.

In April 1919 Hochuli, pointing to "the regrettable situation in the pastoral office here," declared his withdrawal and that of his immediate family from the Reformed state church. Because of the church tax obligations, there arose thereafter a confused back and forth. In this the church administration was forced to consult several lawyers. Barth's attempt to speak personally with Hochuli about this step failed because of the factory owner's refusal.

But the conflict with the church administration continued after this withdrawal from the church. At the beginning of March, the factory set the beginning of its work day for 7:30 a.m., and demanded from the pastor that the children in confirmation class working there be able to begin work at that time. "Otherwise we will be required to prohibit the children in question from participating in the confirmation classes." In his own handwriting, Hochuli added a note to this letter: "Tomorrow and the day after tomorrow the confirmation youth will not be coming. You have no right to set the hours of the class as you wish." (Letter from Hochuli to the pastor's office in Safenwil on March 2, 1920.) On April 12, 1920, we read in the minutes: "Mr. Hochuli now intends to withdraw the girls working in his factory from confirmation classes here and send them instead to confirmation classes in Zofingen with Mr. Geisbühler, lay preacher, which meets on Sunday afternoon, when the girls do not have to work. This involves six children." Barth reported that he had sought for a long time to have some solidarity among his colleagues, so that they could not be played off against one another, but without success. Hochuli was admonished in writing about the illegality of his actions, and the congregation was notified of the situation through a congregational letter. But that, too, was unsuccessful. Already in the confirmation classes of 1919 the number of confirmands was noticeably reduced, to three boys and fifteen girls. It became known that a number of children had gone to the neighboring parishes of Schönenwerd and Zofingen, because their confirmation classes met only once a week. But the parents of many of those children remaining in Safenwil yielded to the pressure of the firm and directed an appeal to the church office in November 1920, to offer the confirmation classes at another time. The church administration accepted this, but insisted that the confirmation classes, in accordance with the new factory ordinances in Switzerland (and not only the church regulations of Aargau) be held *during* the hours of the work day. Hochuli did not agree to this, and the *Freier Aargauer* no doubt was correct with their pronouncement of 1916 that nearly every working family in Safenwil was dependent on this firm, and thus none other than the church administration would dare to speak out against him.

These Hochuli affairs show us the realities of late capitalism. Barth's politically motivated pastorate had its grounds certainly not only in the experience of the brutality of the social situation. But they motivated his socialist decisions again and again and created the possibility for him to persevere through his pastorate even in those places where otherwise deep political oppositions threatened his church administration and destroyed it repeatedly. Already in the sermons of 1913 he condemned child labor, and pleaded with the parents to endure the economic plight rather than deliver their children too early into the world of the factory—this, too, naturally, without success. That he in this situation came to radical, revolutionary convictions and at the same time took reforming, moderating actions can be explained from the objective misery of this situation.

In 1921, as he accepted the call to Göttingen and left Safenwil, the flood gates of hateful polemics and grateful defense were opened about him once again in the press. The *Zofinger Tagblatt* looked back:

> Barely out of his university studies, without any experience of practical life, and blinded by an almost socialist revolutionary spirit, he rubbed everyone in this rural area the wrong way. He and the church people did not understand one another. Only the local socialist party found in him the wished for protector and agitator. The local industrialists on the other hand had in him a tough opponent, though the growing crisis weakened his standpoint. With the years the elementary power of the fiery spirit moved aside, though it did not ever come to a balance or real peace. Many church members stayed away from wor-

ship, although Comrade Barth is a cleaver preacher and an intellectual person of great stature. In social areas he achieved a number of improvements, and could have achieved more in the congregation and the community if his academic lectern socialism had not prevented him from working together with the bourgeoisie.

So: from this side a departure with infamy, as he would have to experience later at his departure from the University of Basel again with a very similar content. Even more infamy was in the *Zurzacher Volksblatt* [Zurzach People's News]: "So, since he was no good as a pastor, he became a professor, in order to make other incapable pastors. Ragaz the Second. And this call can be explained no doubt as simply an act of protection by some socialist bosom friend in the (German) Empire, where such people now rule the higher schools."

But elsewhere people saw it differently. With Barth's departure, it was said, for example, "the most meaningful period for our congregation comes to an end. With the appearance of Pastor Barth a small group of owners lost their strong influence over the large majority of the population, and this influence can . . . never be taken back. This is the explanation for the droppings, which shortly before Pastor Barth's departure appeared in the bourgeois press about him." In another place it was said: "Pastor Barth practiced his office inspired by the principles of a genuine social effectiveness. He did not care about reputation or class position. He taught genuine Christianity . . . When Pastor Barth now leaves our village, threatened by the donkey kicks of this caste, a great part of the population is genuinely saddened at his leaving and remembers with gratitude his sacrificial care for the poor and the oppressed. We wish him all the best for his future work." And in the *Freier Aargauer* from March 4, 1922:

> The big and little yapping papers of the bourgeoisie snapped at him and complained because of his "views stirring up class hatred." But Pastor Barth was doing nothing but teaching Christianity without adulteration and asking for its practical application. He was persecuted by the hate of the capitalists of all religions and those without any because he placed himself on the side of the oppressed, persecuted and the poor . . . We send along our best wishes for happiness and success for one who was not recognized in his homeland, but honored abroad as one who strives for a genuine humanity!

And that, too was naturally—a newspaper!

8

The Idol Totters

The General Attack from the Epistle to the Romans

IT WAS THE SECOND EDITION OF THE *RÖMERBRIEF* [*THE EPISTLE TO THE Romans*] of 1922 that made Karl Barth famous. But it is perhaps with the first edition of 1919 as with nothing else that he can speak to today's generation, open as it is to revolution and intoxicated with the wine of transformation. The period of his work of *theological* construction begins with the second *Römerbrief:* "God is God" and is the Wholly Other over against everything here and now—concepts that are the already worn out keys to his *Kirchliche Dogmatik* [*Church Dogmatics*] as well. But it is in the first *Römerbrief* where Karl Barth sets the tone for his life's labor as a socially and politically relevant endeavor even before he provides specific theological qualification for it. The foundation of Karl Barth's political work is *not* only to be found in the writings of the crisis year 1938: not in *Rechtfertigung und Recht* [E.T. *Church and State*, 1939], nor later in *Christengemeinde und Bürgergemeinde* [E.T. *The Christian Community and the Civil Community*, 1954]. That foundation is laid in the first edition of the *Römerbrief*, in the Safenwil sermons that cluster around it, printed in *Suchet Gott, so werdet ihr leben!* [Seek God and you will live] published together with his friend Eduard Thurneysen in 1917, the *real* crisis year of recent world history, as well as in the speeches delivered in the Aargau during those World War I years. Barth's theology comes into being socially-politically and appears not only in what the man Barth had to say in his parergal writings about politics and church politics or, for that matter, about social ethics. His theology is a social-political event in itself and as such in every detail, something that would need a separate examination. There is no theological profundity and no divine mystery that Barth would not have considered socially relevant, fruitful and subversive.

Of course, one cannot rely on narrow, discipline-specific concepts of politics and social science when one seeks to discern that characterization of Barth's theologizing. Today he is often criticized for that. His theology became not *in* itself politics and social science and thus corresponded neither to the requirements of Ludwig Feuerbach's and his left-wing Hegelian comrades, who wanted to see religion as such transformed into politics, nor to the demands of the unfermented Protestant and Catholic modernism of the day that wanted to see theology established *as* social science, including in the manner theological faculties were to be structured in the reform of the universities. Barth's theology *is* theology. But it *develops* socially-politically, it *constructs* itself within the horizon of society, it *reflects* on its teachings, thought-structures and concepts in terms of an understanding of reality that is shaped by politics and social actuality. Where other theologies construct their concept of reality in terms of *history*—in the wake of historicism, in terms of *being*—in the wake of philosophy, in terms of *existence* or *time* (of *being and time* or *time and history*), Barth does so in terms of society's average experience of social reality. This requires elucidation and can be provided here, of course, only in a fragmentary and rudimentary manner.

But so far we have not really signaled the opening salvo of the *general attack of the Römerbrief*; the true "charge!"[1] yell of Barth's legions of angels (Barth himself liked to use military imagery!) has not yet rung in our ears. Whoever incorporates the first *Römerbrief* and everything preceding and surrounding it into Barth's entire work will find a form of *left-wing* reception of his work a him more appropriate than others that, under the pressure of the Church Struggle, misshaped his theology into a fortress without gates into or out of it. Those interpretations did not even find some dungeon where they could house this highly aggressive, polemical and political master-builder who had joined forces with Western democrats and Eastern communists. When it comes to Karl Barth's social consciousness, there was and still is in the public's mind an unbridgeable difference between the political progressiveness of this man and the seeming orthodoxy of his theological system. Together with the theologically sophisticated Marxists in today's Marxist-Christian dialogue, from Milan Machovec to Ernst Bloch, many theolo-

---

1. Marquardt uses the German term "Urrägeschrei." "Urrä" means something like "start the battle!"—a shout to "move on quickly"—in German "hurren." The term "Urrägeschrei" signals a harrowing shouting.—Trans.

gians trading on this difference declare that it also marks what in their view distinguishes the progressive second *Römerbrief* and the *Church Dogmatics*. Both positions are part of a hardened and hence dominant understanding of Barth. I can regard it only as a misunderstanding since I am persuaded by the unity of his theologizing throughout all its twists and turns and therefore accept the subversive first edition as an integral part of his entire work.

What is at issue? We will insist that both of Karl Barth's *Römerbriefe* are truly understood not only in substance but also in method and in the aggressive tone that marks them both when they are acknowledged as interpretations of *Paul's Epistle to the Romans*. The rank of Barth's two commentaries is to be measured by their exegetical claims. Unlike most of my old Marburg friends, for example, I am not prepared to concede that the file is now closed on the rank of Barth's exegesis. Both books *are* expositions of Scripture. But in interpreting the apostle Paul's *Epistle*, the two books offer more in terms of scholarship: namely *an analysis of the phenomenon of religion in the context of an examination and clarification by Barth of a biblically legitimate concept of "God."* This is a formula for everything left to say now.

The formula has three components. (1) In his analysis of the phenomenon of religion, Barth also touches on the discussion theology was then involved in about history, psychology, sociology and philosophy of religion. In those decades, all of those areas lurked behind more or less every scholarly expression of theology. But he also draws in the swirling *religious situation* at that time of war and revolution. The analysis is the perfect key to unlock the door to an academic future as well as to his contemporary intellectuals among the aficionados and despisers of all religion.—(2) With a huge exertion of will that at its deepest level is barely understandable—something quite unexpected in the man Barth!—he lays a foundation for a powerful theological concept of renewal, of the liberation of theology from philosophy, not to speak of a whole host of other demanding powers, personalities and truths. A *concept* of God is what must be found.

To the average perception of Barth this will sound quite peculiar. Here he is passionately fighting for what he with Hermann Kutter called the *living God*, fighting against all *concepts* of God, for *God-self* and against the human imaginations of *God* that are at play in all concepts of God. But if that is all one knows of the early Barth one knows utterly too little. Later, in his *Anselm*-book (1931) and then in his *Church Dogmatics*, he could do without first establishing, defining and elucidating what he meant when he uttered the ominous word *God* precisely because he had been so overwhelmingly occupied with it in his early years in general and in the two *Römerbriefe* in particular. In those books Barth is *in search of his concept of God*. He will *find* it there as little as later in *Anselm* or in *Church Dogmatics*. But he too cannot do theology without "elucidating" his concepts, as Rudolf Bultmann had demanded of him, the only difference being that Barth had to do theology as such as a never finished process of the ever unsuccessful, ever incomplete elucidation of theology's chief concept: *God*. Others to his left and right always knew what they meant when they said God, from Bultmann's analysis of the existential knowledge contained in the concept of God (the human being's questionable and limited, challenged and transitory condition), to Tillich's formula that "God" is what is of "ultimate concern" to me, and to Braun's "the ground of my being driven about and challenged," etc.

In those early years, Barth shared in the search for and development of formal structures of the concept of God. He also adhered to the theoretical norm that *God* had to be a universal concept that can be related to everyone and everything. But unlike others next to him, he did not test the universal function of a possible concept of God against the possibilities inherent in consciousness so that a person's relation to God—no matter what form that relation took—could and had to be *made plain* to her or him. Barth renounced the normativeness of consciousness, declaring against Bultmann that one's faith is also something that one can only believe; Bultmann responded that this was nonsense. But in Barth's renunciation lies the most profound turning point for a theology that is connected to social, communal, supra-individual reality. The rejection of psychology of religion's individual consciousness included the rejection of Hegel's "spirit," the universal consciousness of humanity proposed by speculative history. This opened the space for the other norm of Barth's concept of God: the third component of our formula, namely biblical legitimacy. Barth did not want to propose a concept of God in the construction of which the biblical proclamation of God and its own structures did not have a direct impact from the very outset. That is the methodological meaning of his much maligned, alleged *biblicism*. The Bible is an *a priori* active participant in Barth's theology, a factor one would not have simply taken for granted. The clarification of his concepts does not occur *before* he uses them but *as* he uses them in doing theology; and doing theology means for him: interpreting the Scriptures. And that is true also in relation to the chief concept of theology: the concept of God.

This should sufficiently clarify the relation of Barth's two *Römerbriefe* to his entire opus, particularly to the *Church Dogmatics*. The *Römerbriefe*, that is therefore exposition of Scripture in general, are the real prolegomena of the Dogmatics; here concepts, certainly the concept of God, are explained, not conclusively but in a preliminary form. That is exactly how the *Church Dogmatics* also proceeded from its beginnings in 1932. The small-print biblical expositions came into being, as Barth stated in reply to questions, *before* he composed the larger-print dogmatic text. One cannot miss what this means for the relation of dogmatics to biblical scholarship in Barth's own work as well. I will say more about that later. In principle with respect to the character of Karl Barth's theology we conclude that the general attack of the two *Römerbriefe* is aimed at the central position that consciousness occupies in every *modern* theology, expelling it from its key function in the construction of theology and filling the vacated place with the exposition of Scripture. *The Bible becomes the consciousness of the theologian Karl Barth.* The domineering position of the modern consciousness is broken with the entry into "the new world of the Bible" that Barth talked about in 1916 and is replaced by what he called a "biblical attitude." Needless to say, this procedure is of momentous consequence. Barth does indeed veer off the over a century old route that all Protestant theology was marching on, exposing himself to the danger of being misunderstood as a pre-Cartesian who henceforth wants *cogito ergo sum* simply to be shoved aside by *credo ut intelligam*. It is true, to the very end there is an objectivism in Barth, not only in the doctrine of God but also in the understanding of the human being. Humans are described entirely from the outside, entirely from the one who encounters them, entirely from the event of salvation, as if they had no problematic self or were functioning figurines that do not understand and testify to the positions of divine action. It is as if they were actors on a stage who must *represent* those positions: Jews portraying the left arm of God and the godless God's patience, all the while doing so without knowledge, indeed, against everything they know of themselves if not *de facto* but surely *de jure*, without a subjective faith yet still truly made righteous by God's actions.

But Barth's meaning is not that of a pre-Cartesian objectivist. Given the origins of his theological thinking, what he means has a societal-socialist orientation. Initially, his critique of the key-function of consciousness is not a critique of epistemology but of society. Self-consciousness is subject to that critique because of its bourgeois class conditioning. For the bourgeois their self-consciousness is their be all and end all, it is their god. Proletarians on the contrary are impoverished not only by their material distress but also by their lack of consciousness of self. They are *unable* to have self-consciousness; they exist in dependency and are defined only from the outside also in the conditions of consciousness without any real connection to themselves. That is why Swiss religious socialism accorded such profound anthropological value to Marxist social democracy: at that time, it was the only effective means of offering proletarians a real connectedness to themselves. *This* way of seeing things became a structural element in Barth's theologizing, irrespective of his changing and developing relationship with socialism and communism. At no time does theology address itself to the soul only; it always has also to do with the body of human beings. God's action encounters and is concerned with humankind just as objectively and externally as class-structures determine it objectively and externally. Before associating with the individual soul in personal biographical action, God acts in world-historical ways making use of great collectives such as the empirical people of Israel, the empirical church, the empirical Judaism, in other words: social and political institutions. Thus, theological objectivity is no longer designed metaphysically or epistemologically but socially. Karl Barth begins with a left-wing Hegelian élan that he does not turn against theology but builds it into it.

The whole *leftist* thought structure reappears in Barth's analysis of religion, but not in the sense of Feuerbach or of the Marxist critique of religion. Barth was well acquainted with both as his works on Feuerbach demonstrate. What he learned from him finds its way not into his analysis of religion—something quite characteristic for Barth—but positively into the structure of his theology. Feuerbach's critique of religion became important above all for Barth's christology. His view of religion is unique even though he describes it in terms of social categories. We note that for Barth the social criterion is not an *external* norm for his critique of religion nor one that is applied after the fact. Barth is no Enlightenment figure. When he depicts religion in terms of social categories, he proceeds much more in a downright Marxist manner. As for Karl Marx so for Barth religion is in itself a social phenomenon.

Barth says that "every attitude a human being takes and every position it gives rise to is a relationship to God," and that comprises its totality. It is not simply an individual (moral, psychic, religious) "attitude" but also an objective "situation," not only a matter between "God and the soul" but also one of [existing social] "circumstances." God's universality is cast *a priori* in social terms. Barth continues: "The only question is: which conditions? We *have* God always, but we have him the way we want to have him" (Rom 1:11). That is how Barth formulates the constellation that starts religion. He himself puts the word "have" in inverted commas, but not in order to put an ironic twist on our human "having" God, but to recall the categorical meaning of "having" in all its forms. Long before, Moses Hess, the Communist Rabbi, spoke of material and intellectual having as a category of bourgeois existence and the young Marx developed that idea analytically in his Paris manuscripts on economy. When Barth puts religion right away within the perspective of the category of having, he determines it socially. We can even now speak of a completely distinct type of theology that is independent of other German theologies if we keep in mind that the system of categories relating to "having" is something wholly different from what was to emerge in Heidegger's reflections on the meaning of the little word "is." And later, proceeding via Heidegger, Bultmannian theology relates itself to ontology and with it to metaphysical inquiry very differently than Karl Barth who is related to that tradition via Marx and Moses Hess. Barth's break with that tradition, resulting from the discovery of the social category, was much more radical than the break the theology made which wanted to accomplish its departure from the tradition by means of historicism. But it could not save itself from historical relativism but by seeking refuge yet again in ontology. For the time being there is *no* road back into the ontological that leads through Marx.

Barth considers "having" God to be as objective and inescapable as the law of having is in bourgeois-capitalistic society. But under the arch of that category there is the illusory freedom of choice: Everything, God included, can be had one way or another as the market permits. And according to Barth religion grows on and from those illusory conditions.

Religion begins to grow when religious greed, the "boundless yearning for God," awakens, which, of course, cannot be stilled because it never leads further than to the edge of the imperceptible, of the transcendent, of the fact that God is not at our disposal. And so this passion, bent as it is on possessing, only creates suffering from the negation that asserts that the highest good is not "to be had." "Yearning" and "suffering" are basic constellations of religion. The early Barth would make use also of Augustine's formula from religious neo-Platonism that the restless heart does not find peace until it "rests in Thee." Bultmann also refers to it several times. Characteristically Barth put aside that neo-Platonic restlessness, declaring it harmless compared to the social and political unrest of the day. He did not look upon that unrest from a cultural-critical perspective that would have seen it as a general phenomenon of the times. Instead and in concert particularly with the religious socialists of Switzerland, he identified that unrest highly concretely as a situation expressing the yearning and suffering of the proletariat. For Barth, the proletariat's circumstances made these basic constellations visibly manifest not only by way of example; they were a real actuality for his own generation. Barth's sermons from Safenwil and Leutwil declare the gospel really *only* in this context relation. The use of the category of having and the analysis of the basic constellation of religion as yearning and suffering from the negation necessarily complement each other in this image of religion.

But the analysis amounts to more than that. Just as the basic constellation of religion within the category of having described the proletariat in particular, so does the reality of religion describe the bourgeoisie. The religious person is one who cannot stand the situation of not having, that is, yearning and suffering, and for that reason turns to self-help, changes the objective religious condition, that is, not having God, into his/her own religious demeanor behavior. Instead of letting God be God in the negation of not-having, they turn to the act of creating God themselves.

> The act of humans who coldly live for themselves and their will is one of *imprisonment*, it is an encapsulation, a misjudgment of the truth they know well enough. They know God but will not venture into that understanding wherein God could actually come *into force*. They know the truth but do not *want* to know it and then it cannot become *actuality*. Indolently and maliciously

> they relate God to their own person. What they ought to think
> of God, they think of themselves, what they ought to give to
> God, they give to themselves, what God ought to be for them,
> they are for themselves. That is how they imprison the truth, rob
> it of its seriousness and magnitude, render it harmless and use-
> less, turning it into untruth. From this act of injustice is forged
> the impiety with which humans then create gods in their own
> image . . . For when humans become God for themselves, their
> lordless world must replenish itself with idols; when the world
> is full of idols, human beings must evermore feel themselves to
> be the sole god among their false gods, the only truth among all
> the phantasms.

This is the story of the ego waking up and of the development of the
power of the human beings' religious productivity. They *create* the possibility of having God, which they do not have otherwise, and create it
by themselves: Religion never gets beyond the religious egotism that
Barth detected not only in Pietism.

We note here in passing that Barth's analysis of the conditions of religious productivity anticipates in conception and substance Bultmann's
problematic of myth. Barth's analysis of religion in many ways corresponds to Bultmann's analysis of myth and his critique of religion
accomplishes, albeit with very different categories, what Bultmann's
demythologization does. I personally think that Barth's critique is more
thorough, but that is not at issue now. In terms of substance, Barth
builds up in his two *Römerbriefe* a continuous structure of the process
of religious production, of bourgeois mythologizing.

To mythologize is to "confuse" God with idols or with humans,
time with eternity; it is "the possibility of appealing to an entity held in
considerable esteem only among humans as if it were God; it is the possibility of projecting what is great in time into eternity and what is great
in eternity into time, to transpose what humans consider greatness as
pre-established justification from the human context into the divine
judgment and what is great in God's eyes as supplementary justice from
the divine judgment into the human context." In the words of Barth's
famous Tambach address *Der Christ in der Gesellschaft* [The Christian
in Society], to mythologize is to clericalize and secularize Jesus Christ.
Or in yet other terms: Every form of socializing Christ is characteristic
of the mythological-religious-bourgeois confusing of God.

To mythologize is to "mix" time and eternity, to produce "divinities that somehow appear in the form of the being, having and doing characteristic of human beings" to produce "a humanity that somehow presents itself in the form of God's being, having and doing." What gets set up are "mysterious in-between regions" and a magic that floats between worlds is being performed.

To mythologize is to "separate" what belongs together; it is to separate God and the human being. Here the analysis becomes most cutting; it is the strongest protest *against* the diastasis, against dualism, against everything Marcionite, precisely against what the vulgar perception of Barth retains in its memory of those years. "Something that God has united separates itself: spirit and form, the inner and the outer. Form stands there empty of spirit and once again the Spirit hovers without form over the waters." "Idea" splits itself off, takes on a "special existence," becomes and "independent entity," a "mere object of cognition," creates a "consciousness" in its devotees of "a unique good" and becomes a "specialty" that loses every touch of "universality." God becomes particular, something the religious "have," the foundation and unique good of the special existence. God becomes a class-god.

Barth described the mythological-religious production conditions of the bourgeoisie using the concepts of the ancient church's two-natures doctrine. To confuse, mix and separate God and the human being was condemned as heretical acts already by the ancient church. They were rejected on the basis of how orthodox teaching determined the relationship between Jesus Christ's divine and human natures. The question is: On what basis does Barth spurn the religious-mythological heresies of the bourgeoisie?

Given the later Barth of the *Church Dogmatics,* one would think that he spurned them on the basis of a clear Christology. But characteristically that is not the case. The famous "christological concentration" of all theology is not the beginning of Barth's ways. Rather, it has a highly revealing pre-history in Karl Barth's early theology of the Bible and revelation that has to be described as a theology of history. Once again, that seems most astonishing, seeing that Barth became important for the Protestant church with his radical rejection of theology of history! But we have no option but to seek an understanding of Karl Barth's own theology of history alongside that rejection and, therefore, must study the connection between his theology of history's position and its negation.

His theology begins with the discovery of that peculiar entity he calls "the new world in the Bible." It was a political discovery in the narrow sense of the word that one can demonstrate biographically from his correspondence with Eduard Thurneysen. That discovery could happen only when (1) the categories of interpretation associated with bourgeois-theological scholarship were failing and (2) when a political hermeneutical interest—or as Thurneysen put it: "relevant interest in what is going on"—just could not be kept away from the Bible any longer. On November 11, 1918, when Germany was caught up in revolution and Switzerland in a national strike, Barth wrote, "One broods now over the newspaper and then over the New Testament and really sees dreadfully little of the organic connection of both worlds about which one ought to be able now to say something clearly and energetically." The World War and the socialist revolution give rise to a new *exegetical* situation. Now the Bible is understood as a "new world" and that means as a holistic entity and totality in its relation to the old bourgeois world that is passing away and collapsing, a "new world" that in itself is clear and consummate. Protestant orthodoxy's marks of Scripture—its *auctoritas normativa, perspicuitas, perfectio* or *sufficientia*—are interpreted within this concept of the "new world" not only in a biblical-apocalyptic but simultaneously also in a social manner. Understood as a "new world," the Bible is quite sufficient, clear and competent not per se but for the presently existing social situation. What the Bible meant for eternal salvation in the sixteenth century is what it now should mean for the social situation of the bourgeoisie's collapse. The Bible must not be held up to a collapsing society in cold, abstract and positivist ways as something *totaliter aliter*, utterly different; what has to be looked for is the "organic connection of both worlds," that is, the organic connection of Bible and society.

Barth finds it in two principal contents of the Bible that occupy him most in the first *Römerbrief*: in its proclamation of the Holy Spirit and in the resurrection. The Bible speaks of the Holy Spirit, but it also makes her[2] effective. The spirit is "that of the self of God and of Christ,

---

2. In German, "spirit" is a masculine noun: *der Geist*. Marquardt uses the masculine pronoun: *ihn*. It is now customary in translating *theological* texts into English to follow the Hebrew denoting of the spirit as a feminine noun and thus use the feminine pronoun *"her"* as is done here. —Trans.

that which waits for us behind the letter of the Bible." Not only behind the letter of the Bible but also behind what the church does: sermon, prayer, eucharist and baptism. "Yes, we may go further still: the Holy Spirit, the spirit of power and life, can wait for us behind *worldly* books and writings . . . Freedom, justice, brother/sisterliness[3] have been and still are today such words, ideals, as we call them, that people give their hearts to because deep down they sense or else clearly feel that those words, were they to become true, would mean a new world." The "new world" in the Bible is the Bible that renews the world. Renewing the world, changing it, is what the Bible is about. "A new world, the world of God is in the Bible. There is a spirit in the Bible, . . . it presses us onto the primary fact, whether we will or no. There is a river in the Bible that carries us away, once we have entrusted our destiny to it—away from ourselves to the sea. The Holy Scriptures will interpret themselves in spite of our human limitations. We need only dare to follow this drive, this spirit, this river, which is in the Bible itself, to grow out beyond ourselves toward the highest answer and reach for it." But as much as God's driving Spirit is in the *Bible,* it *is* also in the *world.* "Ever since Pentecost God's Spirit is in the world and cannot be driven from it any more." The Holy Spirit is a world-historical fact; it is she who creates the organic connection of both worlds.

But how can the spirit be such a fact? By the power of the dynamite of the resurrection! At that time, the resurrection was for Barth *the* theological content that governed everything. It is not yet developed christologically but primarily in terms of its apocalyptic, world-historical substance. Pannenberg is right. Barth calls the resurrection "a power that moves the world."—It creates *spes futurae vitae,* the hope of life to come. Moltmann is right.—In creating hope of life to come, resurrection ever creates in us the expectation that the world is going to be changed, qualifies appearance and does away with resignation. Resurrection throws open the "boundaries of humanity" imposed by death and offers the "emergence of a wholly other *totaliter aliter . . .* order of bodily being in our bodily being." This *totaliter aliter* ["total

---

3. The German word here is *Brüderlichkeit,* literally "brotherliness."—The growing convention among translators today is that only when it can be shown conclusively that males only are designated by a German term will it be translated accordingly. The translator is not persuaded that Karl Barth meant "brotherliness" to denote males only and, therefore, rendered the original as "brother/sisterliness.—Trans.

othereness"] is, therefore, not one of dualistic cosmology, nor one of the Marcionite anti-body and anti-empirical kind; it is clearly a revolutionary total otherness that bespeaks another *order* of bodily being. Resurrection is "*consummatio mundi*, the world's consummation, the abolition of the given, the termination of all becoming, the passing of this world's time." But it is by no means only a negation; rather, it also brings into the world "a peculiar rhythm of progress" that compels us "out of life into death—out of death into life." Resurrection is the truth that "gives up its strange, standoffish, transcendent position vis-à-vis reality" and, like Wisdom in Ecclesiastes, plays on the earth once again and does so "as the living dialectic of all the world's reality, questioning all its alleged answers and answering all its actual questions." The resurrection is "critical potency" and "redeeming movement."

How so? In that it constitutes a "subject of things new." This understanding is of great theological depth. The "new bodily being" comes into being in the "exchange of predicates" between our being sowed corruptible and our being raised incorruptible. The subject remains but is the "subject of things new." Today we would say: Resurrection is our being re-functionalized from death to life, providing "a tremendously new factor in the practical conduct of life." "In the midst of moral-political reality the moral subject is newly constituted by being incorporated into the order of the reign of heaven." It was clear to Barth from the outset that this newly constituted bodily being takes reality collectively. The truly new solid subject established by the resurrection is not the "solitary figure" who goes it alone but the community, the church which in turn is possible only as a "subject of society." For the Barth of the *Römerbriefe,* this once again unambiguously means that in the resurrection the community is constituted as a new, subversive, socially revolutionary subject. The high point of Barth's expectation is that after the "slow dying down of the fire of Marxist dogma," which he acknowledges with regret, there will be "the resurrection of a socialist church in a world that has become socialist." So, here are the criteria on the basis of which the bourgeois nature of religion is rejected. To confuse, mix and separate God and the human being is to sin against the organic and critical connection between Bible and society, is to indulge in the selfishness of *having,* indignant and against what is coming toward us, which upsets and overturns the very foundations of everything.

Barth was serious about revolution in those years. The expression "God's revolution" was common among Swiss religious socialists. Hermann Kutter already used it in connection with the socialist-proletarian revolution at the time against the ruling bourgeoisie. But Barth added a sharp Marxist-Leninist edge to it in the two editions of his *Römerbrief.* As we have discovered now, his exposition of Romans 13 in the first edition was a spirited conversation with Lenin's *State and Revolution* whose mains aspects Barth transferred from the proletarian revolutionary subject to the Christian community as the subversive subject.[4] By choosing Rom 12:21: "Do not let evil overcome you, but overcome evil with good,"—as the headline of the chapter on Romans 13, he can describe the "actual," that is, the bourgeois class-state, as a state of tyranny pure and simple, just as Lenin had described it. "Its name is *violence*" and it is "evil as such." Its wisdom is "red tape and machine guns"; Lenin had said: "bureaucracy and standing army." In that state the idea of all politics is "to defeat by majority vote," that is, "to all intents and purposes to enslave the subjugated." That is so even in a parliamentary democracy. The idea is "to organize one class for the purpose of systematically using violence against another, of one segment of the population against another."

> That people have the temerity to claim that they can confront fellow human beings with an a priori higher *right* to regulate from then on pretty well all their actions and direct them in specific ways deeply wounds the sense of justice, irrespective of which order does this. That sense is deeply wounded when some entity, claiming legitimacy but quickly found out to be a sham, when a multiplicity, having conspired to do so, speak as if they were one voice, when a minority or even a majority (yes, even the greatest democratic majority of all against one!) claims to be the community. When a most fortuitous agreement on the smooth organization of the struggle for existence portrays itself

4. In 1985, when the third edition of his *Theologie und Sozialismus* was published, Marquardt added a postscript, entitled "After Thirteen Years," in which he said: "I take back—but only for the time being—my thesis of a direct literary dependency of Barth on Lenin's *State and Revolution* . . . Still, I need to say here that Lenin's presence in Switzerland, where he worked on that manuscript since 1916, unquestionably had an effect on Swiss socialism. After all, he did not live in Zurich as a solitary recluse . . . So, even if a direct dependency of Barth's exposition of Rom 13 on the work by Lenin cannot be established, it does not at all affect the substantive relation of the arguments; rather, it makes them so much more exciting and does not rule out any historical linkage.—Ed.

to be the peace everyone longs for and ought to be respected, a
horrible wound is inflicted on the sense of justice.

From that perspective, even "a *constitutional* state is beyond correction."
Where Lenin criticized the corrupt practices of revenue officials in his
State and Revolution, Barth criticizes the system of taxation and cus-
toms itself.

Lenin and Barth are at one precisely at the crucial point of Lenin's
reflections: in the struggle against the state turned into a supreme metaphysical value, as if it were the reign of God on earth elevated onto the
philosophical level, the actualization of the loftiest idea. Lenin reminds
us that Engels had already renounced the idolatry of the state. "The state
is not from eternity." The *hypo theou* of Rom 13:1 notwithstanding, Barth
too calls the state "a highly fortuitous arrangement." He too cannot find
it in himself to ordain "a most immanent order with transcendence."
"A human being does *not* have the right to claim objective legitimacy
against human beings. The greater the semblance of objectivity someone is clever enough to convey the greater the injustice done to others.
The task of the Christian community is to *starve* the state *religiously* in
opposition to every form of state metaphysics." "You are to refuse the
state the pathos, seriousness and importance of the divine." And that
does not mean to desecularize the world or to embrace political reti-
cence; it means subversion. "In that process, the state together with its
slaves and admirers may comfort itself that initially we *only* alienate the
souls from it. But should the state come to see the danger of this method
of revolution, there will always be time to prove ourselves as martyrs."
"As Christians, you have nothing to do with the tyrannical state. You
do not belong to it at all as Christians. You do not need it and it cannot
occur to you to desire its preservation and strengthening." Even as a
constitutional state it is none of your business. Leave it to its demise:
despise it radically and all its paraphernalia. "We fight it on principle,
radically" and that means precisely that the "state as it exists now" is "not
to be improved but to be *replaced*, the violence of injustice at the top
and the bottom removed" by "the violence of justice."

But precisely here Barth becomes more radical than Lenin. He
takes the side of the anarchists whom Lenin had combated in *State and
Revolution*. Lenin wanted to replace the "specific power of repression"
of a handful of rich people by a "specific power of repression exercised
by the proletariat," by the dictatorship of the proletariat. But here Barth

says that "more than Leninism" is at stake. It makes no sense to replace the state only by the state. Every new and better state will also be marked by the evil at work in every human being if the revolution does not do away with anthropological evil *also*.

When the subject of anthropological evil comes up, Christian tradition generally becomes anti-revolutionary. It maintains that humans are evil from birth and, therefore, the new world is out of reach. But the Barth of the two *Römerbriefe* does not give in here; he prefers going over to the anarchist side to putting the brakes on revolutionary radicalism. Lenin had postulated new social conditions as the pre-condition for the creation of the "new human being"; so does Barth but, "more Leninistic"; he postulates the new human being, not so much as the precondition of revolution, but as integral to it. Barth accuses Lenin that he believed the revolution could be achieved "with people as they happen to be," which necessarily means with new repressive violence. Leaping over the phase of the dictatorship of the proletariat, Barth envisages directly the phase of the "state in demise" and images it completely in Marxist-Leninist terms: as the automatic "process of dissolution" of a "world that passes away quite by itself." Lenin reckoned that not until the communist phase of the revolution would the liberated masses become accustomed to social life free of repression. Barth wants to see that process of becoming accustomed in the very progress of revolution, at least for the Christian community as the revolutionary subject. The evil is to be overcome with good, [that is] by means of "all people quietly and communally getting used to the atmosphere of the divine, by a common growing more and more at home in God's orders. This must not be disturbed by individual anarchist outbursts," not by "transgressions by individual human beings," something that Lenin, the realist, at least had reckoned with. Evil is overcome with good "only when a new human nature has been built up wherein love replaces duty, and when that nature has been achieved, the present order will collapse on its own. The removal and replacement of moral duties in the world may be seriously considered."

We come to a close.—There are more parallels in Barth to Lenin and anarchistic contradictions against him that one could refer to here in numerous details. But our issue is only to show *which* general attack it was that Barth actually mounted in his two *Römerbriefe*. This theology arose under the sign of the socialist revolution; it is a theology of revolution of an intensity and radical nature that is unparalleled even today also in this respect. It is a theology of revolution, that is, not one occasioned by or that follows after revolution, but one that has internalized and taken it into itself making it its own subject. Of course, here as everywhere else Barth was an eclectic. He did not produce a Marxist theology. The very changes from the first to the second edition of the *Römerbrief* negate that, wherein other authorities, such as Nietzsche, Kierkegaard, Dostoevsky, are part of Barth's arsenal against Lenin.

But one needs to exercise care at this point. The change is no flight from society into literature, into nihilism or existentialism. The second edition of the *Römerbrief* anticipates the absolutely necessary nihilistic and existentialist-personalistic correction of Marxism that Jean Paul Sartre was later to introduce into Marxism and that today separates Western from Eastern communism, the anarchistic-anti-authoritarian from the Leninist-state-servile communism. The second edition issues a warning about the "red brother" that must not be misinterpreted as a turn away from revolution but as a warning *to* the "red brother" who after all is also a red *brother* over there. That change too has its own highly concrete conditions in the history of that time. It was obvious by 1922 that the revolution in Russia, much hoped for and then welcomed, did not lead any further than to the White Russian counter-revolution. Barth addresses this explicitly in the second edition of the *Römerbrief* and relativizes revolutionary and counter-revolutionary one against the other. All groups have to learn to recognize themselves in the other and that is not an ethical-moral law now but a theological one. For God himself encounters us always in the objective other. And the Weimar Republic that had been established in the meantime obviously had to have its place in the second edition of the *Römerbrief*. The subversive exploitation of the present state in *Römerbrief I* makes way for a sober involvement in this, a social-democratic state; of course, it was to be a soberness guided not by some abstract anti-ideological postulate but by radical leftist skepticism *and* goal orientation. The revolution, the reign of God is there in the background, and Barth does not justify such involvement now with a move into reformism or some such thing, but by depicting it as a highly militant "demonstration" for the new that is to come. In the first edition of the *Römerbrief*, the new that is to come spawns total negation while in the second edition—forever falsely perceived as a negative work—it spawns demonstrative analogy. Now the revolutionary method consists in non-destruction, in the sober voiding of existing reality to make room for what is to come. As in the first edition, this method does not at all exclude but indeed explicitly supports the leftist, radical option of the congregation, including—if necessary— its participation in street combat and mounting the barricades.

Be that as it may: for the Barth of the two *Römerbriefe God* and revolution belong together. The shape that Kutter and Ragaz had given to *God's revolution* enters into Barth's theology with a specificity no one could have foreseen; it does indeed determine primarily his *concept* of God. God's transcendence is the transcendence of the underground against all that prevails. (In the second edition of the *Römerbrief* all that prevails is called evil!) God's being-wholly-other is no epistemological, metaphysical, ontological otherness; rather, it is the actual-social-political otherness of what is to come vis-à-vis what is now. God's self-being is the process of this world's passing away, dying off and of the coming of God's reign, a process no dictatorship of the proletariat can deliver. It is that movement which through resurrection and the Spirit's drive brought forth the congregation as the new "subject of society" and now carries it through time. In short, as Barth will later put it in his *Church Dogmatics*: God is the "really transforming fact" where the concept of *real* is Barth's protest against the ontological understanding of reality found in other theologies and the concept of *fact* is intended to signal the empirically real that *God* is all about in Barth's view.

Another paper will deal with the place of exegesis in Barth's theology;[5] here, we conclude with the methodological comment that the socialist radicalism of the *Römerbriefe*, which had become internalized into Barth's theology, was kept in every subsequent phase of his work. (We note in passing that it was no longer the *young* Barth of the historical-critical liberalism of the journal *Christliche Welt* that we meet in the two editions of the *Römerbrief*.) That radicalism can be lifted out, without great difficulty and without doing violence to the text, from its concealment in the language of dogmatics. That is a task that, in my view, future studies of Karl Barth have to accomplish. For without this, the tottering idols of academic, bourgeois theology will not be brought down. But in Barth's theology they *have* already been brought down.

---

5. Cf. Friedrich-Wilhelm Marquardt, "Notwendige Scheidungen und Entscheidungen in der Theologie Karl Barths" (1969), in Marquardt, *Verwegenheiten: Theologische Stücke aus Berlin* (Munich: Kaiser, 1981) 424–38.—Ed.

9

Theological and Political Motivations of Karl Barth in the Church Struggle

> *What we need is a completely fresh reflection the whole structure of which has all the characteristics of a reformation. It is not for nothing that the editors of the Confessing Church's leading journals named it—perhaps with a touch of boldness—"Junge Kirche" [Young Church].*
>
> —Karl Barth
> March 15, 1936, at Schaffhausen

The question just doesn't go away: How are theology and politics related in Karl Barth?

On the night of June 24 to 25, 1933, when he wrote *Theologische Existenz heute!* [*Theological Existence To-day!*], Karl Barth called for a distinction between the theologian and the politician. It was the very act of self-assertion that demanded such a distinction in face of National Socialism's seduction. Anyone wanting to speak "to the situation" as a theologian would "no longer be a preacher and teacher of the Church" but, instead, turn into "a politician and church-politician. It is no disgrace to be a politician or even a church-politician; it holds a special esteem but it is something else to be a theologian."[1]

Five years later, that distinction was turned against him but not by his opponents. Rather, it was the forces in German Protestantism, who seemed closest to him in matters of church and theology. On October 28, 1938, after Barth's famous letter to Josef L. Hromádka had become widely known, the Provisional Board of the German Evangelical

---

1. Barth, *Theological Existence To-day! A Plea for Theological Freedom*, trans. R. Birch Hoyle (London: Hodder & Stoughton, 1933) 16–17.

Church sent a letter to the governing bodies and fraternal councils of the territorial churches. Signed by P. Müller of Berlin-Dahlem, the letter requested that "it be made appropriate use of" and declared that: "With that declaration Karl Barth has left the way which he once pointed as a teacher of the church. It is no longer the teacher of theology but the politician that speaks in his word."[2]

In 1938 and ever after Barth repudiated the claim that he had changed his position. "A conscientious critic would have to conclude that they [Barth's political statements; F.-W. M.] are implicitly accounted for in my entire work and therefore confirm them and in no way render them 'untrustworthy.'"[3] This indicates that from its outset Barth's theology implied a political position.

Conversely, it is clearer today than at that time that the difference the Confessing Church's leadership perceived between itself and Barth was not based unambiguously in the distinction between theology here and politics there. For in their letter the writers set prayer "for our Sudeten-German brethren" over against Barth's support for the army of Czechoslovakia and prayer "for the leaders of our people" against his encouragement of the Czechoslovakian leadership. And whereas Barth rigorously opposed the Munich Accord, the letter praised it as a work of "God's mercy."[4] This is to say: in the Confessing Church's strictly theological self-understanding there actually is a different political argument directed against Barth.

Here we are confronted by a *self-contradiction* in the theology Barth and his friends represented. It surfaced again and again throughout the whole Church-Struggle and grievously impacted on the post-war history of the church in Germany. Its tentacles reach into our own days where people seem to observe a "right wing Barthianism" separating itself from a "left wing Barthianism."[5] This self-contradiction manifests

2. Type-written copy [of the letter]: Nachlass Helmut Gollwitzer, Evangelisches Zentralarchiv, Berlin, EZA 686/7849.—The archive will be identified as EZA for the remainder of the essay.

3. Carbon-copy of a letter by Barth, dated "Basel, October 23, 1938," beginning with "Dear Vicar," from the same file cited in note 2; to date, the letter has unfortunately not been located in EZA.

4. Copy of the letter of "the Provisional Leadership of the German Evangelical Church" of October 28, 1938, in the Gollwitzer file cited in note 2.

5. Cf. Max Geiger, "Karl-Barth-Tagungen auf dem Leuenberg," in Eduard Thurneysen, *Karl Barth: "Theologie und Sozialismus" in den Briefen seiner Frühzeit* (Zurich: Theologischer Verlag, 1973) 45–46.

itself in political differences. But it also signals a difference between Barth and his friends in the understanding of how theology and politics are related and, most profoundly, in how the theology that is done along these lines is itself understood.

What the theological-political struggles of the post-war decades prove is that this self-contradiction cannot be resolved in terms of systematics until it is understood from its roots, that is, in terms of history. Obviously, more is required than renewed attention to Barth's own fundamental discussions such as *Rechtfertigung und Recht*, ["Church and State"], *Evangelium und Gesetz*, ["Gospel and Law"], *Christengemeinde und Bürgergemeinde*, ["The Christian Community and the Civil Community"], *Politische Entscheidungen in der Einheit des Glaubens*, ["Political Decisions in the Unity of the Faith"], etc. For they do not remove the political contradictions which in turn put into question the unambiguousness of the doctrinal statement. If, according to Barth's own declaration, his political statements are implicit in his theological works, then the theological and political motivations present themselves much more intimately that they could be rendered into purely dogmatic unambiguousness. Here everything depends on the perception of the process of how these motivations pervaded one another. And that process was not exclusively or even chiefly one of systematics but of history and politics. Thus, the historical-political motivations of Barth's thought have to be acknowledged as such if they are to be recognized once again as *theological* ones.

I

Barth himself is not without blame for politically abstract interpretations of his theology. Following plausible implications of the socialist-idealist tradition that was his, he proposed—especially in 1933—an identity of the theological and the political that left the political unexplained and made room for it only indirectly in the theological. His position was consciously "untopical and unassailable" "as if nothing had happened," but nevertheless he believed that doing "theology and only theology" unwaveringly "is also a response to the situation: at any rate it is a response befitting Church-politics, and, indirectly, even politics."[6]

---

6. Barth, *Theological Existence To-day!*, 9–10. [Trans. altered.]

"Friend, let us think spiritually and just therefore *realistically*."[7] In the forenoon of October 31, 1933, Barth said in Berlin: "If I were a preacher now, I would have to remind myself anew every Saturday that I have to preach the word of God witnessed to in Holy Scripture, in the text of the day, and that I don't have to name my views of the Third Reich. And because I am convinced that I cannot speak in the name of God but can only serve his word, I shall become modest and be very reticent in regard to concrete matters, so reticent and so abstract that it is perhaps already uncannily concrete again."[8]

After the war, Barth explained to Emil Brunner that it is "a legend void of historical substance" when it is alleged that he "had recommended 'passive unconcern' to the Germans when I counseled them to stick to their task of proclamation . . . 'as if nothing had happened'. If they had done that consistently they would have countered National Socialism with a political factor of the first order."[9] Yet the question remains of how it was possible that this legend could arise at all in the circles closest to Barth. Obviously, too much had remained unsaid in the formula of the identity of the theological and the political, in what else he meant but for which those close by and those far away had not the slightest preconditions for understanding it. And so his theological urgings to remain focused served excellently in their political abstractness as a rallying cry for the Confessing Church's resistance movement and, in Barth's eyes, allowed for the concrete to appear quite clearly in the abstract. But this shows that the meaning and comprehension of the theologically abstract is tied to the substance of a concrete experience. Without it the theological position of abstractness remains open to misunderstanding, indeed, must become meaningless when separated from its experiential context and objectified in terms of dogmatics. That is precisely what happened with the differentiation between "substance" and "the present situation" in 1933 and gets repeated mindlessly to this day. "I asked myself in the most turbulent days this summer when I had

7. Ibid., 81. [Trans. altered.]

8. Type-written, untitled sheets from the Archive for the History of the Church-Struggle, EZA 50/384, sheet 159.

9. Barth, "Theologische Existenz 'heute'! Antwort an Emil Brunner," in Barth, *Christliche Gemeinde im Wechsel der Staatsordnungen: Dokumente einer Ungarnreise 1948* (Zollikon-Zürich: Evangelischer Verlag, 1948), 70. Translated as "The Christian Community in the Midst of Political Change," in Barth, *Against the Stream* (London: SCM, 1954) 19.

to preach whether I did not have to say a rousing word now but then simply chose the text of the pericope and said nothing about the present situation in so many words. But I was told afterwards that the sermon was very much heard as a word to the situation."[10] As long as the sermon brings about such a concrete echo to "the present situation," it does indeed permit that it can restrict itself to addressing the "substance" of theology exclusively. But that depends on specific preconditions based in unmistakable and unrepeatable situations that bestow concrete results on the abstract. But addressing theological "substance" cannot then claim validity apart from "the situation." When in June 1933 Barth said that the Holy Spirit needs no "movements,"[11] he did not mean that the Holy Spirit is a historically immobile power insensitive to the situation. He soon critiqued that it remained unexplained how the political is present in the theological; he recognized the problem and revised it. The situations must be understood that render the abstract effective if its own meaning is to be grasped at all.

Some things can be told about the year 1933.—On October 30, 1933, Barth had delivered an address, entitled *Reformation als Entscheidung* [Reformation as Decision],[12] at the *Singakademie* [Academy of Singing] in Berlin. The next morning, Reformation Day, he met with a number of ministers from Berlin for conversation at the home of Gerhard Jacobi. A transcript of that conversation was subsequently sent hither and yon by Erika Küppers; later it was to play an incriminating role in the process against Barth.[13] In that conversation, Barth outlined why he rejected the notion of "double revelation" in Scripture and *kairos*. "You mustn't think that I am neutral in face of all that is going on. I too have a position toward the Third Reich. But I want to protest against anyone coming along telling us that God's word is this or that, that it demands such and such a response . . . There is no unambiguous word for us in history." That sounds very much like what is held to be Barth's rejection of every kind of theology of history. But in this conversation the emphasis lies not so much on the fundamental freedom of the preaching of the *kairos*

---

10. Untitled sheets, see note 8 above; EZA 50/384, sheet 159.

11. Barth, *Theological Existence To-day!*, 78.

12. Barth, *Reformation als Entscheidung*, Theologische Existenz heute, no. 3 (Munich: Kaiser, 1933).

13. Cf. Karl Kupisch, "Karl Barths Entlassung," in Kupisch, *Durch den Zaun der Geschichte: Beobachtungen und Erkenntnisse* (Berlin: Lettner, 1964) 493.

as on the lack of unambiguousness in what history gives us to understand. Whoever would want to "say something unambiguous" about the problems facing us "would need to be a prophet. Things become quite simple when one adopts the party's stance. But when something is to be said from the word of God, are we not really struck dumb, as it were? Is it really not enough when the church says again and again: But *there is* a commandment spoken into this situation, a commandment independent of every claim and condition: 'You are to serve the Lord your God and no one else!' Do you really believe that any one of us is able to state unambiguously how that is to be interpreted? Won't political passion and political resentment creep up again and again in all of us?"[14]

That statement reveals a twofold dimension of experience. Of course, there is above all the emphatic opposition to the German Christians' theology, its interpretation of history and how it is beholden to that interpretation. It is to be met by abstaining on principle from theology of history altogether. But something more reverberates here: There is in fact no one in the circle around Barth who could say unequivocally how the first commandment is to be interpreted "concretely," that is, in the existing situation. There surely were people in that circle who had not only all sorts of political passion and resentment but also clearer ideas about the Third Reich. We shall see later what these ideas looked like in Barth's head, for example. But it is in fact not (yet?) possible today to discern what the relationship was between those ideas and the first commandment, *the* theological axiom of Karl Barth. And in that situation a theological abstractness commends itself that for the time being has to shoulder everything concrete and make it come to pass.

Let us test that situation-based interpretation of the theologically abstract of that year 1933.—On the very first page of *Theological Existence To-day!*, Barth writes: "I have ample reasons for being content to keep within the limits of my vocation as a theological professor."[15] There is a story, told by Hellmut Traub and Helmut Gollwitzer, about an angrily withdrawn first draft of that pamphlet that seemed much too political to the friends and that imposed on Barth those "reasons" for self-limitation. Is that story hidden in those words?[16] (Later on, we

14. Untitled sheets, see n. 8 above, EZA 50/384, sheets 158–59.

15. Barth, *Theological Existence To-day!*, 10.

16. Helmut Gollwitzer, *Reich Gottes und Sozialismus bei Karl Barth*, Theologische Existenz heute, n.s., no. 169 (Munich: Kaiser, 1972) 59.

shall touch upon another example of the withdrawal of an initially politically direct argumentation in favor of one "within the limits of my vocation.") Given the circumstances of those years, there were obvious risks and dangers related to political argumentation. Barth learned after that discussion in Berlin what far-reaching consequences could follow even from private conversations. Hellmut Traub goes on to tell that he and Charlotte von Kirschbaum talked Barth out of the first version of *Theological Existence To-day!*, not only out of consideration for Barth himself and his circle of students, but also above all for the publisher of that manuscript.[17] Thus, the theologically abstract is surely also an expression of the situation and—of the language of slaves. Speaking in that language became customary and gradually also came to be understood in the Confessing Church having become virtually typical for its preaching-style. One of these days someone ought to work on this matter.

The argument Barth made in the Reformation Day conversation in response to H. Böhm is of greater weight. The latter had spoken of the possibility of "reflecting from the perspective of the second article [of the Creed] on the aspects that come under the purview of the first article." He said: "On the basis of the decision taken, we must say 'yes' or 'no' to very specific things, perhaps even to the order of society as a whole, which in certain aspects is demonic indeed but in others has to be affirmed." Barth replied: "I agree completely. Indeed, we have to address the domain of the first article on the basis of the second. Everything would be in order if *only that* were the issue here. But the intervention a moment ago indicated that the real intent is to say that we must say 'yes.'"[18] What Barth wants to resist is precisely the politically affirmative interpretation put on the drift of the theological argumentation which in itself is correct in terms of dogma. In its "Barthian correctness" that interpretation functions exactly in the way the theologically impossible revelation of history the German Christians were propagating. What in Barth's opinion has to be taken cognizance of and to be decided upon now cannot be taken cognizance of and decided upon in terms of what is theologically correct, in the formalities of dogmatics. "It *might* be" that sometimes one has to say "yes." "But is the same church prepared to say something about what is happening in our concentration camps

---

17. Oral communication from H. Traub.

18. Untitled sheets, see note 8 above, EZA 50/384, sheet 158.

and who has done that? Who is saying something about what has been done and is being done to Jews? Or what is to be said when the word 'the total state' is uttered? What happened when the Reichstag was burning? And what will happen on November 12—will it be an honest election or a cunning maneuver? Taking a stand would surely also mean taking a stand on *those* things."[19] Obviously, correct doctrine meets its limits also in what the *kairos* demands.

Barth conceded in the pre-trial proceedings against him that he uttered those words in "tones of agitation."[20] This was to have serious repercussions during the actual trial. But his heart was in what he said. Here was the essence of the critique not only of theological errors but also of precisely the correct aspects of a theology of the second article. Here was the companion-piece—perhaps even the original motive?—to the theology that is given purely theological treatment in *Theological Existence To-day!* in "perhaps a slightly increased tone but without direct allusions."[21] It is quite possible that a series of politically *gravamina*, such as those raised in the Jacobi residence, were suppressed in *Theological Existence To-day!* There are two reasons for the theological abstractness, the reduction of the political argument into theology and the identification of the theological and the political in 1933. One is that no common political conviction could be reached between Barth and his friends and that as a result one was "struck dumb" when "something had to be said from the word of God." The other is that those factors were meant concretely to prevent the political affirmation of the "yes" to Hitler, the "yes" of the church to the National-Socialist "promise" that seemed still unavoidable at that time among even Barth's closest allies in spirit. Radical political abstinence, total concentration on theology alone could meet that danger.

Put positively: Barth sought to arouse resistance. In April 1937 he said this: "I remember as if it were today that when I gave an address in Berlin and came to its climax, I uttered—unintentionally I

19. Ibid.

20. Copy of the judgment rendered in the "criminal process against Professor Karl Barth in Bonn" in the file "Karl Barth and the German Church-Struggle," 14. [The document has unfortunately not been found to date in the EZA. But cf. the printed version of it in Hans Prolingheuer, *Der Fall Karl Barth: Chronographie einer Vertreibung 1934–1935* (Neukirchen-Vlyun: Neukirchener Verlag, 1977, 2nd ed. 1984) 286–96, where the author deals with the judgment of the Cologne service-court against Karl Barth.]

21. Barth, *Theological Existence To-day!*, 9.

presume—this single word: resistance! I could not have anticipated the huge response to that word; I even had to interrupt my address for a few minutes. Resistance!"[22] Well, Barth did not toss that word into the Academy of Singing unintentionally; it is part of the text of his address "Reformation as Decision." Those who do not wish "to become guilty of the neo-Protestant unfaithfulness to the Reformation have to offer *resistance*, strengthened by what the Reformation has to say to us precisely at this moment."[23] "And resistance is to be offered *joyfully*" because the opponents' spears are hollow!—citing the famous words of the battle of Sempach.[24] A "no!" without any "yes!" whatsoever is what is required now. And Romans 13 cannot be used without reference to Revelation 13. A decision is called for now. "Confessing Church means to be church in the act of decision."[25]

For Barth, this encompassing will to resist applied not only to the church but right from the outset also to politics. The question is how is this will compatible with the commandment of theological abstractness? We said that theological abstractness was the expression of resistance. Given the way things stood in 1933, resistance could gather itself only in such theological abstractness. But is it the final word that "when something has to be said from the word of God" we are "struck dumb" when it comes to being concrete? Is the first commandment's concreteness in 1933 really only indirect? Must not the abstract and the concrete be related after all?

22. Barth, "Vom Kampf und Weg der Evangelischen Kirche in Deutschland: Vortrag von Prof. Dr. Karl Barth (Universität Basel) in der Schweiz im Jahre 1937 gehalten." Type-written copy in the Archive for the History of the Church Struggle, EZA 50/936, 049–056.—The same address, also in type-script and under the same signature but with a divergent title "Der deutsche Kirchenkampf. Vortrag gehalten im Volkshaus in Basel am 23. 4. 1937" is also in that archive. We quote from the manuscript named first, 053, p. 9.

23. Barth, *Reformation als Entscheidung*, see n. 12 above, 23.

24. Ibid., 24.

25. Barth, "Die Bekennende Kirche im heutigen Deutschland: Vortrag von Karl Barth; Gehalten am 15. 3. 1936 in Schaffhausen." Type-written copy, EZA 50/936, 048–049, pp. 9–10.

II

By Reformation Day 1933, indeed already earlier that summer when he composed *Theological Existence To-day!*, Barth had no doubt that the church's statements had to be "also truly" political statements. But he did not find in the Confessing Church "the people needed for that"—in Luther's phrase. In his farewell letter of June 30, 1935, to [Pastor] Hermann Hesse and the German Confessing Church, Barth writes: "After the judgment in Cologne and why it was rendered and after the explanation of its reasons"—on December 20, 1934, Barth was dismissed from his teaching position—"at a time and in a situation when a confessing church was faced with really different problems, people asked me about my political thoughts and actions. Without any reasons based in Christian confession of faith, I was chided for those thoughts and actions and they were turned against me as incriminations . . . A huge fuss was made of my indeed not careful but also not world-shaking remark about the 'Northern border.' [In an interview in Switzerland Barth counseled that the border of Switzerland and Germany be fortified; F.-W. M.] It was spread by word of mouth and in writing all over Germany. But hardly by the German Christians and, as far as I know, by the state or the party; it were the people of the Confessing Church right up to the prominent members of the National Council of Brethren."[26] Since its synod of Augsburg in June 1935, Barth no longer feels at one with the Confessing Church in terms of church politics. But he also explicitly cites the political differences in this context. "My thoughts about the present system of government in Germany were negative from the start but, as my publications show, I was initially able to restrain myself in a certain way. But over time and as events unfolded, my thoughts became increasingly pointed so that my continued existence in Germany became physically impossible, so to speak, seeing that the Confessing Church is unable to support me and those thoughts as a whole."[27] This means: Barth's existence had been made impossible precisely by the church that could not support the motive of political resistance. It means furthermore that time and "the course of events" forced him finally to give up theological abstractness. It cannot be sustained in the

---

26. Barth, Letter to Hermann Hesse, June 30, 1935, type-written copy, EZA 50/936, 041, p. 2.

27. Ibid., EZA 50/936, 042, p. 3.

Third Reich. It was an option at a specifically limited moment, at best of the years 1933 and 1934 and not a timeless, general and objectifiable option without connection to existing circumstances. Abstractness is no option, not for Barth the "politician" nor for the church as a whole if everything is as it ought to be. "I have no doubt that very many of its members quietly think as I do. And I am also convinced that sooner or later the Confessing Church as such will have to face the question whether it must not also think exactly the same on the basis of the confession of faith and then speak up or act accordingly." To be sure: "At the present time, the Confessing Church as such . . . does *not* stand there. It does not occur to it that in addressing a word to the 'rulers' [*Obrigkeit*] it would have to say something else than request the preservation of its existence which the Reich's government had guaranteed, grounding that 'urgent' request in a solemn declaration of political trustworthiness . . . But [the Confessing Church] has not spoken a single word to the simplest questions of public honesty. It speaks, when it speaks, still only about its own thing." But Barth formulates this often repeated critique of the Confessing Church as a critique of himself as well. "It is and will remain a troubling memory of the past two years that I myself did not push forward more energetically in the direction indicated here."[28] That realization weighed heavily upon him for the entire Nazi period. He restated it again explicitly as late as July 1945 to German theologians who were prisoners of war. "I openly confess to you: if I, looking back on my years in Germany, accuse myself of something, it is that when I concentrated on my theological-ecclesiastical tasks and shied away from getting mixed up as a Swiss in German affairs, I failed to sound the alarm—not only implicitly but explicitly—against the signs that I noticed since my arrival on German soil in 1921 in the church and world around me, signs that became more and more uncanny . . ."[29] Barth knew already in 1937 that ecclesiastical and political resistance, the theological and political motive, could "no longer be neatly separated later," that is, after 1933/34, "and that a distinction between them would be difficult to establish today."[30] Time and unfolding events

28. All excerpts from ibid., EZA 50/936, 042–043, p. 3–4.

29. Karl Barth, "An die deutschen Theologen in der Kriegsgefangenschaft," in Barth, *Karl Barth zum Kirchenkampf: Beteiligung, Mahnung, Zuspruch,* Theologische Existenz heute, n.s., no. 49 (Munich: Kaiser, 1956) 91.

30. Barth, "Vom Kampf und Weg der Evangelischen Kirche in Deutschland," see note 22 above, EZA 50/936, 053, p. 5.

demand that the political implications of theology be made explicit. But for Barth that does not mean that ethical consequences have to be drawn from the premises of dogmatics. What it does mean is this: a new determination has to be found of the relation of the divine abstract to the political concrete. "Would it be possible to wean future German theologians from swearing an oath to the 'God of history' *as well as* from the flight from politics?"[31]

Barth now replaces the reduction of the political into the theological that he had made in 1933 by the explication of the theological in terms of the political. The God of revelation must effectively be put as a "counter reality"[32] over against the "God of history." The "conduct of the Old Testament prophets" is now said to be "decisive"[33] even if what had caused impediments in 1933: prophetic unanimity and a common mind in the church, should still not have been reached by now. If one could not speak in 1933 "in the name of God," political speech in God's name is now unavoidable. But "in God's name" now has to mean: In the name of the God who according to the Scriptures' testimony manifests Himself in Jesus Christ. Hence, Jesus Christ must now replace the lack of unambiguousness and of common understanding. He Himself is the power of resistance now against whatever idol is affirmed in both the German Christians' heretical and doctrinally correct theologies. "Every Czech soldier who will fight and suffer will do so also for us and—I say without any reservation—for the church of Jesus Christ as well . . ." For: "One thing only is sure: whatever humanly possible resistance has to be offered today at the boundaries of Czechoslovakia and the good conscience in which it is offered—and with it the final victory!— depends on as many people as possible placing their trust not in human beings, statesmen, canons and airplanes but in the living God and father of Jesus Christ."[34]

31. Photocopy of a letter by Barth to Sergeant Werner Koch, Basel, June 22, 1945, second sheet.

32. Cf. Dieter Schellong, *Karl Barth als Theologe der Neuzeit*, Theologische Existenz heute, n.s., no. 173 (Munich: Kaiser, 1973), 90; cf. also 100.

33. Barth, Letter to Hermann Hesse, June 30, 1935; see note 26 above, EZA 50/936, 042, p. 3.

34. Barth's letter of September 19, 1938, to Josef L. Hromádka, reprinted in Barth's essay "Fürchtet Euch nicht! Ein Brief," in Barth, *Der Götze wackelt: Zeitkritische Aufsätze, Reden und Briefe von 1930 bis 1960*, ed. Karl Kupisch (Berlin: Käthe Vogt, 1961) 157–58.

Those climactic sentences of the Hromádka letter of 1938 caused huge excitement[35] which obscured the fact that those were not exceptional utterances but examples of the typical manner of Barth's argumentation at that time. The struggle for Swiss resistance against the power in the North is also conducted "In the name of God the Almighty!"[36] In the same year, 1941, Barth writes from Switzerland a letter to Great Britain; in it he says: "Dear Christian brothers in Great Britain, I would ask you to understand that in the fight against Hitler we are on truly solid ground only when we oppose him unambiguously in the name of the singularly Christian reality, unequivocally in the name of Jesus Christ."[37] Once again the demand for unambiguousness, except that by now there is no more doubt that one has this unambiguousness "in the name of Jesus Christ." What constitutes it?

First, the reference to "the living God" in the letter to Hromádka alludes to a basic motif of the political theology of Barth's early socialist period.[38] The Letter to Great Britain plays it out in full: The political decision can be definitive "because the world in which we live is the place where Jesus Christ rose from the dead"[39] and the appeal to the resurrection of Jesus Christ is "the ultimate reason" for fighting against Hitler and for "the necessity of resisting him."[40] This is an argument from the fundamental theological-political understanding of reality in Barth's theology. According to it, God is "not a second reality distinct from a supposed first reality here and now, and therefore necessarily exposed to the suspicion of being merely ideal and therefore unreal."[41] Rather, God is the fact that "materially changes all human beings and everything in all things."[42] That fact was for Barth always the most pro-

---

35. Cf. Karl Kupisch, "Sommer 1938," in his *Durch den Zaun der Geschichte* (Berlin: Lettner, 1964), esp. 519ff.

36. Cf. Barth, "Im Namen Gottes des Allmächtigen!," in Barth, *Eine Schweizer Stimme 1938–1945* (Zollikon-Zürich: Evangelischer Verlag, 1945) 201ff.

37. Barth, *A Letter to Great Britain from Switzerland* (London: Sheldon, 1941) 32.—Referred to as *Letter*.

38. Cf. Marquardt, *Theologie und Sozialismus: Das Beispiel Karl Barths* (Munich: Kaiser, 1972; 3rd ed. 1985) esp. 169ff.

39. Barth, *Letter*, 9.

40. Ibid., 15.

41. Barth, *Church Dogmatics*, vol. IV/3, trans. G. W. Bromiley (Edinburgh: T. & T. Clark, 1962) 489.—Referred to as *CD* plus the relevant volume number and translator.

42. Barth, *CD*, II/1, trans. T. H. L. Parker et al. (1957), 258. [Trans. altered.] Cf. also F.-W. Marquardt, *Theologie und Sozialismus*, 242ff.

found point of mediating theology and politics; it was so also during the Church Struggle and remained so to the last. But the question is: Why did this argument not catch on particularly in the crucial years of 1933 and 1934, the way it had in the earlier Safenwil years in face of the proletariat's misery, World War I and the Bolshevik revolution or the way it would once again later, e.g., in face of the threat of nuclear weapons and the War in Vietnam?

The answer is that in those first two years Barth's analysis of National-Socialist reality had not yet advanced far enough for him to present it in a theologically compelling form, conceptually clear and unequivocal. He clearly recognized the phenomena and, as the conversation at the Jacobis shows, let nothing escape his precise observation. The concept of "the total state" already conveyed to him the utter incompatibility of Christianity and National Socialism. But, as we shall see later, it was precisely the concept of totality as such that designated the contrast only that he saw and not yet its substance. And thus the issue was which social realities would deliver the political categories that would in turn provide the requisite unambiguousness also for theology. Strictly theological deductions would not suffice for the dialectical structure of Bart's realism; they seemed too formal and void of substance as he indicated in speaking with H. Böhm. At that point, a discussion about the problems of the state would have been out of the question. While in Germany, Barth clearly steered away from that issue and certainly did not make it a crucial point of the struggle. The question of the church had priority for the constitution of the resistance seeing that it had greater practical urgency. Only after he was outside of Germany, in writings such as *Rechtfertigung und Recht* ["Church and State"] and *Evangelium und Gesetz* ["Gospel and Law"], did he look for new ways while the text of the fifth article of the Barmen Declaration had to suffice precisely in its sparse wording against the German state metaphysics.

This is no accident. What we have here reflects the conditions for a free political reflection that cannot develop itself and reach conceptual unambiguousness under the conditions of total opposition and struggle. The political concept must be capable of dialectical application to other, still somewhat more differentiated conditions and it is, in the final analysis, not a negative but a positive reflection on Barth's theology that he was able only after his departure from Germany to achieve the decisive transposition of the theological into the political.

The understanding that resistance had to be offered unequivocally "in the name of Jesus Christ" was something Barth could not derive categorically from the conditions of total *Gleichschaltung* existing in Germany; only those of the still open Western European societies could yield it. The letter to Great Britain expresses this in a peculiar way when Barth, "united" with the English "for all practical purposes in the attitude toward this war which we as Christians have to take up,"[43] engages at the same time in a dispute with them about the motives for the resistance. "But it is not so clear to me if and to what extent we are agreed on the foundations of our attitude."[44]

> You may have been struck by the fact that the ultimate reason which I put forward against Hitler and for the necessity of re-sisting him was simply the resurrection of Jesus Christ. But I have been struck, on my side, by the fact that in your pro-nouncements various other conceptions have been put forward as primary and ultimate reasons—such as "civilization", "the liberty of the individual," "freedom of scholarly research," "the infinite value of the human personality," "the brotherhood of all humans," "social justice," etc. Now, my question is this: are our intentions really identical, even though the ultimate reasons for them are described in terms which differ so widely from each other?[45]

Barth readily concedes that with those "terms" the English have some-thing basically Christian in mind. But he asks whether the struggle against Hitler can be seriously sustained by the struggle for the values of bourgeois society, for the "ideology of the eighteenth century,"[46] for that is the issue for the British. Barth questions this with vehemence by identifying the inner weakness of bourgeois society vis-à-vis Hitler by name.

He does this in a highly curious way: by positive characterization of "Jesus Christ" as the political power that is not infected by those weaknesses. If liberal bourgeois society is marked by the desire to avoid

43. *Letter*, 14–15.
44. Ibid., 15. [Trans. altered.]
45. Ibid., 15–16. [Trans. altered.]
46. Ibid., 17.

conflict, then Jesus Christ is the power of compelling decisiveness that leaves open no "line of retreat on which we could once again withdraw from our obligations."[47] If bourgeois society, having decided to offer resistance, needs hypertrophic crusade-ideologies for its self-legitimization, then Jesus Christ is the power of sober reflection precisely about the tasks and options of the state who takes up arms in order to defend itself.[48] If the world's bourgeois society immerses itself in utopias of war-aims and new world orders touching upon economic and social, national and international conditions and wastes energies that would sap those needed today for full-fledged resistance, then Jesus Christ is the sobering power that lifts us from our concerns for the coming day and commits us to the work of the hour.[49] If indifference toward the world, unengaged "spectator curiosity" about the chaos round about, and habitual compromising that led to church-bells being rung "when Mr. Chamberlain and Mr. Daladier returned from Munich as if what happened there had been a great revelation," if all that is typical of bourgeois society and expresses nothing but arrogance toward the rest of the world, then Jesus Christ is the power that teaches us humility and therefore participation in the life of the world.[50] If bourgeois society looks with optimism and harbours illusions about the power of evil in the world and, for that reason, nourishes highly superficial self-confidence in its aircrafts and tanks, the inexhaustible resources of the system, and also its wit and morality, then Jesus Christ is the power of freedom from illusions which knows "that the devil was always a bit cleverer, quicker and stronger than one had imagined," and the far more practical power that does not slacken until Hitler has been overcome.[51]

All this means that Jesus Christ functions directly as a principle of political radicalism and reality. It is an idea that always corresponded to Barth's theological intentions, to the sobriety of his understanding of reality derived from the resurrection, and to the directly political nature of his concept of God. Yet he could not develop that idea concretely and assert it in the church in the same manner at all times and places. He could concretize it between 1911 and 1921 in relation to the socialist

47. Ibid., 19.
48. Ibid., 20–21.
49. Ibid., 22–23.
50. Ibid., 24.
51. Ibid., 26.

movement but not in the same way in Germany during the first years of National Socialism. He engages the idea and forms new concreteness in the discussions with societies of the West and their lacking or insufficient will to resist the Third Reich. Therefore, this idea is thoroughly society-dependent. It arises in different functions—in fact in materially different substance—under different historical conditions. In National-Socialist Germany the reality principle Jesus Christ signifies political abstinence, yes: abstractness, the reduction of Jesus Christ into theological form. And under the social and political conditions in which an open society makes its decisions the principle means explicating and introducing the substance of theology directly into political argument. Barth's Christological realism is a concept of social dialectics. But as such it can be won only in societies that are still in the process of dialectical, contradictory movement. By joining the Confessing Church in Germany, Barth had hoped to gain access to a power of social movement and political resistance. But that was exactly what the Confessing Church could not be. And since Barth observed other forces of society—the university, the arts, the political parties—collapse even before the Confessing Church did or being eliminated from the social process of movement through Hitler's *Gleichschaltung,* he much to his disappointment had to remain politically "irrelevant" in Germany, abstract, that is, without concepts. It was only outside of Germany that he found his way to that political concept which he then also used for the formation of his theological concepts, the formation of concepts for a gospel that is "not struck dumb."

In terms of its substance, the theological or, more accurately, the Christological reality concept: the "name of Jesus Christ," is conceived as a political power of resistance in contrast to liberal bourgeois society. That society it is that is lacking in face of National Socialism. It must be excelled "in the name of Jesus Christ." Its ideals, ideologies and virtues, the modes of conduct developed in its systems of existence, have to be contradicted "in the name of Jesus Christ."

This leads us to the materially political motive without which Barth's theological motivation in the Church Struggle may, in my view, not be understood as well.

III

On April 23, 1937, Barth spoke at the House of the People in Basel on "Vom Kampf und Weg der Evangelischen Kirche in Deutschland," [On the Struggle and Way of the Evangelical Church in Germany].[52] It is an astonishing document insofar as it is an in-depth analysis of the social "presuppositions of the German Church Struggle" that is hardly presented anywhere else. One of those presuppositions is "the modern world that is best characterized as the world where the human being is her/his sovereign." This modern world as such is "as old as the world in general. But one may also claim that it got the face we see today only two hundred years ago. The world of that human being was not destroyed, as we believed then, by the World War we all still hold in vivid memory." There was a time when Karl Barth thought of WW I as a turning point bar none. The failure of the three "powers of the mind": science, socialism and church, a failure he experienced as a portent, could not destroy the web that the system of the last two centuries had woven.[53]

National Socialism is part of that "modern world" and is not to be stared at as a historically or socially isolated phenomenon. "Not only National Socialism and its great antagonist, Communism, belong to that world, we all do. As do the ideals that move and drive all of us, some more, some less," like "democracy, Socialism, natural law and historical development, common sense and freedom of conscience . . ."[54]

"This modern world presents itself chiefly in two forms, one of which is the *liberal* one." The other is the authoritarian form. Barth describes the "*liberal world*" as the world of

> free competition of persons, systems and ideas under the slogan: Make way to the fittest! in the open and sometimes clandestine fight of all against all. The road to power in this liberal world is built by getting the majority of people or of capital or both together on side. The wisdom of government consists here in balancing majority and minority as much as possible until there is once again a reversal of the relation between the parties and a new balancing act has to be set up. That is what the

52. Barth, "Vom Kampf und Weg der Evangelischen Kirche in Deutschland," see n. 22 above, EZA 50/936.

53. Ibid., EZA 50/936, 050, p. 2.—One is taken aback how the whole text confirms Dieter Schellong's analysis of Barth's concept of modernity; cf. n. 32.

54. Ibid., EZA 50/936, 050, p. 2.

competition between the conservative and the progressive, between the national and the international idea, between matter
and idea, between optimism and pessimism looks like in the
modern world; sometimes it is a hostile and at other times a
merry relationship.[55]

"That is roughly what it looked like in Germany before 1933,"
Barth continues, thereby signaling the continuity of liberal, bourgeois
society and National Socialism. The authoritarian National Socialism
grew up "in the same house and in the same world" as the liberal world
and then "took its place." "The road leading up to this was relatively
simple. The authoritarian world tends to win when the tendency found
in all human beings and all systems to put themselves into a position
of absoluteness"—which, as we saw, was particularly the tendency of
liberal, bourgeois society of "the last two hundred years"—"is conjoined
with the determination and the power actually to do this and act upon
it.""Hitler and his people . . . had that power and determination; not even
greatest aversion to them can deny that."[56] And how could he prevail?
"Because people came from liberalism, because they had so many lords
or none; that is why they fell also in the church, in this liberal church,
for the one who knew how to set himself up as lord."[57]

In a different context Barth goes into political detail citing external
factors for the success of National Socialism.

We must remember the victorious powers' behavior in the years
after the War and how it could not help compromising every
liberal German government in the eyes of the people . . . In
Germany Europe reaps today what it had sown. Had the foreign
governments dealt differently with a Stresemann and a Brüning,
we would have no Hitler today. We must note furthermore the
world's economic crisis among whose victims Germany was
also and in a particular way. Finally, the example of Italy and
Russia demonstrated to the German people how a desperate
people can under certain circumstances help itself with desperate means. Germany has imitated that example with German
thoroughness.[58]

55. Ibid., EZA 50/936, 051, p. 3.

56. Ibid., EZA 50/936, 051, p. 3.

57. Ibid., EZA 50/936, 053, p. 5.

58. Barth, "Die Bekennende Kirche im heutigen Deutschland," see n. 25 above, EZA
50/936, 044, p. 1.

But it is the inner dimension of the social development that carries more weight for Barth. "That is what happens when liberalism ripens and turns into its natural opposite."[59] In his eyes, this is a necessary development. "Does that transition in the life of Germany from the modern world's first into its second form, from liberalism into authoritarianism perhaps manifest a general law in the historical life of the present time?" And, full of shrewd insight, he continues: "Do we perhaps have to anticipate that an international fascism will arise, fighting against or perhaps someday in alliance with Russia, its greatest antagonist? Is that so unthinkable?" It is in 1937 that he ponders whether military readiness may possibly come to grief from the inevitability of such a development. "In Germany too people talked about the hard fists of the workers that would show Hitler where to go but then it turned out otherwise." It all adds up to this: "We cannot deny at all that we are moving about in the modern world's liberal chambers which, as we saw, represent the slippery slope that some day will end up down there in authoritarianism, a world that at any rate is itself already full enough of evil, misery and struggle."[60]

Communism has no role of its own in Barth's analysis here. Its place is that of National Socialism's antagonist within the "authoritarian," anti-liberal floor of the modern edifice of being. But what cannot be ignored is that the structure of Barth's analysis, irrespective of all its unconventional details, is a Marxist view of historical development. To this day, bourgeois interpretation passionately rejects the idea that there is an inherently necessary connection between capitalistic liberalism and fascism. Only the Marxist view of history talks of liberalism "turning" into fascism as its "natural counterpart." This is where we would find confirmation—were we looking for it—that Barth held on to basic elements of Marxist thought from his Safenwil days and still after he relinquished revolutionary Socialism. Those elements also impacted on his political stance toward National Socialism. With such a background of understanding society he developed a completely different position vis-à-vis the Third Reich than most of his friends in Germany including many closest to him in church and theology. That understanding gave Barth a wholly different scope of insight into the development of the

59. Barth, "Vom Kampf und Weg der Evangelischen Kirche in Deutschland," see n. 22 above, EZA 50/936, 053, p. 5.

60. Ibid., EZA 50/936. 055–056, pp. 7–8.

new situation and, hence, a different possibility of stressing what was then called for. It yielded a different radicalism in diagnosis and prognosis as well as greater staying-power for a strategy of resistance. As a result Barth steadily got into conflicts over the hasty and mostly rather superficial-tactical reactions of the "church-politicians" among his like-minded comrades. His understanding also allowed him to relativize the enemy and, accordingly, attack him more pointedly. "The resistance that came into being then was genuine and strong only when its focus was not only on the incidental opponent the movement faced at the moment, that is, on National Socialism and its terror, but when it was rooted in the understanding that it was aimed at the *entire* world of the modern human being, including liberalism."[61] It was obvious that Barth could not find acceptance in Germany for this Marxist accent in his critique of fascism. In the first years of the Third Reich he would have been associated on account of it with the communists who were persecuted even before the Jews and Christians and immediately jailed. Even more, he would have been discredited in the circles of the Christian bourgeoisie from which a good part of the Confessing Church's membership had derived and which he wanted to win over for the resistance. But if it is true that he could not make use of this basic structure of his political understanding in Germany, then we can see also why he could not succeed in developing the theological-political concepts and the "unambiguousness" that he was always looking for at the time whose most important constitutive element would have been an unambiguous and commonly held conviction in the Confessing Church's Circle of Brethren. But, conversely, one can understand the actuality of the political position he took in Western liberal and capitalist-bourgeois societies. It similarly helps us understand the directness of his various theological-political arguments "in the name of Jesus Christ" in conditions that he recognized and could address as conditions in contradictoriness and as still free societies, on the one hand, but also defenselessly at the mercy of fascism, on the other, because they are potentially fascist themselves. That contradictoriness gave rise to the dialectical political concept that seemed essential to him in the formulation of an unambiguous theological concept. His Marxist understanding of history left him no room in Germany any longer to move forward in terms of a concept of unambiguous theological-political mediation; only outside Germany

61. Ibid., EZA 50/936, 054, p. 6.

was such room left open to him. Those who understand Barth's theology only in terms of his German experience need to grasp that they understand it only in its most restricted, restrained, armor-plated defensive form, robbed of its free dialectics and banned into the rigidity of the antithesis and not in its sharp, mobile attacking form. They see it in the same apologetic form that distinguishes the second edition of his *Römerbrief* from the attacking form of the first edition in which political decisions also shaped the formation of concepts. In the second edition, diastatic antithesis implicitly holds and critiques Socialism, in the first, dialectics explicates theology in terms of Socialism.

Karl Barth's struggle against theological liberalism was the context that helped him give at least a theological-ecclesiastical framework for the comprehensive struggle against bourgeois society carrying fascism within itself. There is no need now to restate the well-known fact that he considered the emergence of the Confessing Church and, in particular, the Theological Declaration of Barmen to be fundamentally a liberation movement of the Christian church as a whole from its at least two hundred year long Babylonian captivity in natural theology. Just as in society in general so in theology and the church people went along with "the inherited theological indifferentism or liberalism, with that spirit that has governed Protestants in Germany and elsewhere for two hundred years and in accordance with which the church has basically nothing any more of its own to represent over against the world."[62] It is no coincidence that these are the same two hundred years that are of such crucial consequence also in the political-social aspect of the "modern world." The only thing to be emphasized in this connection is that, at least in Barth's view, the rejection of liberal theology is integral to his historical-social judgment of bourgeois society and that neither of the two critical components: theological and social development, can be analyzed abstractly in separation. It is *one and the same* critique, theological-social, and its explosive force comes from the Marxist conviction: fascism is the immanence of the conditions of bourgeois capitalism.

That explains why Barth's attack on National-Socialist "authoritarianism" and on the "totalitarianism" of the fascist claim was not launched from a position of democratic pluralism. Nothing was more mistaken

---

62. Barth, "Die Bekennende Kirche im heutigen Deutschland," see n. 25 above, EZA 50/936, 046, p. 4.

than the assertion Barth had fought against the Third Reich as a Swiss and Western democrat. For then he would have delivered the democratic critique of totality. Instead, he acted as a theological and political radical by opposing fascist totality with the totality of the gospel and attacked those who did not want to react totally to fascism. "People could not see the necessity of asserting the totality of the Christian message of God's reign against that system."[63] With words such as that Barth attacked the Confessing Church and, at the same time, depicted the radicalism of the total confrontation that he simply could not find precisely among the democratic forces of Europe who, other than socialists and Marxists, shied away in their liberalism from the category of totality.

IV

The way we have depicted the relation of the theological and political motives in Barth's contribution to the Church Struggle has thus far hardly been considered in this manner. A host of especially systematic questions is raised by our depiction. The history of how Barth's theologizing developed shows us already for the second time mutually contradictory theological base constellations. Just as one has to manage the—crudely put—difference between the first and second editions of the *Römerbrief* in relation to Socialism, so one has to deal with the difference in relation to National Socialism between the position Barth held in 1933 and 1934 in Germany and the position he held outside Germany as of 1937 the latest until the end of the War. Does the history of his theological development permit a systematic decision between the respective forms? Does it permit at least relatively clear conclusions about where Barth's actual and deepest intention is most clearly apparent? And what does it mean systematically speaking when the theology of this theologian, a man who apparently completely abhorred the spirit of the times, the *Zeitgeist*, and links to the *kairos*, over the course of time and depending on the "unfolding events" confronts us in different forms that are determined of all things by prevailing events? We ought not yet close the files dealing with the topics of theology and history, theology and society and, yes, theology and socialism in Barth. Given this context, what does a methodological principle such as the following from the old Barth mean for the understanding of his theology as

63. Ibid.

a whole? "The difference between the times and situations in which the theological act of knowledge is carried out opposes any thoroughgoing and consistent systematization."[64] This surely is to be applied not only to epochal historical differences such as those between Ancient Church, Middle Ages, Reformation, Modernity, etc., which have long been in use to explain—from great historical distance—theological differences. The course of how Barth's theologizing developed shows that there are also differences that are based in the experiences of "day-to-day politics." One could speak of aspects in Barth's theology that are of epochal historical significance at best only in light of the fact that the acceleration of social development is today "epoch making" more rapidly. We now experience epochal significance in "day-to-day political" events more immediately than before and the customary disqualification of the actuality of day-to-day politics in sermon and theology ignores the objective law of history's development. The forms of Karl Barth's theological-political expression changed ever so rapidly over the course of ten and later of only five to two years. They give us an insight into the acceleration of historical processes and are thereby a forceful example of "modern" theologizing attentive to the times. The option of an abstractly dogmatic, purely intra-theological exploration of the relation between theology and politics in Barth surely becomes an insoluble problem when the relatedness of the theological act of knowledge to "the difference between the times and situations" is not acknowledged and systematically attended to. As far as basic principles are concerned, much extensive work is still needed on adequate categories of a theology today. But in relation to Barth a historical-social categorization and classification of his theology is required. This endeavor is today still very much in its infancy and the dispute about how meaningful, useful and appropriate an undertaking this will be is only just starting.

Barth was fully cognizant of the problem of the political-doctrinal contradictoriness of his theologizing but he did not turn it into a consistent system. Indeed, systematic inconsistency, breaks in argumentation and contrasts left unmediated were his means of giving this formal expression. The substantive meaning of that unsystematic form was openness to the historical change that Barth expected "from above," from "the living God" but for which he also had a "human" and then

---

64. Barth, *Evangelical Theology: An Introduction*, trans. Grover Foley (New York: Holt, Rinehart & Winston, 1963) 89.

above all political perspective without which the "from above" would have remained unreal for him. This is because for him the living God just was never a "second reality," something different "from an entity allegedly real here and now."

In closing we explicate this by means of a highly problematic example.—In the Archive for the History of the Church Struggle, located in Berlin-Zehlendorf, there is a type-written document called "A Short Commentary on the First Article of the Theological Declaration of the Barmen Synod of May 31, 1934."[65] On closer scrutiny it turns out to be identical to a large extend with the text of *CD* II/1, pp. 172ff. In the type-written version there are some very slight merely stylistic deviations in addition to a longer item of argumentation that was obviously left out of the *Church Dogmatics*. The text in the Archive may well have been a document of the way Barth's theology was disseminated in National-Socialist Germany. There is another example of that in the Archive; it is about Jesus as the *homo judaeus* in *CD* I/2. The relation of our texts one to the other is presumably that of the one he delivered in Basel to the printed, published version of the *Dogmatics*. What is of interest is just where that originally oral text goes beyond the published one.

In his addresses of April 23, 1937, at the *Volkshaus* in Basel and March 15, 1936, at Schaffhausen, Barth raised the question of the "preconditions" of the Church Struggle. In exactly the same way he addresses the "genesis of Barmen" in that "Short Commentary" but not only concerning the theological and church-political preconditions but also and more inclusively the social-political ones. "Why is it that in the long series of similar experiences the church has had it was just at that time and—of all places—in Germany" that there arose opposition in the church against the error of natural theology?

> Why not earlier, why not, for example, at the end of the eighteenth century when what was expected of the church then was outwardly no less crazy than what is expected of it at the present? Why not somewhere else, in some church that had the time and leisure fundamentally to clarify the situation of theological history for itself in peace and quiet and then proceed calmly to such a far-reaching decision? Why right now and why in

---

65. Barth, "Kurze Kommentierung des ersten Satzes der Theologischen Erklärung der Barmer Synode vom 31. Mai 1934," EZA 50/224, pp. 187–91.

Germany where what is basic and concrete actuality, where the protest against an old and general error and the protest against the present German error, had to be brought together in such a confused and moreover highly dangerous way?[66]

"One of the causes of this event, seen from a human perspective," Barth says, "is that the form of the opponent, that is, of the natural theology the church had to deal with, was completely different from the one it had faced hitherto. To put it plainly: it was the totalitarianism of the neo-German politics and *Weltanschauung* that compelled the church to cleanse itself even though it did not know or desire it at first."[67] Just as Hitler's success in the development of society lay simply in that he consistently and with violence did what everyone in the liberal system had always wanted to do, so in the domain of theology "the discovery of the idea all of its predecessors had missed, namely that one can achieve everything with the means of the stage of siege imposed on the nation's public and private life was quite simply what turned that power into the now ruling power." "All of a sudden the animal bared its fangs." And the *modus operandi* was "no longer the force of reasoned argument but the force of physical violence pure and simple." "What weight did eighteenth century reason still carry? Or the spirit and freedom of Idealism? What about the *aesthesis* [the perception of reality through the senses] of Romanticism? And what weight did the noble thoroughness and science of the nineteenth century still carry?" and by implication: what value did the substance of bourgeois society have? "All of these may have had their time and fulfilled their service but now they were all tossed aside, none of them left as an option," offering no line of retreat, as Barth was to put it in the 1941 letter to Great Britain. "The only option was the barbaric horror figure of the new god who had surpassed and devoured all of them . . ."[68] In a word: "The new feature of the situation in Germany 1933 was that the church was forced to make this choice but not as the result of theological instruction but by harsh pressure from outside."[69] "Whatever theological reflection there was notoriously came afterwards."[70]

66. Ibid., EZA 50/224, 189, p. 5.
67. Ibid., EZA 50/224, 189–190, pp. 5–6.
68. Ibid., EZA 50/224, 190, p. 6.
69. Ibid., EZA 50/224, 190, pp. 6–7.
70. Ibid., EZA 50/224, 190, p. 7.

In the printed version Barth left out this briefly sketched section dealing with the historical "preconditions" of a major theological statement and, conversely, the notoriously after-the-fact reaction of theology to political reality. If we were dealing here with a single, isolated argument by Barth, it would not be worthy of making a fuss over it. But that is not the case as those two addresses of 1936 and 1937 show. Barth basically reverts here to one of his very early theological-social ideas: the "insight into the secondary character of the religious idea" which has "praxis" for its precondition.[71] Here we have confirmation that induction from political experience to the formulation of theological knowledge—sketched out elsewhere[72] as Barth's "thinking toward God" [Denken auf Gott hin]—remained a virulent option in his thinking.

The presence of that understanding here raises question upon question. One surely does Barth no injustice when in explaining the deletion referred to earlier one looks initially to purely personal considerations. He had to defend himself throughout the Church Struggle against the view that the phenomenon of the Confessing Church was the product and issue of "Barthian theology" only. "I was given to understand over there (in England) that the dispute about the Barmen Statement was a domestic question of Germany or even an arbitrary specialty of Barthian theology."[73] Or "It was said: One ought not to think that the Barmen Declaration was a confessional statement of the nature of the Nicene Creed or the Augsburg Confession. One can look at things slightly differently. There is too much of Barth's theology in it."[74] Barth adds this comment: "It would be ridiculous to confuse the result with the causes and to resolve this puzzle by laying the blame for or the merit of the matter at the feet of a certain theological orientation that unfortunately or luckily prevailed in those years and especially at Barmen."[75]

That is why it was important for Barth to leave aside and delete subjective idiosyncrasies of his thinking and untypical matters that

71. Barth, "Der Glaube an den persönlichen Gott," Zeitschrift für Theologie und Kirche 24 (1914) 22. Cf. Marquardt, Theologie und Sozialismus, 276ff., esp. 282.

72. Ibid., 181–82.

73. Barth, "Eine Frage und eine Antwort," in Karl Barth zum Kirchenkampf, 70.

74. "Barths Gedanken über die Lage in einer Bekenntnisversammlung evangelischer Studenten am 1. Dezember 1934," type-written ms in the EZA 50/936, 035, p. 2.

75. Barth, "Kurze Kommentierung," see n. 65 above, EZA 50/224, 189, p. 5.

had no import for the church. As we already noted in connection with *Theological Existence To-day!* Barth sacrificed public expression of his political judgment to that decision. He did so also in this case. Political argumentation in connection with theological questions was a "hallmark" precisely of his theology. When the need arose he could do without it. But that raises a highly critical question: Did Barth in so doing not set aside a form of presentation that was so characteristically his own and that he could not do without?

Leaving theological methodology aside for the moment, one wonders whether a feature that identified Barth's dogmatics, namely its historical-political dimension, is not being abandoned here and the church-political pugnacity that he clearly intended it to have.[76] Barth's political analyses in particular, in their partially Marxist base structure, are not neutral-historical-scholarly presentations at all; they are forms of the fight historical consciousness wages against existing reality. It makes sense that just such analyses and their deliberate actuality were not to claim space in a set of church dogmatics which itself sought to be ecumenical in orientation and did not intend to be a direct fight-manifesto of an individual church in specific situations. Yet the question remains whether Barth did not thereby sacrifice too much to the objectivity of dogmatics.

One can ask the same in a theologically less fundamental way: Are we to assume that there exists a difference in Barth between the form of cognition and the form of presentation? That would parallel the same, famous difference in Marx' *Das Kapital.* The inductive way of cognition that forms itself from the real detail of politics and history would disappear from the presentation of dogmatics. Were there to be such a difference, this would help explain many a puzzling implication for example, of historical-critical insights and historical-political judgments found in the dogmatics text. In addition, it would *justify* what we believe to be a necessary task: to read Barth's "pure" theological texts too with an eye to their non-theological implications—as palimpsests, as it were. It was precisely in the middle years of the National-Socialist

---

76. Cf. the foreword to *CD* I/1; Marquardt, "Exegese und Dogmatik in Karl Barths Theologie. Was meint: 'Kritischer müssten mir die Historisch-Kritischen sein!'?" in *Registerband zur Kirchlichen Dogmatik* (Zurich: Theologischer Verlag, 1970) 654–55. See also the reprint of that article in Marquardt, *Verwegenheiten: Theologische Stücke aus Berlin* (Munich: Kaiser Verlag, 1981) 381–406, esp. 384ff.

era, between 1936 and 1938, when Barth felt more and more ready to explicate his theology politically, that he emphasized the implication, indeed the immanence of the political in the theological. A sentence from the letter addressed to Franz Hildebrandt in London, written the same day as the letter to a vicar [see note 3 above] October 28, 1938, confirms this interpretation. "The 'political protest' that is raised in the name and in defense of a human ideology and that can be neither identified nor combined with the gospel is one thing. The 'political protest' that is immanent in the preaching of the gospel is another as surely as the church has to announce the whole word of God to the whole human being. When, where and how that takes concrete form belongs to the particular responsibility of the church in every particular situation. Were the church to abandon the word, it would abandon itself."[77]

How are we to judge Barth's setting aside the political and historical induction process that he did indeed not relinquish when he formed his own judgments and concepts? Is it escapism into the self-movement of the objective spirit on the part of a theology that must be regarded as being unhistorical and unpolitical after all?

What we are saying here is not altogether impossible; in fact, in this form it corresponds to the average understanding of Barth's theology. That weighty motive can be detected also in our own presentation. Not knowing what a far-reaching substantiation has been left out at this juncture, the reader of the text in the "Church Dogmatics" reads the following at the relevant place: "It was not the new political totalitarianism, nor was it the methods of beleaguerment which precipitated this event [of Barmen; F.-W. M.]." We now know that Barth plainly took back one of his explicit ideas; it is a self-contradiction. What follows then is there only parenthetically: ". . . That this could be the case certainly has its spiritual-historical, theological and political presuppositions and determinations . . ." However nothing is concretely detailed by Barth. But we learn from this very passage what he intended in this self-correction. He does not rule out historical determination, yet goes on: "But all the same it was impossible, and in the end a miracle, in the eyes of those who saw it at close quarters."[78] The deletion of the political argumenta-

---

77. Type-written copy in Helmut Gollwitzer's file: "Karl Barth and the German Church Struggle." Not yet found to date in the EZA, unfortunately—Ed.

78. CD, II/1, 176.

tion serves to praise the theology of Barmen as a theology of the word of God, as a miracle void of historical derivation.

This would amount to a highly dubious church-historical mysti-fication and the entire effort Barth spent repeatedly on the miraculous dimension of his presentation of the Church Struggle would be a deeply suspicious undertaking if it did not describe an unmistakable experi-ence of Barth—and of many of his friends. This experience would be beyond external critique, on the one hand, if not, on the other, Barth's presentation itself were mediated through critical-historical categories and sought to explain the miracle from its very lack of historical deriva-tion, that is to say, if Barth did not try to explain it historically.

And so we read: The Christian faith

> was confessed in Germany in those years against a power that got rid of all its opponents with ease. What happened with the conservative and radical parties? And what became of the German press, the German universities, the German theater, German science and art, the German school and the German economy? What are Goethe, Fichte and Hegel today? How their pupils have fallen, all of them! How all these blades bent with the wind! This state knew how to subject everything under its will! There is no more freedom in today's Germany except one: the freedom of faith. The freedom of faith was not crushed even though it, and it in particular, was meant to be crushed. That is a promising portent.[79]

> In a Germany where everything, really everything had collapsed under the violence of the state: science, art, university, school, the Confessing Church represents a truly singular phenom-enon; it is in fact the sole agent that again and again dares to declare both orally and in print: We reject the total state.[80]

We leave it to the historians what historical weight they wish to give to that depiction. It will not escape them that this document comes out of the very heat of the struggle, that it is an interpretation of history

---

79. Barth, "Not und Verheissung im deutschen Kirchenkampf: Aus einem Vortrag (K.B.)," type-written ms., EZA 50/936, 062–068, here 067, p. 7.—We could not follow up on the relation between this ms. to a publication with the same title of the BEG-Verlag Bern, 1938.

80. Barth, "Die Bekennende Kirche im heutigen Deutschland," see n. 25 above, EZA 5/936, 048, p. 9.

"from the front lines." But it will be good to acknowledge at least this mode of Barth's communication.

The phenomenon of a confessing church in Germany is "miraculous" also in that it gained "political significance" quite against its declared will and that the state was impacted by its resistance. It was not for naught that the state "mobilized the secret police against the Confessing Church, imprisoned numerous ministers or expelled them. And it is not for naught as well that the state curiously was ready again and again—not completely but at least partially—to back off in face of the stance taken by the Confessing Church. Whether the political significance of this will have far-reaching results cannot be predicted. It is undoubtedly of great political relevance that through this the German public is becoming accustomed . . . to the fact that resistance against the total state exists in the very territory of Germany."[81]

The story becomes the more "miraculous" the more one is constrained by historical judgment to acknowledge that it was not the "politically dissatisfied," the "old Social Democrats and German Nationals [*Deutschnationale*] who came together in the Confessing Church and launched their protest under its cover,"[82] as people outside Germany were inclined to believe when trying to explain the "phenomenon" of the Confessing Church. "I can only attest to the fact that it was *not* so. In fact, those who were part of this church-based resistance—certainly in those days—still believed politically in the goodness of National Socialism. The resistance movement did not grow from political opposition . . ."[83] Barth goes as far as to say: "I would be guilty of false pretense were I to assert that this struggle was initially and decidedly" one of political resistance.[84] "I have sufficiently intimate knowledge of what took place and know the leading figures of the Confessing Church well enough in order to say: It is no true that among the leaders, especially those of more radical orientation, there was even one whose politics was disguised . . . The danger that faces the Confessing Church is certainly not that it might be seduced by politics but that it might be scared

---

81. Ibid.

82. Barth, "Vom Kampf der Evangelischen Kirche in Deutschland," see n. 22 above, EZA 50/936, 053, p. 5.

83. Ibid.

84. Ibid., EZA 50/936, 049, p. 1.

of the necessary political consequences to be drawn."[85]—The "miracle" is so much greater indeed in light of these considerations.

But all these historical de-facto-conditions that Barth gathers up in the theological "miracle" also signify that the church, "when all its other counselors and helpers have fled" had "God for its comforter in the one word of God that is called Jesus Christ." "The cause that led to the birth to the Confessing Church within the German Evangelical Church was, indeed, the victory of National Socialism and the quandaries, temptations and afflictions it burdened the church with. But one would misunderstand things were one to believe that what happened was simply a reaction. What happened here was something new."[86] "That the church still had left the one word of God called Jesus Christ when nothing else was left for it, that it could not let itself fall into an abyss as it was surely expected to do, but that it could and had to prepare a new stand for itself and that what those on the other side took to be an unstoppable logic of things came just this time to a fundamental halt in he church: all this is the other, spiritual dimension of what happened, something that as such can indeed be appraised only spiritually."[87] For Barth the "miracle" itself follows a "logic": the logic of contradictory historical factuality. But this clearly demands that a "spiritual side" of the entire event be also depicted spiritually, that is to say, in terms of the logic of the self-movement of the objective spirit of Barth's theology. That happens in the praise of Jesus Christ as the "word of God." In addition, it compels the recognition that there is no "spiritual side" without a historical flipside and a different form of understanding corresponding to it, namely historical-political understanding. This in turn compels conceptualization of "the name of Jesus Christ" as the real and radical principle of political resistance. If, on the one hand, one comes to see that the unyielding nature of theological theory is simply indispensable in face of the coma of a bourgeois church that remained even "after 1918 a still rather privileged religious society with strong connections to right-wing bourgeoisie,"[88] allowing the theological concept to stiffen

85. Barth, "Die Bekennende Kirche im heutigen Deutschland," see n. 25 above, EZA 50/936, 048, p. 9.

86. Ibid., EZA 50/936, 045, p. 2.

87. Barth, "Kurze Kommentierung," see n. 65 above, EZA 50/224, 190–191, sheets 7–8.

88. Barth, "Die Bekennende Kirche im heutigen Deutschland," see n. 25 above, EZA 50/936, 045, p. 2.

itself into something of mere affirmation, then one learns from Barth, on the other hand, that the theological concept becomes fluid only when it is formed in relation to resistance, not in relation to affirmation but in relation to revolutionary praxis, which is to say, when theological concept-formation refuses to escape into the self-movement of its own absolute spirit but nestles up to "the living God's" ways in the social development and contradictions of everyday life.

Political concept-formation and its subsequent dogmatic transformation into theology become comprehensible only within this field of tension. The theological concept is no longer endowed with eternity. Only in the process of overcoming her or himself day in and day out, of entering into and passing through the theological-political contradiction, can the theologian still lay hold of the concept.

It is therefore false to justify in strictly theological-dogmatic terms Barth's deletion of social analysis from his *Dogmatics*. It is correct to historically-socially and hence systematically verify the immanence of the social concept in the *Dogmatics*.

Epilogue

Friedrich-Wilhelm Marquardt
A Theological-Biographical Sketch

Andreas Pangritz

> "And they that are wise (the teachers) shall shine as the bright-
> ness of the firmament; and they that turn many to righteousness
> as the stars for ever and ever."
>
> —Daniel 12:3

On May 25, 2002, Friedrich-Wilhelm Marquardt, professor emeritus for systematic theology at the Free University (FU) of Berlin, was called out of life, as the death announcement of his family put it, "in the midst of a happy spring walk."

The readers would have known him above all as a tireless worker for the renewal of the relationship between Christians and Jews. The reflections concerning the encounter between Christians and Jews, the recognition of the shared responsibility of Christians for the national-socialist murder of the Jews, but also the meaning of the return of Israel to her land and the founding of the state of Israel were pulled by Marquardt into the center of his dogmatics perhaps more than by any other Christian theologian. It was a long journey to that point.[1]

---

1. Quotations with dates, but without page numbers in the following refer to un-published, autobiographical lectures of Marquardt's from the winter semester, 1994/95, an interview from February 5, 1995, and an oral reflection about his work on the dog-matics from the summer semester, 1995.

Childhood, Nazi Years and War, Liberation

Friedrich-W. Marquardt was born on December 2, 1928, in Eberswalde, in the Mark Brandenburg. When he later, despite the darkening of his youth during the Nazi years could look back at lighter, happier remembrances of his childhood, that was not least because of his experience of music. He had a strong musical imprint from his mother, who was moved by the *Wandervogel* (a current of the German youth movement of the 1920s). The old Christmas carol "From Heaven Above, Oh Angel, Come . . . ," that his mother chose to wake him with on his birthday left a lasting impression on him. In addition to the utopian, musical *glossolalia* ("eia, eia, susani, susani, susani") contained in it, lines like "Come not without instruments, bring your lutes, your harps and violins!" had a long lasting effect on his musical education, his playing musical instruments, his youthful pleasure in composition, his enthusiastic participation in choirs, etc. Later the last verse became very important to him also on account of its message: "Sing peace to people far and wide . . . Give God praise and honor eternally." ("My Childhood and the Nazi Years," October 21, 1994). The early musical training also found its clear echo in his later theological works.

Marquardt experienced his parents as "old Nazis, from the so-called battle time before 1933." The noise of the so-called "Night of Crystal" (November 9, 1938) in his hometown belonged to his early memories. The father put on his SS Uniform, and went out to see what was going on; the next morning at breakfast he reported, "the police took care of it." But on his way to school, the son saw the destroyed Jewish shops, and then "the burned out synagogue, which I had not noticed before." The charred remains of texts in a language unknown to him became a lesson, so that he later decided to make "the Night of Crystal" into "a foundational date" for his theologizing.[2]

Literally on his own person Marquardt had his first experience with the ruling racism, as the "Aryan proof" (*Ariernachweis*), required by the Nuremberg Laws of 1935 could not be fully realized. For his Nazi parents, the "Jewish great-grandmother" meant a catastrophe that had

---

2. Marquardt, "Mich befreit der Gott Israels" [The God of Israel sets me free], in *Zum Frieden befreit: Predigthilfe und Texte zum Gedenkjahr*, ed. Aktion Sühnezeichen Friedensdienste (Berlin: Aktion Sühnezeichen Friedensdienste, 1985) 23–29.

to be hidden.[3] Marquardt had no recollection of his confirmation sessions with the pastor, who was one of the "German Christians" (those Protestants who approved the Nazis and the "nazification" of the Church, in contrast to the "Confessing Church"). He later found his confirmation text from 1 Corinthians 16:13 ("Watch ye, stand fast in the faith, quit you like men, be strong.") awful, not least because of the key word "like men," which bothered him. For the most part he considered himself to be a "religious heathen" in the sense of a "very deeply imbedded natural religion," a kind of "belief in fate," as mediated by Goethe ("My Religion—and What Happened to It," November 11, 1994).

Marquardt's youthful experience with National Socialism had, according to his remembrances,

> . . . a very strong bodily component . . . It was not only the pressure for the uniform. I wanted the youth group uniform as a matter of fact in order to be included, but probably also partly because of the dagger—what could today be explained psychoanalytically. It was no problem to get into the uniform. But then to *be* uniformed. The young Nazis (*Jungvolk*) were primarily concerned with body conformity . . . One became a marching unit, ordered according to body size, drilled according to body measurements, and grasped the mindlessness of it all. One was a moving body unit for propaganda. Reaction to a parental home, which deviated politically from this norm, was a physical, sadistic torture. The body was taken over by the state for marching, for standing rank on rank and shouting for hours, made into a tool for war. The feeling of "being lived" in this way made a very deep impression on me.[4]

Finally, the regular flag ceremony on the street in front of the school since the beginning of the war served the "psychological rearmament." As the bombing attacks of the Allies mounted on Berlin, the school children had to take part again and again in the nightly air-raid exercises. At the same time Marquardt traveled occasionally to Berlin to take part in the cultural life, especially the musical life of the city. After one bombing raid, the grand street, Unter den Linden, "in flames," made a lasting impression, "burning Berlin." After he had undertaken a trip in summer 1944, in Mozart's footsteps, to Salzburg, he was required with other students to dig anti-tank trenches in Nazi-occupied Poland.

3. Ibid., 24.
4. Ibid., 26.

He found this to be totally senseless. In November 1944 Marquardt had to attend a "defense training camp" in Bad Freienwalde, where he learned to use rifle, machine pistol and bazookas. If he had not been prior to this, this experience caused Marquardt to become an "anti-militarist." He was deeply marked by the last essay theme assigned to him in his German class shortly before Christmas 1944: "How do you intend to lead your life to the point of death for the fatherland?" ("My War," October 28, 1994). Later this theme released in him the chain of thoughts: (1) Anything but "fatherland," (2) Never again "death for . . . ," (3) What must one do, to be able to "lead" his life, and (4) What can I "intend" to do?[5]

In March 1945 Marquardt, as a 16-year-old youth, was drafted into the work force (*Arbeitsdienst*), that is, actually to military training and war duty, in the hinterlands of Cuxhaven, as part of the "last German storm" to save the fatherland, as it was explained to him. After a fire-fight with Canadian troops, he came on April 25 to a British POW camp in Schleswig-Holstein ("My War," October 28, 1994). In his red diary he noted, on the occasion of the British victory celebration on May 12, 1945, thoughts of suicide because of the "collapse" of Germany. He didn't know whether to interpret the defeat as a "wise leading" or as "blind raging fate."[6] Later he remembered the "ambivalence" between the "feeling: we have lost everything." and the "feeling of liberation," which he had experienced in the post-war period. ("My Freedom," November 4, 1994).

After his release from the POW camp in July 1945, Marquardt came next to Elberfeld to two old aunts. After an interim residence in Bavarian Partenkirchen he came near the end of 1945 to Hesse, and was able in October 1946 in Gießen to pass the "Special-Abitur" (high school comprehensive exam that permitted one to apply for study at the university level) for those who had been involved in the war and had their studies interrupted. Before being admitted to the university, he began to learn Hebrew in order to be able to begin studies in Evangelical (Protestant) Theology. Martin Niemöller's (1892–1984) sermons about "German guilt" became a liberating experience for him. He followed Niemöller "from village to village" in order to listen to his sermons. He was fascinated at first by the Niemöller's sermon style. He presented

5. Ibid., 29.
6. Ibid., 25.

"the language of the Bible," without any translation, "directly into the present" of the Germans. Certainly he also knew that this preacher had survived years in the German concentration camps. But he was fascinated by the fact that Niemöller never spoke of his experience in the concentration camp nor about the guilt of others, but solely "about his own personal guilt," his lack of solidarity with the victims of the Nazis, the communists, the Jews, the sick. "I had to learn, that, in my betrayal of the communists and the Jews, I betrayed my Lord Jesus." This recognition from Niemöller fell on Marquardt's soul "as a blow directly across my 'natural religion'" ("My Religion—and What Happened to It," November 11, 1994).

Theology Study in Marburg and Berlin, the First Trip Abroad

Marquardt began his study of theology in May 1947, after failed attempts to be admitted to Heidelberg or Göttingen, as a "native of Hesse," which he had become in the meantime, in Marburg an der Lahn. With Marburg he bound together continually "the feeling of a great good fortune and a great thankfulness, to have teachers at all!" ("My Marburg Teachers," November 18, 1994). But "deeper" than the studies for him at first though were the conversations with older "officer colleagues," in which he took part solely as an auditor, as they shared their war experiences, talked about the high church liturgical renewal efforts of the "Berneuchner," as also re-establishing the "student clubs," which the Americans forbade (because of the role these groups had played as strong nationalistic German organizations since the nineteenth century, and which had been easily recruited for support of the Nazi programs.) In Marburg he found then in the *Evangelische Studentengemeinde* (Student Christian Movement) with its choir "Kurrende" a living community, out of which, despite the trend of the times, "without me," friendships could develop. This experience of "the possibility of a free, communal humanity," awakened in him the desire to become a campus minister himself ("My Religion—and What Happened to It," November 11, 1994).

In Marburg Marquardt became acquainted with late representatives of the *religionsgeschichtliche* school, and neo-Kantianism. Especially Rudolf Bultmann (1884–1976) became important to him, with his program of "de-mythologizing," which determined much of the theological discussion of Germany at that time, along with his "existential interpretation" of the New Testament, which accompanied his program. In the library, Marquardt copied every page of Bultmann's booklet, *Offenbarung und Heilsgeschehen,* into his own notebook, because there was no place anywhere to purchase the book. The essay about de-mythologizing, from 1941, contained therein, which he to a great extent memorized, had him "hugely liberated," because in it the dogmatic tradition seemed to be, to a large extent, "finished." Marquardt found that "fabulous," and quickly became an "apostle" of de-mythologizing. Likewise the "keyword, decision," taken over from Heidegger, as decision, made possible by the "kerygma" for the "actualization" of the self, worked convincingly on Marquardt. Existentialism corresponded to the life feeling of one returning from the war. Its "esthetic style," which could go "to the boundaries of madness," seemed though, in the end, to be "sterile" for Marquardt ("My Marburg Teachers," November 18, 1994).

Perhaps the most important "disturbance" happened to Marquardt's theological thinking at the time through his first trip abroad, which he made to the Netherlands. At the invitation of the Union of Dutch Theology Students he took part the end of October, beginning of November 1949, in a European student conference at the conference center of the religious socialists in Bentveld. The meeting had as its purpose the evaluation of the World Assembly of Churches in Amsterdam, at which, under the motto, "The Disorder of the World and God's Plan of Salvation," the ecumenical World Council of Churches was formed. The conference in Bentveld gathered around the theme of "social disorder" in the constellation of the beginning Cold War, with Karl Barth's document, "Christian Community and the Civil Community"[7] at the center of the discussion. Marquardt, because of theological grounds, immediately placed himself on the side of the "eastern Christians," against the thought of the western faction, who thought they could give European society a new order with "Christian programmatic." After Niemöller's sermons had already moved him in the direction of Marx's teachings, the discussions in Bentveld contributed further to his "formation of a social consciousness." ("My First Trip Abroad," November 15, 1994).

---

7. Cf. Karl Barth, *Christengemeinde und Bürgergemeinde*, Theologische Studien 20 (Zollikon-Zürich: Evangelischer Verlag, 1946).

Marquardt was invited for a weekend to a family in Amsterdam, where the "great indignation" among the passengers on a streetcar at his conversation in German with his hostess became a "key experience" concerning "nationalism." The next weekend, the beginning of November 1949, Marquardt was a guest in a Jewish family in Leyden, which was spared by the Nazis—his first "shared life and encounter with Jews," ("My First Trip Abroad," November 25, 1994).

> Their hospitality overwhelmed me. Nothing was left out of the necessary thoughts between a Dutch Jewish family and a student who had grown up in Nazi Germany. But they did not put me to shame, as I remember it, at any time . . . My hosts in Leiden saw me no longer as a German. They accepted me as a Christian. I can remember it to this day: An appeal to the unconscious in my future . . . a Christian at a Jewish table—this, alongside the event on the Amsterdam streetcar, was for me a second Dutch primal experience![8]

The "infection" of his "German identity" through the confrontation with reports of suffering under the German occupation and the "great amazement" at the "Jewish openness, generosity and hospitality" became a "psychically healing" lesson ("My First Trip Abroad," November 25, 1994).

In 1950 Marquardt left Marburg, as the "unpolitical" nature of its existentialist atmosphere, in its bourgeois self-centeredness, had become in the meantime "no longer bearable" for him. He went to Berlin, to complete his studies at the Kirchliche Hochschule (Seminary of the Evangelical Church of Berlin-Brandenburg), because he saw his future tasks in the German East. Many of his Marburg friendships were broken off because of this decision. Marquardt hoped that, in Berlin, he would "see himself over against the political and social realities differently" than in the province of Marburg ("My Marburg Teachers," and "My First Trip Abroad," November 18 and 25, 1994).[9]

---

8. Marquardt, "Zwischen Amsterdam und Berlin" [Between Amsterdam and Berlin], in *Abirren: Niederländische und deutsche Beiträge von und für Friedrich-Wilhelm Marquardt*, ed. Susanne Hennecke and Michael Weinrich (Wittingen: Erev-Rav, 1998) 97–147.

9. On Marquardt's Berlin professors, Martin Fischer, Karl Kupisch and Heinrich Vogel, see the essays, "Ein Nachhall auf Deutschland: Martin Fischers politische Theologie" [An echo on Germany: Martin Fischer's political theology], in Marquardt, *Verwegenheiten: Theologische Stücke aus Berlin* (Munich: Kaiser, 1981) 29–54; "'Die

Karl Barth as Teacher, Founding of the Family

On the day of his first theological examination in the summer of 1951, the GDR closed the borders to theologians from the West, so that Marquardt had to give up his intention of becoming a pastor in the East. So he traveled—decisive for his further theological development—to Basel, to continue his studies for three semesters with Karl Barth (1886–1968) as a "Bultmann-corpse, driving upstream on the Rhine from Germany, in a remarkable way," as Barth later formulated it.[10] Naturally Marquardt presented himself, before he sought Barth out, first to Karl Jaspers, whose existential philosophy seemed to Marquardt to be of more immediate relevance. Barth, about whom Marquardt at first had serious reservations, began in the Winter Semester 1951/52, after concluding the section on Christology, to lecture on the doctrine of justification, which was of special interest to Marquardt as a Bultmann student. Barth's dynamic interpretation of justification, with its aim at the practical life of the Christian was at first "alien," but yet "stimulating" for Marquardt. It was a similar new experience then for Marquardt in the following semesters with the positing of the faith of the congregation, the church, ahead of the faith of the individual ("My Teachers: Karl Barth," January 13, 1995). These were the semesters in which Barth wrote "the first volume of his doctrine of the atonement, 'with continual consideration of the . . . raging Bultmann controversy.'"[11]

In his seminar in the winter semester 1951/52, Barth concerned himself, with uncommonly great interest on the part of his hearers, expressly with the questions raised by Bultmann in his "Kerygma and Myth," but also with the "questions that ought to be turned around and placed to him (Bultmann)."[12] In the summer semester 1952 Marquardt

---

Juden unter uns': Über Karl Kupischs Beitrag zur Judenfrage" [The Jews among us: Karl Kupisch's contributions to the Jewish question], ibid., 91–113; "Solidarität mit den Gottlosen: Zur Geschichte und Bedeutung eines Theologumenon" [Solidarity with the godless: On the history and meaning of a theological concept], ibid., 120–42.

10. Karl Barth, Letter to Friedrich-Wilhelm Marquardt, September 5, 1967, in Barth, *Briefe 1961–1968*, ed. Jürgen Fangmeier and Hinrich Stoevesandt (Zürich: Theologischer Verlag, 1975) 419.

11. Cf. Eberhard Busch, *Karl Barths Lebenslauf: Nach seinen Briefen und autobiographischen Texten*, [Karl Barth's Life: According to his letters and autobiographical texts], 3rd ed. (Munich: Kaiser, 1978) 402.

12. Cf. ibid., 403. As one of the results of this seminar see Barth's essay, *Rudolf Bultmann: Ein Versuch, ihn zu verstehen* [Rudolf Bultmann: An attempt at understanding him] (Zollikon-Zürich: Evangelischer Verlag, 1952).

took part in Barth's seminar on Melanchthon's *Loci Communes*, in which he worked out the connection between Bultmann and young Melanchthon. In the weekly evenings in "The Charon Cellar," Marquardt perceived Barth as a radical political ethicist, who decisively followed the line of Gustav Heinemann and Martin Niemöller.

Marquardt became a "student" of Barth's, but "without becoming a 'Barthian,'" in Barth's colloquium over the *Prolegomena* (*Die Kirchliche Dogmatik*, vol. I/2), in which Barth was "prepared for every self-criticism." Here Marquardt understood Jesus Christ himself as "our pre-understanding" ("My Teachers: Karl Barth," January 13, 1995). In the spring of 1952 he also participated in helping prepare the first part of Barth's doctrine of the atonement (*Die Kirchliche Dogmatik*, vol. IV/1) for publication.[13] The problem of the relationship of "Exegesis and Dogmatics in Barth's Theology" must have interested Marquardt, as a theologian schooled exegetically by Bultmann, intensely. Barth's early requirement "The historical critical theologians need to be *more* critical for me!" became for Marquardt one of the guiding threads for his reception of Barth.[14]

In late summer 1952 Marquardt made the personal acquaintance in Bonn, as "Barth's messenger," of Brigitte and Helmut Gollwitzer (1908–1993). Marquardt had received Gollwitzer's book about his Russian POW experiences, . . . *und führen, wohin du nicht willst*[15] [. . . and lead you where you do not want to go], alongside Bonhoeffer's *Letters and Papers from Prison*[16] as "the spiritual event of the year

13. Cf. ibid., 405–6.

14. Cf. Marquardt, "Exegese und Dogmatik in Barths Theologie: Was meint: 'Kritischer müßten mir die Historisch-Kritischen sein!'?" [Exegesis and dogmatics in Barth's theology: What is meant by 'the historical-critical theologians need to be *more* critical for me!'?], first in the index volume to Barth's *Die Kirchliche Dogmatik* (Zürich: Theologischer Verlag, 1970), also in *Verwegenheiten* (see n. 9 above), 404: "It is precisely the unpredictable, in-breaking, grounded in nothing but its own necessity, the *alien* in the biblical expressions which give them the priority in a system, which conceives of history in the political categories of alienation, aggression and revolution (but not in the philosophical existentials of non-being and being, decision and losing or winning oneself)."

15. Cf. Helmut Gollwitzer, . . . *und führen, wohin du nicht willst: Bericht einer Gefangenschaft* (Munich: Kaiser, 1951); English ed.: *Unwilling Journey: A Diary from Russia*, trans. E. M. Delacour with help from Robert Fenn (London: SCM, 1953).

16. Cf. Dietrich Bonhoeffer, *Widerstand und Ergebung: Briefe und Aufzeichnungen aus der Haft*, [*Letters and Papers from Prison*], ed. Eberhard Bethge (Munich: Kaiser 1951).

1951."[17] Since his intention of taking a pastorate in East Germany could not be realized, Marquardt went in 1953 to Bavaria, to serve his vicariate in Lindau on Lake Constance. After his ordination in Munich, he moved "in the winter of 1954/55, newly married, to Bonn, entrusted by Barth to Gollwitzer's care," in order to dedicate himself—endowed with a graduate study grant arranged by Karl Barth—to the theme: "Understanding and the Church's Proclamation."[18] His wife Dorothee, whom Marquardt had gotten to know in Gießen, as she was still studying in Wetzlar, had, in the meantime, started her studies in France in the field of economics and literature. She interrupted her studies then to work as a staff member in the French embassy in Bonn in order to support the young family ("Cold War," February 3, 1995). Marquardt's doctoral project at the time fell apart—apparently through his return to his earlier "Bultmannitis," occasioned by the "hermeneutical subject matter."[19] Hans-Joachim Iwand had requested changes that Marquardt no longer could or would take on—not least because of the birth of their first child, a daughter, which forced him to undertake himself the support of the family. Later there came additions to the family of another daughter and a son. Marquardt became pastor in Euskirchen, where he because of an explicitly "political sermon" opposing Adenauer's western orientation met approval, but also opposition. He then took up a pastorate in Langenfeld (Rhineland) ("Cold War," February 3 and 10, 1995).

Pastor to Students in Berlin

After Marquardt was called to be pastor to students at the Free University (FU) of Berlin (West), newly founded in 1948, the family moved on May 10, 1957, to Berlin, even before the Gollwitzers moved to the city. Helmut Gollwitzer was drawn by the newly established position as professor of systematic theology on the philosophical faculty of the FU. He began there in the fall of 1957—despite Barth's warning

17. Marquardt, "Genosse meiner Niederlagen," [Comrade of my defeats], in *Begegnungen mit Helmut Gollwitzer,* ed. Ulrich Kabitz and F.-W. Marquardt (Munich: Kaiser, 1984) 88–89.

18. Ibid., 95.

19. Ibid., 96.—There is a fragmentary result on hand: Marquardt, "Geschichte und kirchliche Verkündigung" [History and the church's proclamation], in *Antwort: Karl Barth zum 70. Geburtstag am 10. Mai 1956* (Zollikon-Zürich, 1956) 620–29.

against this "so expressly 'western' university," at which he would lose his "independence" and so also his "credibility."[20]

In March 1959 Marquardt, as campus minister, together with Rudolf Weckerling, the campus minister at the Technical University of Berlin-Charlottenburg, accompanied the first group of German students invited to Israel on their journey to the Near East. The group traveled not from the west, but from the east, by way of Lebanon, Syria and Jordan, to Israel.[21] The group had the assignment of seeking possibilities for the work of "Aktion Sühnezeichen" (Action Reconciliation) in Palestinian refugee camps. The friendliness that the group experienced from the Arabian side aroused uncertainty among the students as to whether they could even undertake the difficult encounter with the Israeli side ("The Story of my Dogmatics," July 4, 1995).[22] They were surprised then at the curiosity on the part of the Israeli conversation partners about the group's experiences, especially in the refugee camps of Damascus and Jericho. In Israel the students worked first in a kibbutz, before an encounter with Martin Buber (1878–1965), Schalom Ben-Chorin (1913–1999), and others.

Theologically and spiritually this journey brought "total confusion" to Marquardt. There was, first, "the experience that Judaism is not at all a religion, but a real, living people!," the experience of an "identity connection" between *this* people and *this* land, "not mediated through any sort of theology, not mediated either through any sort of feeling of guilt," but communicated through living people as "witnesses of the relationship between the people of today and the people of the Bible." He began to ask, "How can one read the corresponding texts in the Bible when that about which the Bible speaks is immediately present and I can be a real contemporary of the biblical reality?" Marquardt's

20. Cf. Barth's letter to Helmut Gollwitzer of June 25, 1956, quoted by Andreas Pangritz, *Vom Kleiner- und Unsichtbarwerden der Theologie* [On theology's becoming smaller and invisible] (Tübingen: Theologischer Verlag, 1996) 115 n. 58.

21. On this first Israel-trip cf. Marquardt, "Begegnungen mit Juden," [Encounters with Jews], *Verwegenheiten* (see n. 9 above) 145–51.

22. Cf. Marquardt, "Ein Brief," in *Verwegenheiten*, 117–18: "We experienced in Beirut and Damascus and in the Old City of Jerusalem a glowing Arabian friendship . . . The Arabian part of our journey was what one today would call a 'trip' . . . a 'high.' And it broke now on the stone walls of Jerusalem, at the Mandelbaum Gate, with the question: Do we cross over to the Jews or not? . . . the 'high' of the Arabian *eros* seemed to have taken from us the necessary discipline of the *agape* for the meeting with the Israelis."

hermeneutics, gained in Marburg with Rudolf Bultmann, according to which it was a case of relating the Bible immediately to "my existence," was "completely turned topsy-turvy." He also found the hermeneutics learned with Barth turned upside down, according to which the Bible has meaning only when it "relates to Jesus Christ." It was a new experience for Marquardt, to have the Bible related to present day people.

Marquardt's "spiritualized" theologizing up to this time was "totally shattered" by the "material experience" of the "meaning of the physical land for the self-understanding of the Jewish people." The meaning and sense of the category "land" had become "suspect for him as a German," but here it was precisely "this land," Israel, in which people "existed as rescued," and "this land," for whose "making it fruitful" they labored. Added to this was "the experience of the state." The "daily pledge of allegiance to the flag" in the kibbutz was at first alienating to the group—Marquardt had had "more than enough" of flags. Also the arming of the kibbutz—"our kibbutz lay in the north, along the Lebanese border"—was for him an extraordinarily "politically shattering experience." ("The Story of my Dogmatics," July 4, 1995). Later Marquardt characterized this journey—the "actual, deep unrest, . . . which the encounter with the Jewish state had brought to me"—as "a key to my theological existence," which then marked his whole further theologizing ("Memorial Day for the Liberation of Auschwitz," January 27, 1995).[23]

The first practical result of this journey to Israel was the formation of the working group, "Jews and Christians," connected with the *Deutscher Evangelischer Kirchentag* (German Protestant Church Congress), which met in Berlin in 1961. Here Marquardt worked with Helmut Gollwitzer[24]

---

23. Cf. Marquardt, "Mein Israel," in *Mein Israel: 21 erbetene Interventionen*, ed. Micha Brumlik (Frankfurt am Main: Fischer, 1998), 35–44; published again in Marquardt, *Auf einem Schul-Weg: Kleinere christlich-jüdische Lerneinheiten* (Berlin: Orient & Okzident, 1999), 191–201.

24. For Gollwitzer's contribution, cf. Marquardt, "Hermeneutik des christlich-jüdischen Verhältnisses: Über Helmut Gollwitzers Arbeit an der 'Judenfrage'" [Hermeneutics of the relationship between Jews and Christians: On Helmut Gollwitzer's work on the "Jewish Question"], in *Richte unsere Füße auf den Weg des Friedens: Helmut Gollwitzer zum 70. Geburtstag*, ed. Andreas Baudis et al. (Munich: Kaiser, 1979) 138–54. Cf. also Andreas Pangritz, "Helmut Gollwitzers Theologie des christlich-jüdischen Verhältnisses: Versuch einer kritischen Bilanz" [Helmut Gollwitzer's theology of the relationship between Jews and Christians: An attempt at a critical balance], *Evangelische Theologie* 56 (1996) 359–76.

and Rabbi Robert Raphael Geis (1906–1972)[25] and others.[26] Geis had allowed himself to be encouraged to return to Germany in 1952 by Leo Baeck and Karl Barth. The living encounter with Jews, which was made possible by this working group, represented since then the most important "setting in life" (*Sitz im Leben*) for Marquardt's theologizing. It was no longer the conversations with the academic theology of the professional colleagues, but the conversations with the Jews and the people of the church who provided for Marquardt the bulk of his theological "improvements in thought."

As one of the first theological consequences of his journey to Israel, Marquardt saw himself faced with the question of the meaning of God's relationship to the Jewish people for Christians. He began by confronting "the meaning of the Biblical promise of the land for Christians." It was surprising to him that the promise of the land is not considered superseded or obsolete even in the New Testament.[27]

Soon he moved on past the theological to concern himself with the political dimension of the Israel experience and the history of Zionism, in which especially his right-wing Zionist Berlin friend Jochanan Bloch (1919–1979) was both stimulating and exciting for him. Bloch charged the German Old Testament scholars with creating a Christian "scientific" bias,[28] and Marquardt agreed with him. Later Marquardt characterized the temporary "daily relationship" to Jochanan Bloch, who showed his "aggressive interest" in Marquardt's theological work, as his "most intensive, most dynamic relationship with a Jew." Marquardt here encountered "simple Zionism in this man for the first time." Marquardt began

25. On Robert Raphael Geis, cf. Marquardt, "Ein Lehrer aus Israel" [A teacher from Israel], in *Verwegenheiten* (see n. 9 above) 55–68.

26. Further Jewish founding members of the working group were Schalom Ben-Chorin, Ernst Ludwig Ehrlich (whom Marquardt had met already during his time in Basel), Eva Reichmann and Eleonore Sterling.—With regard to the history of the working group, "Jews and Christians," cf. Gabriele Kammerer, *In die Haare, in die Arme: 40 Jahre Arbeitsgemeinschaft "Juden und Christen" beim deutschen evangelischen Kirchentag* (Gütersloh: Gütersloher Verlagshaus, 2001).

27. Cf. Marquardt, *Die Bedeutung der biblischen Landverheißungen für die Christen* [The meaning of the biblical promises of the land for the Christians], Theologische Existenz heute, n.s., no. 116 (Munich: Kaiser, 1964).

28. Cf. Jochanan Bloch, *Das anstößige Volk: Über die weltliche Glaubensgemeinschaft der Juden* [The offensive people: Concerning the worldly faith community of the Jews] (Heidelberg: Lambert Schneider, 1964).

also to seek to enlist Christians to grasp the meaning of Zionism.[29] In 1970, Marquardt was invited to a colloquium at the Hebrew University in Jerusalem, on the theme "People, Land, State," as a guest speaker. His later book, "Die Juden und ihr Land," (The Jews and their land)[30] became his "best seller." (Interview, February 5, 1995).

Till the building of the Berlin Wall in 1961 (August 13), the *Evangelische Studentengemeinde* (Student Christian Movement) formed a bridge between students at the Humboldt University in East Berlin and the Free University in West Berlin. They presented public "Day of Repentance" programs for both parts of Berlin with prominent speakers such as Martin Niemöller and Gustav Heinemann in Berlin's Congress Hall. It was in the East-West conflict a "great experience" for Marquardt that a "congregation" could here "come into being as a singular political subject," without simply joining one or the other political party. He reckoned this "coming of age" of the congregation later to the "pre-history" of the student movement ("Cold War," February 3, 1995).

The Free University was at that time "a jungle for the recruitment of students, some in need of money, some blinded by ideology, for both west and east secret service."[31] As Marquardt in one of his first pastoral duties had to inter the ashes of a Free University student, who had died in a prison in East Germany, he asked the Rector of the University to warn students against activity in the secret services, but met with his request only with total misunderstanding. In the face of the production of "totalitarian" portraits of "the enemy" on the basis of the anti-communistic basic understanding of those living in the "frontier city" of West-Berlin, and the consequently practiced "forced capture of the souls," Marquardt saw himself forced into a "political ministry." ("Cold War," February 10, 1995). So he fell quickly into the "ins and outs of the 'underground' of the time . . . in order to help students free themselves from their bonds, which destroyed both soul and life itself."[32] The then Lord Mayor of Berlin, Willy Brandt, on the occasion of a visit to the *Evangelische Studentengemeinde* in Dahlem, had to admit that

29. Cf. Marquardt, "Christentum und Zionismus" [Christianity and Zionism], in *Verwegenheiten* (see n. 9 above), 165–201.

30. Cf. Marquardt, *Die Juden und ihr Land* [The Jews and their land] (Hamburg: Siebenstern, 1975; Gütersloh: Gütersloher Verlagshaus, 1978).

31. Cf. Marquardt, "Genosse meiner Niederlagen" (see n. 17 above), 98.

32. Ibid.

he was powerless in the face of the activities of the Allies who shared authority in Berlin, and the activities of their secret services. At this time Marquardt experienced the strongest attacks in both western and eastern media against his work in the *Studentengemeinde*. ("Cold War," February 10, 1995)."

Marquardt became a member of different "fellowship" groups, such as the *Unterwegs-Kreis*, (underway, "on the road" circle) and the *Weißenseer Arbeitskreis*, (Weißensee working group, in East Berlin), which, in opposition to the positions of the church hierarchy, sought to overcome the confrontations of the Cold War and thereby make the experiences of the Confessing Church (the church opposed to the "German Christians,"—cf. the Declaration of Barmen) fruitful in a divided Germany ("Cold War," February 10, 1995). Marquardt was engaged as West Berlin representative in the executive committee of the Arbeitsgemeinschaft Kirchlicher Bruderschaften, a working group of theologians in the tradition of the Confessing Church, in protest against the atomic armament of the German army. In June 1961 he took part—against the general advice of the hierarchy of the church—in the first All-Christian Peace Conference in Prague, organized by the Czech theologian Josef L. Hromádka (1889–1969), which set as its goal the overcoming of the East-West conflict.

The first "Marquardt case" also came in 1961. "Against his better judgment," Marquardt let himself be persuaded by his colleagues in the West German Campus Ministry Conference, "to take part in a visit by the German Army School for internal leadership in Koblenz." There he became acquainted with "the portraits of propaganda," with which the military chaplaincy provided "life instruction" lessons "quite clearly" integrated into "psychological warfare."[33] After this Marquardt sent a confidential letter to (Church) President Kurt Scharf (Berlin-West) (1902–1990), in which he expressed his sorrow over the use of the church for military purposes. The situation was at that time such that the military chaplaincy represented, according to Marquardt, "the decisive component" of the "psychological warfare:" "Faith and Christianity" here were "totally integrated into the military and psychological goals of the German army." From the point of view of the military leadership, Germany was "already in a condition of war." The "friend-enemy sche-

33. Ibid., 102.

matic" made, for the military chaplaincy, "any real Protestant protest in individual parts of this development totally impossible."[34]

The "confidential letter" to Kurt Scharf landed, under to this day not completely explained circumstances, in East Berlin, and from there through the GDR Christian Democratic Union (political party in East Germany, allied with the Communist Party) to all Protestant (Evangelical) pastors in the German Federal Republic, and with that into the West German public ("Cold War," February 10, 1995). The letter unleashed a political storm, which can hardly be fathomed today. Marquardt stood as an example of the "communist infiltration," as it was called in the over-heated atmosphere of the Cold War.[35] Marquardt was not up to the publicity and the concerns stirred up "by the West German secret police (equivalent to the FBI)." He became ill, "extremely disturbed," and had to take a semester off from his duties.[36] The invitation from Brigitte and Helmut Gollwitzer, "to share with them their life in their vacation house in Wallis in the winter of 1962," helped him to get over "the effects on his health from the public uproar that arose about him."[37]

Examination of Barth's "Doctrine of Israel"

In 1963 Marquardt assumed the assistantship to Helmut Gollwitzer at the Free University. He made a second run at his doctorate, this time motivated by his journey to Israel in 1959. His dissertation was to be about Karl Barth's so-called "doctrine of Israel"—a project that Marquardt had

---

34. Marquardt, Letter to (Church) President Kurt Scharf, from April 16, 1961, quoted by Gerd Klatt, "Von Bruder- zu Genossenschaft: Ein kleines, aber bedeutsames Kapitel ESG-Geschichte," in *Störenfriedels Zeddelkasten: Geschenkpapiere zum 60. Geburtstag von Friedrich-Wilhelm Marquardt*, ed. Ute Gniewoß et al. (Berlin: Alektor, 1991) 261–76, 268. [From brotherhood to comradeship: A little, but important chapter of the history of the Student Christian Movement, in Notebox of "disturber of the peace": Papers on the occasion of the 60th birthday of Marquardt.—Wordplay on Marquardt's name: Friedrich = rich in peace, Störenfriedel = disturber of the peace.]

35. Ibid., 270.

36. Marquardt, "Genosse meiner Niederlagen," 103. In view of the erection of the Berlin Wall, August 13, 1961, Marquardt asked himself: "How will you answer your children about the present situation of Berlin, when war breaks loose?" ("Cold War," February 10, 1995).

37. G. Klatt (see above note 34), 274.

touched upon during his recuperation staying with Gollwitzers on their island in Lake Champex in the winter of 1962.[38]

But first there was a difficult conflict within the working group "Christians and Jews," which had to be settled. An attempt by Gollwitzer, which had not been talked through in advance with the working group, to mediate between the working group and conservative Lutheran representatives of the "Mission to the Jews," provoked Robert Raphael Geis to an outraged observation at Purim,[39] which at first met with a lack of understanding on the part of Gollwitzer. Over against his appeal to the discipline of friendship, Geis insisted: "The church had the chance to confess Christ once in relationship to the Jews: in the Third Reich. They didn't take advantage of the opportunity . . ."[40]

Marquardt tried to mediate in the later so-called "Purim controversy," in which he took Geis's side. After he had let Geis know that he did not take the position of Gollwitzer, Geis was prepared to take a more conciliatory stance toward Gollwitzer (Interview, February 5, 1995). On the other hand Gollwitzer later was able to admit that he had been "struck by a blindness," which evidenced a "hardness of heart." So the crisis was a "storm that cleared the air."[41] Marquardt for his part saw in the letters that went back and forth in the months of the controversy documents of a painful Christian learning process in which, "confronted with Jewish self-understanding, some of the oldest Christian statements had to be shattered when they came in contact with real people!"[42]

Marquardt received his doctorate in 1967 from the Kirchliche Hochschule (Berlin-Zehlendorf) with his study about Israel in the

38. Marquardt, "Genosse meiner Niederlagen," 103.

39. Cf. Robert R. Geis, "Judenmission: Eine Purimbetrachtung zur 'Woche der Brüderlichkeit'" [The mission to the Jews: An reflection on Purim for the "Week of Brotherhood"] in the weekly newspaper of the Jews, *Allgemeine Wochenzeitung der Juden,* March 8, 1964: "The mission to the Jews is no longer strictly rejected by this systematic professor of Protestant theology. It is just not to be carried out by 'the cavalry.' The infantry is the repentance for the silence of the church at the murder of millions of Jews. It could become something to make me vomit. But it is Purim after all: Give me a cognac, please!" Translated from *Leiden an der Unerlöstheit der Welt: Robert Raphael Geis 1906–1972; Briefe, Reden, Aufsätze,* ed. Dietrich Goldschmidt, in cooperation with Ingrid Ueberschär (Munich: Kaiser, 1984) 244.

40. Ibid., 253.

41. H. Gollwitzer, in *Leiden,* 227–28. Concerning the "Purim controversy," see also G. Kammerer, *In die Haare, in die Arme* (see n. 26 above) 43–56.

42. Marquardt, "Ein Lehrer aus Israel," in *Verwegenheiten* (see n. 9 above), 63.

thought of Karl Barth.[43] In his dissertation he worked out "the double profit" of Barth's teachings, that Barth namely "(1) in opposition to the tradition was able to affirm not only biblical Israel, but also that Judaism that does not accept Christ"; and "(2) that he undertook this not only with the help of a biblical-hermeneutical reconstruction, but out of the Christological center of his theologizing." Marquardt concluded his work with the critical question, "whether Barth perhaps made himself guilty of not drawing the proper Christological consequences, when he sought to see post-biblical Judaism as witness of the crucified, but not as witness as well of the Risen Christ, and whether he perhaps thereby might still hold unnecessary anti-Judaic undertones."[44] Free from every trace of "Barthianism," Marquardt had thereby laid open a potential in the theology of his teacher, of which Barth himself till that point had not been so clearly aware.

Barth's amazed agreement was then also paired with a word of caution about heretical tendencies in Marquardt's future development. On September 5, 1967, he wrote to Marquardt, "You have very artfully and very well opened and presented my 'doctrine of Israel.'" He now looked forward "happily, but not without a certain concern" to that which Marquardt "in this issue . . . might have to say further." Barth was also prepared to accept the criticism that Marquardt brought to his doctrine: "You had every occasion for this criticism. There is indeed an omission at the point on which you have touched." Barth could "not to excuse it, but perhaps to bring something to its explanation, say two things: (1) Biblical Israel as such gave me so much to think about and to digest, that I simply did not have or find the time, nor the mental capacity, to concern myself in detail with Baeck, Buber, Rosenzweig, etc." For the second part, Barth took Marquardt's criticism as an occasion for the amazing confession that he had "in personal encounters with living Jews (even Jewish Christians) always to swallow something like a completely irrational aversion." To this "somewhat allergic reaction" he himself could now only say "Pfui!" But it might be the case that this "anti-Jewish" affect, which precisely on the basis of his own theologi-

43. Marquardt, *Die Entdeckung des Judentums für die christliche Theologie: Israel im Denken Karl Barths* [The discovery of Judaism for Christian theology: Israel in the thought of Karl Barth] (Munich: Kaiser, 1967).

44. Marquardt, *Die Gegenwart des Auferstandenen bei seinem Volk Israel: Ein dogmatisches Experiment* [The presence of the risen Christ in his people Israel: A dogmatic experiment] (Munich: Kaiser, 1983) 7 (Foreword).

cal presuppositions needed to be contradicted, could have "worked in a retarding fashion" in his doctrine of Israel.[45]

For the work on Barth's "doctrine of Israel," which appeared as volume 1 in the series edited by Helmut Gollwitzer, "Treatises toward a Christian-Jewish Dialogue," Marquardt was honored, together with Friedrich Heer, with the first Buber-Rosenzweig Medal awarded by the Societies for Christian-Jewish Cooperation. In the years 1968 to 1971 Marquardt took over the chair of the working group "Jews and Christians" with the *Deutscher Evangelischer Kirchentag*.

Barth's curious agreement and at the same time word of caution in view of Marquardt's own way into the "doctrine of Israel" was not without grounds: Marquardt had at this time already undertaken a first attempt in his own dogmatic reworking of the theme in expansion of the gaps he had found with Barth. In the winter of 1966/67 he wrote, as a sort of "addendum" to the dissertation a study on "the presence of the risen Christ with his people Israel," for the publication of which though, given its experimental character, at first "the courage" was lacking. There was also in the still very youthful working group "Jews and Christians" at the time just "not enough time" for "difficult dogmatic work."[46] The study was published finally in 1983—expanded by an afterword in which Marquardt fit this "dogmatic experiment" into the Christological discussion that had gone on in the meantime within the Christian-Jewish relationships.[47] The "goal" of this study was "the deter-

45. Barth, Letter to Friedrich-Wilhelm Marquardt, 5. September, 1967, in Barth, *Briefe 1961–1968*, 420–22. The evaluation of Barth's confession in the letter to Marquardt, since both famous-infamous, is to this day hotly contested in the literature. Cf., e.g., John Updike, *Roger's Version* (1986), where the place is used as evidence of the suppressed anti-Semitism in Barth's often imputed Philosemitism. Eberhard Busch, *Unter dem Bogen des einen Bundes: Karl Barth und die Juden 1933–1945* [Under the arc of the one covenant: Karl Barth and the Jews, 1933–1945] (Neukirchen-Vluyn: Neukirchener Verlagshaus, 1996), on the other hand seeks to take Barth in defense of himself, and perhaps thereby does too much of a good thing.

46. Marquardt, *Die Gegenwart des Auferstandenen bei seinem Volk Israel*, 7 (Foreword).

47. Ibid., 9 (Foreword), from a "theological crisis" under the "impression of the Holocaust," which forced itself upon him "first through the contact with the postwar Jewish experience of suffering and becoming conscious of this in the so-called Holocaust theology, was in this study "nothing yet to trace." He was in this work "again and again concerned with the question of defining Judaism theologically, developing a portrait and parable of 'the essence' of Judaism and to shape theological measures of judgment about Israel."

mination of a Christological relationship between Jesus and the Jewish people in which Jesus Christ could be understood as the *actualization of Israel among us goyim*."[48] In his later dogmatics, Marquardt "distanced himself from the 'resurrection' book," by going beyond its Christology. He wanted to "recall" the approach of the "resurrection" book, formulated in the thought structures taken from the early Christian church, "but not, however, the faith in the Risen Christ." More and more the Christological question was "forced into the background through the eschatological question." (Interview, February 5, 1995).

Theology and Socialism

In the years of the student protest movement Marquardt undertook numerous attempts at mediating between "the students," the church public, the church hierarchy and various Berlin political units, in part together with Bishop Kurt Scharf, the composer Hans-Werner Henze and the Free University professor for Judaic Studies, Jacob Taubes (1923–1987). Such mediation also was the intention of Marquardt's book, *Students in Protest*, which appeared in 1968.[49] Marquardt's much recognized and hotly contested book about *Theology and Socialism* can also be seen as a spiritual fruit of the student movement.[50] As Marquardt's dissertation on Barth's "doctrine of Israel" was primarily an attempt to work out the experience of his first journey to Israel, so his book *Theology and Socialism* had the situation of the Berlin theology students as its background, who in the course of their socialist politicization were alienated from theology and left especially the Kirchliche Hochschule in droves in order to study social sciences at the Free University.

The thesis of Marquardt's book *Theology and Socialism* was something like this: Barth's socialist activity had a recognizable influence on

---

48. Ibid., 207 (Nachtrag, 1982) [Addendum].—Marquardt was very much aware here "that Jews cannot draw any direct recognition value from this work." It serves only as an "inner-Christian" understanding, and insofar, is "no work in dialogue with Judaism, but only a work in relationship to it." Ibid., 204.

49. Cf. Marquardt, *Studenten im Protest*, Mit einem Geleitwort von Helmut Gollwitzer [Students in protest, with a preface by Helmut Gollwitzer] (Frankfurt: Stimme, 1968).

50. Cf. Marquardt, *Theologie und Sozialismus: Das Beispiel Karl Barths* [Theology and socialism: The example of Karl Barth's], 1st and 2nd ed. (Munich: Kaiser; Mainz: Matthias Grünewald, 1972); 3rd exp. ed. (Munich: Kaiser, 1985).

his theological thought, not only in the early phases, but even into the *Church Dogmatics*. Already the first sentence, "Karl Barth was a socialist," provoked the bitter protest of the theological guild.[51] As his qualification to become a member of the faculty at the Kirchliche Hochschule, which had just received the right to award tenure (*Habilitationsrecht*) in 1970, the book was rejected in 1971. Out of solidarity with Marquardt, Gollwitzer resigned his teaching position at the Kirchliche Hochschule, which he had up to that point in addition to his professorship at the FU. The colleagues at the Kirchliche Hochschule saw themselves, in order to justify their position, needing to make the files public,[52] without thereby clearing away the suspicion that the rejection was somehow finally politically motivated. As Marquardt in 1972 finally was made a professor in the department of philosophy and social science at the FU in systematic theology, he became once again "a case," about which especially the anti-communistic press in West Berlin was outraged. Elsewhere, among students in many theological schools in West and East Germany, but also in all the theological schools of the Netherlands, in Rome, Paris, Vienna, Basel and Bern and in the United States, where Marquardt was invited to give lectures and to take part in colloquia, Marquardt's "socialism" book earned him acclaim, which continues to this day.[53]

The book *Theology and Socialism* was not merely an episode in Marquardt's thought which was left behind after the echoes of the student revolution but expressed a continuing theological interest. The fact alone that Marquardt up to the last again and again concerned himself with the "leftist" Barth speaks for this.[54] The publication of his edition of

51. Cf. Marquardt, "Genosse meiner Niederlagen" (see n. 17 above), 104. "Right at the first sentence there was 'Karl Barth was a Socialist.' My sensitive wife protested against this sentence: it is provocative! I knew that, too, but I relied on the evidence, which still is available today."

52. Cf. *Gutachten und Stellungnahmen zu der Habilitationsschrift von Dr. Friedrich-Wilhelm Marquardt "Theologie und Sozialismus. Das Beispiel Karl Barths"* [Records and positions concerning the Second Dissertation by Dr. F.-W. Marquardt, "Theology and Socialism," etc.], ed. W. Schmithals (Berlin: Kirchliche Hochschule, 1972).

53. The internationally observed controversy about Marquardt's book *Theology and Socialism* book is, among others, documented in the volume *Karl Barth on Radical Politics*, ed. George Hunsinger (Philadelphia: Westminster, 1976).

54. Cf. Marquardt, "Der Götze wackelt: Der Generalangriff aus dem Römerbrief" ["The Idol Totters: The General Attack from the Epistle to the Romans"] (1970), first as introduction to a "reprint without copyright" of the first edition (1919) from Barth's *Römerbrief* [Epistle to the Romans], then in *Verwegenheiten*, 407–23, also in this vol-

"Socialist Speeches" from the years 1911–1919 from Karl Barth's estate, on which Marquardt had worked since 1971, did not, however, come to pass, after these speeches for the most part "disappeared" from the Karl Barth Archives.[55] According to Marquardt's recognition, these speeches show that Barth had developed, during World War I, from a religious socialist into a rigorous social democrate and, in the revolutionary phase at the end of the war, into a radical socialist, with a tendency toward anarchy, along the lines of the "second and one-half" International.[56]

It is quite another question, as to whether or not the theme of socialism might not have led Marquardt astray, and distracted him from the work on the renewal of Christian-Jewish relations. So, for instance, Michael Wyschogrod, who had found "undivided enthusiasm" over Marquardt's book about Barth's "doctrine of Israel," later expressed his deep skepticism about Marquardt's political positions in view of his "socialism" book.[57] Robert Raphael Geis, however, spoke vehemently in favor of the „socialism" book, as soon as it appeared, because he found there an internal connection to the earlier one about Barth's "doctrine of Israel." He found that "the conversation between Jews and Christians," in its "biblical radicalism," pointed to a political radicalism as well.[58]

---

ume. Cf. also Marquardt, *Der Christ in der Gesellschaft 1919–1979: Geschichte, Analyse und aktuelle Bedeutung von Karl Barths Tambacher Vortrag* [The Christian in society: History, analysis, and actual meaning of Karl Barth's Tambach lecture], Theologische Existenz heute, n.s., no. 206 (Munich: Kaiser, 1980); Marquardt, "Erster Bericht über Karl Barths 'Sozialistische Reden'" ["First Report on Karl Barth's 'Socialist Speeches'"], in *Verwegenheiten*, 470–88, also in this volume; Marquardt, "Der Aktuar: Aus Barths Pfarramt" ["The Secretary of the Church Administration: From Barth's Pastorate"], in *Karl Barth: Der Störenfried?*, Einwürfe, no. 3 (Munich: Kaiser, 1986) 93–139, also in this volume. Cf. also in a more general perspective: Marquardt, "Muß ein Christ Sozialist sein?" [Must a Christian be a socialist?] (1975), in *Verwegenheiten*, 491–510.

55. Marquardt's edition was finished in 1978, but not published. Instead the "Socialist Speeches" were later distributed in other volumes throughout the Karl Barth *Gesamtausgabe* [complete works]; "Meine Lehrer: Karl Barth," January 13, 1995.

56. Cf. Marquardt, "Erster Bericht," in *Verwegenheiten* (see n. 9 above), 478–85.

57. Cf. Michael Wyschogrod, "Lieber Friedrich-Wilhelm" (1988), in *Störenfriedels Zeddelkasten* (see n. 34 above), 34.—Wyschogrod is disturbed there by "the lack in Barth, and in a certain measure also in Marquardt . . . of a clear distinction between democratic and totalitarian socialism." Concerning Marquardt's book about Barth's "doctrine of Israel," on the other hand, he says: "This is a brilliant study about Barth's views on Israel and Judaism, written from a broad perspective, which analyzes Barth's doctrine of Israel in the context of his whole theology, but also in the context of Judaism's self-understandings, for which you are unusually sensitive."

58. Cf. R. R. Geis, Letter to Hans-Joachim Kraus, (April 15, 1972), in *Leiden an der Unerlöstheit der Welt* (see n. 39 above), 363–64. "What disturbs the theologians so much

With that he certainly corresponded to Marquardt's self-understanding in which the theme of socialism belonged structurally to his life-theme of Israel.[59] The displacement of his emphasis in his later dogmatics from the Christological center into the eschatological was for him the result both of the conversations with Judaism and also with socialism. (Interview, February 5, 1995).

In the years 1973 and 1974 Marquardt participated in consultations of the World Council of Churches in Beirut (Lebanon) and Cartigny (Switzerland), dealing with the questions of the Christian-Jewish relationships in the Near East. As an outcome of the conversations there was a meeting with Yassir Arafat, where the situation of the Palestinians, especially the question of the education of the next generation, was discussed. Marquardt got the impression from Arafat of "a personally sympathetic appearance," even when the conversation with respect to "the credibility of the PLO seen through the eyes of the Israelis was not terribly soothing." (Interview, February 5, 1995).

In the early part of the 1970s it came to a bitter quarrel with members of the Bultmann school among German New Testament scholars, because of Marquardt's essay, "The Jews in the Epistle to the Romans."[60] Proceeding from the thesis that it was not the doctrine of justification, but "the relationship of Judaism and non-Judaism" as a Christological question that was actually the theme of the Epistle to the Romans,[61] Marquardt came to the conclusion, that, according to Paul, the Torah declared to the Jews "that you should not separate yourselves from the others," while, "to the gentiles . . . Christ removed their separation from

---

about the clarifications of Marquardt's about Barth? That God is understood as the radicalism of everything political . . .? Yes, that must be it, for it is biblical reality, and theologians are not up to this confrontation. We have two of Marquardt's books before us. In 'Israel in Karl Barth's thought,' the attempt is undertaken, to dismantle the deep gulf to Judaism . . . The second, much contested Barth book would not be thinkable without the first. The so-called 'one-sidedness' is really biblical radicalism . . . A genuine conversation between Jews and Christians can only occur in biblical radicalism. One ought to think it over, before criticizing Marquardt and his book."

59. Cf., e.g., Marquardt, "Martin Buber als sozialistischer Zionist" ["Martin Buber as a Socialist Zionist"] (1975), in Marquardt, *Auf einem Schul-Weg* (see n. 23 above), 147–72, also in this volume, 48–67.

60. Marquardt, *Die Juden im Römerbrief* [The Jews in the Epistle to the Romans], Theologische Studien 107 (Zürich: Theologischer Verlag, 1971). The study was printed again in the exegetical journal, *Texte & Kontexte* 20 (1997) no. 73/74, 11–49.

61. Ibid, 6.

the Jews."[62] Methodologically Marquardt wanted to move beyond the historical-critical method to a "historical-materialistic" interpretation of the Bible (as he called it) that could get through the theological ideas to the "social relationships" that came to expression in them.[63] Only when the relationship of the Jews to the non-Jews was recognized as the theme of Romans, could "the social character of justification" be won back.[64]

Three years later Marquardt's earlier Marburg student colleague and roommate Günter Klein became the spokesman for the Bultmann school, in the meantime professor for New Testament in Münster. In his sharp polemic, "Mercy for the Jews!" he accused Marquardt that, by denying the mission to the Jews, he was withholding from "the Jews" that "which he especially was charged to give, concrete liberation through the word of the cross."[65] Marquardt answered Klein's abuse at the time with silence,[66] but in his later dogmatics he repeated and deepened the essential themes from the essay under the heading, "Jesus between Jews and Greeks," in the context of his Christology as a "journey through the Epistle to the Romans."[67]

In 1974 Marquardt was invited to be visiting professor on the theological faculty of the University of Amsterdam. During this guest

62. Ibid., 41. Paul did not "found Christianity, nor reject Judaism." Ibid., 42.

63. Ibid., 45. The "displacing of Judaism" from the Christian theology was, according to Marquardt, "an especial danger of the Bultmann school." Ibid., 47.

64. Ibid., 48.

65. Cf. Günter Klein, "Erbarmen mit den Juden! Zu einer 'historisch-materialistischen' Paulusdeutung" [Mercy for the Jews! To a "historical-materialistic" interpretation of Paul], *Evangelische Theologie* 34 (1974) 218. Klein was not ashamed to make his plea for the mission to the Jews as "mercy for the Jews," in which he claimed to want to provide protection for "the survivors" from "unwashed sympathy."

66. But see Helmut Gollwitzer, Michael Palmer, and Volkhard Schliski, "Der Jude Paulus und die deutsche neutestamentliche Wissenschaft. Zu Günter Kleins Rezension der Schrift von F.-W. Marquardt 'Die Juden im Römerbrief' [The Jew Paul and German New Testament studies: Concerning Günter Klein's review of the essay by Marquardt, "The Jews in Romans"], *Evangelische Theologie* 34 (1974) 276–304. Cf. also Marquardt, "Abirren," in *Abirren* (see n. 8 above), 158–59.

67. Cf. also Marquardt, *Das christliche Bekenntnis zu Jesus, dem Juden* [The Christian confession to Jesus, the Jew], vol. 1 (Munich: Kaiser, 1990) 180–297, For example, "For the good Jew Paul the oneness or unity of God hangs on the union and unification of Israel with the *goyim*, and the *goyim* with Israel," 201; or "In the common praise of God from Jews and gentiles, i.e., in their 'community of justification,' Paul sees the meaning and goal of the Torah of Moses, for it testifies to the oneness of God," 295.

semester he lived with a Jewish family and so experienced along with them "what was set loose, as at that time—primarily by the request by some of the leading figures of our church—for the release of three of the war criminals imprisoned in Breda."[68] His successful teaching work in Amsterdam earned him the offer from Queen Juliana of the Netherlands to be professor for the history of Christianity and Christian doctrine in the nineteenth and twentieth centuries, at the University of Amsterdam.

To the great disappointment of the Amsterdam faculty Marquardt declined this invitation in favor of Berlin, despite the advice of his friend Jochanan Bloch: "One does *not* disappoint a Queen!" As the basis for his decision Marquardt later gave the impression that, "for the Jewish-Christian instruction," where he saw his primary task, there was a more crucial need in Germany. He resolved, as "repentance" for turning down the Queen of the Netherlands to undertake to work out a dogmatics as "radical self-criticism" of the Christian tradition with its anti-Judaism, regardless of the danger that this might "turn the entire tradition upside down." ("The Story of my Dogmatics," July 4, 1995).

Work on the Dogmatics and Beyond

In 1976 Marquardt was called to be the successor to Helmut Gollwitzer as professor of systematic theology at Berlin's Free University. From that time on, in his weekly lectures and the accompanying colloquia, which he always enjoyed, he developed his dogmatics that critically illuminated the central themes of the theological tradition in order to pull the rug out from under the Anti-Judaism in Christian theology. In the form published between 1988 and 1997, his dogmatics contained seven volumes, in which the themes of eschatology received a relative over-emphasis over against the tradition. The dogmatics reached their

68. Marquardt, "Christsein nach Auschwitz" [Being a Christian after Auschwitz], in Marquardt and Albert H. Friedlander, *Das Schweigen der Christen und die Menschlichkeit Gottes: Gläubige Existenz nach Auschwitz* [The silence of the Christians and the humanity of God: Faithful existence after Auschwitz], (Munich: Kaiser, 1980), 13. "I will never forget how the very thin veil of the salutary time with my hosts was torn open and in those days and nights of a sleepless week their dark fate emerged again in every detail." Cf. also Marquardt, "Zwischen Amsterdam und Berlin," in *Abirren* (see n. 8 above), 100.

high point—something new in the history of Christian dogmatics—in a "theological utopia."[69]

According to Marquardt's own statement, his dogmatics was "basically nothing more than the explication of a journey," the Israel journey of 1959, "nothing but an attempt to untangle the confusion" of that experience. He hesitated a long time, thinking over "whether he wanted to or should treat that which he wanted to work out, really in the form of a dogmatic." He saw "the problem . . ., that it would not be a classical dogmatic, neither in form nor content." It was Helmut Gollwitzer who encouraged him, despite all the departures from the tradition, to hold fast on his claim, really to do dogmatics ("The Story of my Dogmatics," July 4, 1995).[70] Measured by the traditional theological schools however, to use an expression of Karl Barth's, Marquardt's dogmatics had to seem "irregular."[71] With a conscious rejection of comprehensiveness in the themes, Marquardt went against the grain of the tradition (went against the stream.).

69. Cf. Marquardt, *Von Elend und Heimsuchung der Theologie: Prolegomena zur Dogmatik* [On the misery and visitation of theology: Prolegomena to dogmatics] (Munich: Kaiser, 1988); 2nd rev. and exp. ed. (Munich: Kaiser, 1992); Marquardt, *Das christliche Bekenntnis zu Jesus, dem Juden: Eine Christologie* [The Christian confession of Jesus, the Jew: A Christology], 2 vol. (Munich: Kaiser, 1990 and 1991); 2nd ed. (Gütersloh: Gütersloher Verlagshaus, 1993 and 1998); Marquardt, *Was dürfen wir hoffen, wenn wir hoffen dürften? Eine Eschatologie* [What may we hope, if we were permitted to hope at all? An Eschatology] 3 vol., (Gütersloh: Gütersloher Verlagshaus, 1993, 1994, and 1996); Marquardt, *Eia, wärn wir da—eine theologische Utopie* [Oh, if we were only there! A theological utopia] (Gütersloh: Gütersloher Verlagshaus, 1997).

70. Cf. also Marquardt, "Zwischen Amsterdam und Berlin," in *Abirren* (see n. 8 above), 140.

71. Cf. Barth, *Die christliche Dogmatik im Entwurf*, vol. 1: *Die Lehre vom Worte Gottes: Prolegomena zur christlichen Dogmatik* [Christian dogmatics in outline, vol. 1: The doctrine of the word of God: Prolegomena to Christian dogmatics] (Munich: Kaiser, 1927), also as vol. 14 of Karl Barth *Gesamtausgabe*, ed. Gerhard Sauter (Zürich: Theologischer Verlag, 1982) 151. Under "irregular dogmatics" Barth wanted to understand a "reflection on the word of God," which is practiced "unmethodically, chaotically, as in guerrilla warfare, rather than as a regular soldier," and which works against the danger inherent in the regular scholastic practice of "dogmaticizing, becoming hardened and wooden." In such dogmatics theological work might be practiced "often in an infinitely more fruitful manner" than in the "accomplishments of dozens of the all too methodical theologians." In the "Prolegomena" of his *Church Dogmatics* Barth in 1932 expressly emphasized that such "irregular dogmatics" are not necessarily in any way less scolarly than the regular school dogmatics (*Die Kirchliche Dogmatik*, vol. I/1, 294).

When Marquardt started on his dogmatics, the "situation after Auschwitz" had not yet fallen into the center of his thinking. The "whole question of Christ" was still in the foreground, whereby Marquardt now was asking about the meaning of "the Jewish No" to the Messiahship of Jesus for the Christians. As he put it, "We will only then have the Christian anti-Judaism behind us, when we are able theologically, to do something positive with the Jewish "no" to Jesus Christ."[72]

At the presentation of the working group, "Jews and Christians" on June 14, 1979, at the *Kirchentag* in Nuremberg Marquardt then went a decisive step further. In his lecture "Being a Christian after Auschwitz" he began with the question: "'What then should we do?'— after Auschwitz."[73] This was the year in which in January the American TV Series "Holocaust" ran, and opened in many families discussions between the generations about the responsibility of the Germans for the mass murder of millions of Jews.[74] Surprised now, Marquardt asked himself how it came about, "that Auschwitz only now begins to enter our consciousness—that above all we older ones just now have reached the point where we can allow the facts of Auschwitz to get close to us, just now finally are ready to face our guilt and co-responsibility." With this question Marquardt now began to reflect, along with the story of the victims, which he had faced before, also on the story of the perpetrators. And Marquardt could not get around the position: "Auschwitz concerns us today as a judgment on our Christianity."[75]

Then Marquardt reported on the Jewish "Holocaust theology" coming from North America:

> A spell that had lain over the victims was broken. A 30-year-long incubation period of horror has ended. Now, only very slowly that is being said which had paralyzed the souls, the understanding, speech itself since Auschwitz. Only now people are beginning to articulate their experiences, to organize them, to stutter the words, 'How could that have happened? How could

72. Marquardt, "'Feinde um unsretwillen': Das jüdische Nein und die christliche Theologie" ["'Enemies for Our Sake': The Jewish No and Christian Theology"] (1977), in Marquardt, *Verwegenheiten* (see n. 9 above), 311, also in this volume.

73. Marquardt, "Christsein nach Auschwitz" (see n. 68 above), 9.

74. Cf. ibid., 16, "The structure of the lie on which marriages and families had been built totally collapsed. Young people received at last true and honest fathers and mothers, that is, guilty fathers and mothers."

75. Ibid., 9.

that have been permitted? Where were the people who could have and should have helped? Why did not at least the Messiah come, to save? Where was the righteousness of God? Where was God?' Only now does one begin to sink in the whirlwind of these unanswerable questions. Only now is it beginning to be determined, whether faith must be still, or perhaps is no longer possible."[76]

For Richard Rubenstein the conviction expressed by Propst Heinrich Grüber, friend and helper of the Jews in the Confessing Church that, Auschwitz was "the will of God," was "the turning point in his own conviction" that "one could no longer believe in this God, who not only allowed Auschwitz to happen, but *willed* it to be!"[77] Emil Fackenheim on the other hand took from Auschwitz "the commanding voice," that he could not, "after the fact, prove Hitler right," so that the survivors now would be in the position of giving up on God.[78] Marquardt contrasted these Jewish positions with the cynical "untouchableness of the Christian faith," as it had been expressed in his closing sermon by then Berlin Bishop Otto Dibelius in 1966: "Since Auschwitz, you have only lost your nerve; that's all!"[79]

So, for the time being, there remained for Marquardt nothing but his "consternation at our lack of experience of God" to be expressed as the characteristic of "Christian existence after Auschwitz."[80] He bristled against the possibility of seeking, with John Paul II "Golgotha in Auschwitz," or recognizing "Auschwitz as the Golgotha of our time," for: "Even the key of a theology of the cross works too easily . . . We always

---

76. Ibid., 26. Cf. also Marquardt, "Kann man nach Auschwitz noch von Gott reden?" [Can one still speak of God after Auschwitz?] (1979), in Marquardt, *Verwegenheiten* (see n. 9 above), 511–23.

77. Marquardt, "Christsein nach Auschwitz," 27.—Cf. also Richard L. Rubenstein, "Some Perspectives on Religious Faith After Auschwitz," in *The German Church Struggle and the Holocaust*, ed. Franklin H. Littell and Hubert Locke (Detroit: Wayne State University Press, 1974) 256–68. [Probst Grüber was commissioned by the Confessing Church especially to help Jews who had been baptized into the Christian church.—Trans.]

78. Marquardt, "Christsein nach Auschwitz," 28–29.—Cf. Emil L. Fackenheim, "The Commanding Voice of Auschwitz," in Fackenheim, *God's Presence in History: Jewish Affirmations and Philosophical Reflections* (New York: New York University Press, 1970) 67–98.

79. Marquardt, "Christsein nach Auschwitz," 29.

80. Ibid., 30.

know what it is we have to say."[81] Where then was there in Auschwitz "the witness of the humanity of God," in which Christians have always believed? Central theological answers of the Christian tradition must collapse after Auschwitz. So Marquardt closed his Nuremberg lecture with the last words of a lecture by Robert Raphael Geis at the *Kirchentag* in 1967: "The word of faith in our time can and will no longer be pompous or declamatory, it is the 'perhaps' of a timid hope. But the word of God's merciful love is also: perhaps. Perhaps? . . . Perhaps."[82]

After this lecture, which was perceived by many as a turning point in Marquardt's theological development, "the situation after Auschwitz" came to expression anew in the title of the *Prolegomena* volume, "Of the misery and visitation of theology," in which Marquardt reflected "on the connection between theology and crime." The word of Luther helped him, that a theologian came into being not through disputation, but through "dying" (*moriendo*), which Marquardt understood in the sense of the dying of one's own tradition. No "affirmative theology" could appear any more, but only a "self-critical attempt." ("The Story of my Dogmatics," July 4, 1995). Nevertheless he could look back in this volume, in addition to the Jewish "Holocaust theology," also to new developments within the evangelical theology in Germany, such as those which came to expression in the resolution of the synod of Rhineland in January 1980, "Toward the renewal of the relationship between Christians and Jews."[83]

In the two volumes on Christology it showed how far Marquardt's thinking had grown in the meantime, from the dogmatic attempt of his "resurrection" book, in which he still had rejected a "denial of Christological possession." Now the traditional "two nature doctrine" had been transformed into a "working community" between God and Jesus. "The Jew Jesus" was for him not simply "the historical Jesus." He sought rather to understand "Israel itself" as a "Christological fact," in which he—in acceptance of Karl Barth's understanding of Israel as "the natural environment of Jesus Christ"—creatively misused Hans Urs

81. Ibid., 33.

82. Ibid., 34. Cf. Robert Raphael Geis, "Der biblische Friedensauftrag" [The Biblical mandate to peace], in Geis, *Gottes Minorität: Beiträge zur jüdischen Theologie und zur Geschichte der Juden in Deutschland* [God's minority: Contributions to Jewish theology and to the history of the Jews in Germany] (Munich: Kösel, 1971) 119.

83. Cf. Marquardt, *Von Elend und Heimsuchung der Theologie* (see n. 69 above), 397 and 418ff.

von Balthasar's language about Israel as "structural Christology." In the Christological understanding of time[84] he was following Barth, in that he—beyond Barth—even sought to bring in atheism Christologically. (Interview, February 5, 1995).

By closing his Christology with the paragraph, "Amen, that is: May it come to pass!"[85] Marquardt showed how much the Christological question in the meantime "had been forced into the background by the eschatological question" (Interview, February 5, 1995). In the relationship between Jews and Christians, the Messiahship of Jesus had to be placed in question, and in a transformed sense come to expression over against the tradition. Above all the eschatology, the question of "the new reality" had to be addressed, since the Jews were asking, what actually had been changed through Jesus ("The Story of my Dogmatics," July 4, 1995).

So the "imbalance" of the parts within the dogmatics came into being, which was motivated by the word "perhaps" at the end of Marquardt's Nuremberg lecture at the *Kirchentag* of 1979: The tradition was questioned self-critically not only by the experience of the living encounters with Jews, but also under the impression of the Christian co-responsibility for the murder of the Jews. Christian faith is, at least since Auschwitz, no longer a "possession" of the Western world; it can at the most be expressed as an object of hope, if it is permitted to hope at all. Karl Barth did not get to the writing of his intended eschatology—not least because of the breadth of his Christology, spilling over all boundaries. Marquardt's eschatology, if one counts also objectively the "Utopia," claims alone four of his seven volumes, and therewith the largest part of his dogmatics. Barth's "ounce of chiliasm"[86] had become, under the effect of "the influence of Judaism" on his thought "a very large dose of chiliasm." At the same time he saw here the effect of his

84. Cf. Marquardt, "Vom Kommen, Gehen und Bleiben Jesu von Nazareth" [On the coming, going and staying of Jesus of Nazareth], in *Das christliche Bekenntnis zu Jesus, dem Juden*, Bd. 2 (see n. 69 above), 238ff.

85. Ibid., 439ff.

86. Barth, "Das Problem der Ethik in der Gegenwart" [The problem of ethics in the present] (1922), in Barth, *Das Wort Gottes und die Theologie* (Munich: Kaiser, 1924), 139–40.—Here Barth formulated that "without an ounce of Chiliasm ...," there could be ... "no ethics," whereby for him the question of "the socialistic hope for the future" was set at the same time on the agenda.

"socialism" work on the dogmatics: "Forward, and not forgetting!" (Interview, February 5, 1995).

Finally there was for Marquardt, under the title, *Eia, wärn wir da!* (Oh, if only we were there!) the theme of "utopia," to be questioned from the Christian side, whereby, in opposition to the tradition, God very self had become a "utopian reality," expressed thematically only at the very end of the dogmatics, as a "reality for which we cannot yet point to a place in our world, which first seeks a place in the world." There God is "just as utopian" as paradise and the new Jerusalem, the "new social reality in the world, which also has no place, no location, in the present world." Here also Marquardt saw a connection between his work on the Jewish-Christian relationship and his socialist work ("The Story of my Dogmatics," July 4, 1995).[87]

After it came to a political "quarrel" in the working group "Jews and Christians" because of the Gulf War, 1991, that resulted in the resignation of the whole executive committee,[88] Marquardt became once again, from 1991–1994 a member of the executive commission. A mediation of the conflicting positions seemed no longer to be possible. Marquardt saw the purpose of the working group, in view of the conflict in the Middle East not so much that of cooperation with the Israeli peace movement, despite his sympathy for it, but rather to create understanding in Germany for the traumatized Israeli majority. In so far, he remained consciously on "the politically reactionary side." (Interview, February 5, 1995).

On the occasion of his sixteeth birthday, 1988, Helmut Gollwitzer said about his successor, "Friedel always went a step further than I did. He was more courageous. I was more bound to the tradition. Friedel was bolder; he stepped over the borders of the tradition, even beyond the boundaries of orthodoxy."[89] Marquardt himself once described his

87. For Marquardt's Utopia, cf. also Marquardt, "Gott—Utopie?" in *Die Welt als Ort Gottes—Gott als Ort der Welt: Friedrich-Wilhelm Marquardts theologische Utopie,* ed. Magdalene L. Frettlöh and Jan-Dirk Döhling (Gütersloh: Gütersloher Verlagshaus, 2001) 14–35.

88. On this "quarrel," because of the Gulf War, see also G. Kammerer, *In die Haare, in die* Arme (see n. 26 above), 137–49. See also Edna Brocke, "Dreißig Jahre in Folge: Erfahrungen einer Jüdin beim Kirchentag" [Thirty years in succession: Experiences of a Jewish woman with the *Kirchentag*], *Kirche und Israel* 17 (2002) 86–100.

89. H. Gollwitzer, "Laudatio (2.12.1988)," in *Störenfriedels Zeddelkasten* (see n. 34 above), 10.

steps "beyond orthodoxy" like this: "I cannot any longer represent the 'two-nature doctrine' and have my problems with the doctrine of the Trinity ... From my perspective perhaps I have even gone too far away from Barth ... There will probably be, when I am ready, a self-judgment." (Interview, February 5, 1995).

He carried out the "self-judgment" on the occasion of his achieving emeritus status on February 7, 1997, as he took a very careful look, under the heading "Wanderings," at the "manifestations of the heretical" in his theology.[90] First he reminded himself of Barth's warning once upon a time about the danger of himself becoming heretical in his attempt to close the loopholes in Barth's doctrine of Israel. But he thought to avoid this danger by developing himself "no theological doctrine of Israel at all." "The theological dimension does not surface in a divine definition of the Jewish people, but in the working out of my own Christian self-understanding, in my practical and spiritual relationship to this people, above all therefore in the carrying out of a Christian self-criticism of this relationship and in a hope for its renewal."[91]

Then Marquardt is reminded of the "verdict of heresy" expressed by his former student friend Günter Klein on the occasion of his paper "The Jews in the Epistle to the Romans." Finally he confronts the charge of heresy: "Auschwitz received in the layout of my theological work the position of a second source of revelation—alongside the biblical revelation of God, and thereby I was also guilty of that same church-destroying error of which the Confessing Church once charged the 'German Christians' as these in Hitler celebrated the Savior of God sent especially to the German people"—a charge that Marquardt understood to be "impertinent and especially poisonous and vulgar."[92] For he "never explained Auschwitz theologically." When I think about Auschwitz, I think of the people, not of God, of the tortured and murdered, their abandonment by humankind, and the torturers and murderers and their godlessness." Traditional theology rather insisted much more on squeezing some theological "meaning" from Auschwitz, as a "rod of di-

---

90. Cf. Marquardt, "'Abirren': Zu Erscheinungsformen des Häretischen in meiner Theologie"["Wanderings": Concerning the manifestations of the heretical in my theology], in *Abirren* (see n. 8 above), 151–74.

91. Ibid., 157–58.

92. Ibid., 161.

vine anger," in order to avoid the commanded theological repentance.[93] The grounding of the state of Israel also, through which the Jewish people seek "to revise the date of August, 70 CE," which was often interpreted in Christian tradition as the punishment of God, Marquardt did not want to treat as "a historical-theological revelation case," but rather "as a condition of my present consciousness, which I cannot exclude from the horizon of my hermeneutical understanding."[94] However that might be: Marquardt sought finally to leave open the question of whether "heresy" was "error," or "divine leading," tying it to the passage in Gen 12:1–3: "God's might commanded me to wander from my father's house . . ."[95]

As with hardly any other theologian, the living encounters with Judaism and the situation "after Auschwitz" worked their way into the heart of Marquardt's theology, so that dogmatics could only be done "irregularly." In a conversation in Amsterdam with Wessel ten Boom he named as the "starting point" for his "departure" from the dogmatic tradition "the criticism of spiritual violence, which I saw in the traditional ordering of dogmatics." This was "an oppressive system of the truth that Christianity passed on, which had so much systematic within it, that something also violent was passed on as truth." In contrast to that, Marquardt understood his dogmatics as "an attempt, to deliver a criticism against the violence in the Christian tradition." So he chose for his dogmatics "alone those topics . . . where the greatest intellectual, spiritual, and then finally also physical violence was exerted against Judaism." In conclusion, Marquardt saw his dogmatic task as "a 're-translation' of important Christian doctrines in the questions to which they once saw themselves as providing an answer." Insofar, "the doubt, the gaining of the question" was "the most positive thing" he could imagine—"because, if I did not know the question, the answer would not mean a thing to me."[96]

---

93. Ibid., 162ff.

94. Ibid., 188ff.

95. Ibid., 172ff.

96. Cf. "En dan val ik stil . . ." [And then I become quiet], an interview with Marquardt on September 25, 1996, originally in Dutch, in Wessel H. ten Boom, *Alleen GOD kan spreken: Een inleiding op het werk van Friedrich-Wilhelm Marquardt* (Kampen: Kok, 1997) 164–87.

So, finally then, Marquardt remained until the last a student with Judaism. The Israel trip of 1959 gave him continuing impetus again and again to new theological directions, as for instance—twenty years later—to the mentioned as a crossroads at the Nuremberg *Kirchentag* of 1979. In contrast to the "harmony model" and the emphasis of "commonalities" in the beginning phases of the working group "Jews and Christians," the remaining differences came later into the foreground ("The Story of My Dogmatics," July 4, 1995). Finally, consciously taking back all the euphoric expectations from the beginning years of the Christian-Jewish Dialogue, he gave his last collection of essays, with "little Christian-Jewish learning units," the title *Auf einem Schul-Weg* [On a way to school] (1999): "Learning from Judaism seems to me to be a more appropriate assignment for Christians than that which under the heading of a 'Christian-Jewish dialogue' had become at the end an all-too naïve and empty label, used everywhere for propaganda . . . Without a basic and elemental historical and theological 'learning,' I do not see any prospect of getting ahead."[97]

What such "learning" could mean in Judaism will be kept in remembrance thankfully by those who in the last ten years were able to take part in one or more of the annual meetings "Learning from the Talmud," in the Evangelical Academy in Berlin, which Marquardt, together with the Jerusalem Talmud scholar Chana Safrai developed, to give the participants access to the Talmud. These, despite all what at the beginning was so alienating, were able to open also for Christians a path to the understanding of the "oral Torah," as the center of the Jewish faith world. The suspicion of heresy was not excluded, naturally, even with this last "turning toward Jerusalem."[98] "You break through the boundaries of the canon in your theology and thereby leave the church." And indeed: What other Christian theologian would be willing to take seriously the unsystematic Talmudic thinking, and to "make a place for the Jewish tradition of the Halacha . . . in the formulation of Christian theological knowledge"?[99] The growing number of footnotes from volume to volume of quotations from the Talmud and Midrash document how

97. Marquardt, *Auf einem Schul-Weg* (see n. 23 above), 7 (Foreword).

98. Cf. *Wendung nach Jerusalem: Friedrich-Wilhelm Marquardts Theologie im Gespräch* [Turning toward Jerusalem: F.-W. Marquardt's theology in conversation], ed. Hanna Lehming et al. (Gütersloh: Gütersloher Verlagshaus, 1999).

99. Marquardt, *Abirren* (see n. 8 above), 170.

the question finally came through in Marquardt's dogmatics: "Are we in the position, to take up the competition of the Talmud with the New Testament?" ("The Story of my Dogmatics," July 4, 1995)[100]

∼

Despite all the criticism for his teacher Karl Barth, Marquardt was finally of the opinion: "Barth is still ahead of us" (Interview, February 5, 1995). Similarly it is the case that Marquardt is ahead of us. To be sure, a number of "Marquardt circles" have formed at the level of the local congregation, but the academic theology has scarcely concerned itself with his dogmatics. Over against criticism of his theology, which recently has been expressed very sharply from the younger generation, Marquardt showed himself quite open.[101] As long as it could be recognized that the questioning moved in the direction of a repentance of theology "after Auschwitz," Marquardt could say contentedly, "The road goes on!"

At a conference in the [Catholic] Bishop's Academy in Aachen, on the theme "the ecclesiastical culture of guilt," (November 17, 2001), Marquardt got the attention of his listeners as he began his lecture with the words, "As I once more took my sick heart walking in Dahlem . . ." This was surely meant also in a figurative sense, as Marquardt sometimes could speak of the necessity of "heart surgery on Christian theology."[102] But it could also, as his death while on a walk through Dahlem showed, be heard as an indication of his physical health.

100. Cf. also Marquardt, "Warum mich als Christen der Talmud interessiert" [Why the Talmud interests me as a Christian], in *Auf einem Schul-Weg* (see n. 23 above), 257–76, also in this volume.

101. Cf. Barbara Meyer, "'Der Andere des Anderen ist ein Anderer': Kritische Anmerkungen zur Theologie Friedrich-Wilhelm Marquardts" ["The Other of the Other is Another": Critical remarks on the theology of Friedrich-Wilhelm Marquardt], in *Von Gott reden im Land der Täter: Theologische Stimmen der dritten Generation seit der Shoah*, ed. Katharina von Kellenbach et al. (Darmstadt: Wissenschaftliche Buchgesellschaft, 2001) 110–22. Cf. also K. Hanna Holtschneider, "Der Holocaust und die Verhältnisbestimmung von ChristInnen und JüdInnen in Deutschland: Eine kritische Untersuchung der Theologie Friedrich-Wilhelm Marquardts" [The Holocaust and the determination of the relationship between Christian and Jewish men and women in Germany: A critical examination of the theology of Friedrich-Wilhelm Marquardt], ibid., 123–42.

102. Marquardt, "Zwischen Amsterdam und Berlin," in *Abirren* (see n. 8 above), 113.

In his sermon at the memorial service, his younger brother pointed out that Friedrich-Wilhelm Marquardt was "Sunday's child" (born on a Sunday) and died on a Sabbath. From Sunday to Sabbath—an indication of, as with his seven volume dogmatics, a dogmatic week? A completed theological life?—Perhaps!

Sources

Friedrich-Wilhelm Marquardt

"'Enemies for Our Sake': The Jewish No and the Christian Theology." Originally published as "'Feinde um unsretwillen': Das jüdische Nein und die christliche Theologie," in *Treue zur Thora: Beiträge zur Mitte des christlich-jüdischen Gesprächs; Festschrift für Günther Harder zum 75. Geburtstag,* edited by Peter von der Osten-Sacken, 174–93. Berlin: Institut Kirche und Judentum, 1977. Again in Marquardt, *Verwegenheiten: Theologische Stücke aus Berlin* (Munich: Kaiser, 1981) 311–36.

"Elements Unresolved in Leo Baeck's Criticism of Adolf von Harnack." Originally published as "Unabgegoltenes in der Kritik Leo Baecks an Adolf von Harnack," in *Leo Baeck—Lehrer und Helfer in schwerer Zeit,* edited by Werner Licharz (Frankfurt am Main: Haag & Herchen, 1983) 169–87. Revised version in Marquardt, *Auf einem Schul-Weg: Kleinere christlich-jüdische Lerneinheiten* (Berlin: Orient & Okzident, 1999) 39–58; second edition edited by Andreas Pangritz (Aachen: Orient & Okzident, 2005).

"Martin Buber as a Socialist Zionist." Taken from a tape transcript of a lecture given at the Jewish Adult Education Center, Berlin, on February 5, 1975. Originally published as "Martin Buber als sozialistischer Zionist," in *Leben als Begegnung: Ein Jahrhundert Martin Buber (1878–1978): Vorträge und Aufsätze,* edited by Peter von der Osten-Sacken (Berlin: Institut Kirche und Judentum, 1978) 93–107. Revised version in Marquardt, *Auf einem Schul-Weg,* 47–172.

"Why the Talmud Interests Me as a Christian." Paper presented at the twenty-fifth German Protestant Church Congress (Deutscher Evangelischer Kirchentag), Munich, June 10, 1993. Published as "Warum mich als Christen der Talmud interessiert," in *Rundbrief* Nr. 34 des Studienkreises Kirche und Israel der Evangelischen Landeskirche in

Baden (December 1993) 10–16. Revised version in Marquardt, *Auf einem Schul-Weg*, 257–76.

"When Will You Restore the Kingdom for Israel?" Lecture given at the Jewish-Christian Bible Week, Graz (Austria), July 24, 1992. Originally published as "Wann stellst du das Reich für Israel wieder her?" in Marquardt, *Auf einem Schul-Weg*, 173–90.

"First Report on Karl Barth's 'Socialist Speeches.'" Originally published as "Erster Bericht über Karl Barths 'Sozialistische Reden,'" in Marquardt, *Verwegenheiten*, 470–88.

"The Secretary of the Church Administration: From Barth's Pastorate." Originally published as "Der Aktuar: Aus Barths Pfarramt," in *Karl Barth: Der Störenfried?* Einwürfe, no. 3, edited by F.-W. Marquardt et al. (Munich: Kaiser, 1986) 93–139.

"The Idol Totters: The General Attack from the Epistle to the Romans." Paper presented at a conference on Karl Barth at the Evangelische Akademie Baden, Bad Herrenalb, December 12–14, 1969. Originally published as "Der Götze wackelt: Der Generalangriff aus dem Römerbrief," in *Porträt eines Theologen: Stimmt unser Bild von Karl Barth?* Edited by Willi Gegenheimer (Stuttgart: Radius, 1970) 11–28. Again in Marquardt, *Verwegenheiten*, 407–23.

"Theological and Political Motivations of Karl Barth in the Church Struggle." Originally published as "Theologische und politische Motivationen Karl Barths im Kirchenkampf," in *Junge Kirche* 34 (1973) 283–303. Again in Marquardt, *Verwegenheiten*, 439–69.

Andreas Pangritz

"Friedrich-Wilhelm Marquardt—A Theological-Biographical Sketch." Originally published as *"Mich befreit der Gott Israels": Friedrich-Wilhelm Marquardt; Eine theologisch-biographische Skizze.* Berlin: Aktion Sühnezeichen Friedensdienste, 2003. First publication in English, translated by Don McCord, in *European Judaism: A Journal for the New Europe* 38, no. 1, issue no. 74 (Spring 2005) 17–47. Revised version for this volume.

Index of Names